A TEXT-BOOK

OF THE

HISTORY OF PAINTING

BY

JOHN C. VAN DYKE, L.H.D.

PREFACE.

The object of this series of text-books is to provide concise teachable histories of art for class-room use in schools and colleges. The limited time given to the study of art in the average educational institution has not only dictated the condensed style of the volumes, but has limited their scope of matter to the general features of art history. Archæological discussions on special subjects and æsthetic theories have been avoided. The main facts of history as settled by the best authorities are given. If the reader choose to enter into particulars the bibliography cited at the head of each chapter will be found helpful. Illustrations have been introduced as sight-help to the text, and to avoid repetition, abbreviations have been used wherever practicable. The enumeration of the principal extant works of an artist, school, or period, and where they may be found, which follows each chapter, may be serviceable not only as a summary of individual or school achievement, but for reference by travelling students in Europe.

This volume on painting, the first of the series, omits mention of such work in Arabic, Indian, Chinese, and Persian art as may come properly under the head of Ornament—a[viii] subject proposed for separate treatment hereafter. In treating of individual painters it has been thought best to give a short critical estimate of the man and his rank among the painters of his time rather than the detailed facts of his life. Students who wish accounts of the lives of the painters should use Vasari, Larousse, and the *Encyclopædia Britannica* in connection with this text-book.

Acknowledgments are made to the respective publishers of Woltmann and Woermann's History of Painting, and the fine series of art histories by Perrot and Chipiez, for permission to reproduce some few illustrations from these publications.

JOHN C. VAN DYKE.

INTRODUCTION.

The origin of painting is unknown. The first important records of this art are met with in Egypt; but before the Egyptian civilization the men of the early ages probably used color in ornamentation and decoration, and they certainly scratched the outlines of men and animals upon bone and slate. Traces of this rude primitive work still remain to us on the pottery, weapons, and stone implements of the cave-dwellers. But while indicating the awakening of intelligence in early man, they can be reckoned with as art only in a slight archæological way. They show inclination rather than accomplishment—a wish to ornament or to represent, with only a crude knowledge of how to go about it.

The first aim of this primitive painting was undoubtedly decoration—the using of colored forms for color and form only, as shown in the pottery designs or cross-hatchings on stone knives or spear-heads. The second, and perhaps later aim, was by imitating the shapes and colors of men, animals, and the like, to convey an idea of the proportions and characters of such things. An outline of a cave-bear or a mammoth was perhaps the cave-dweller's way of telling his fellows what monsters he had slain. We may assume that it was pictorial record, primitive picture-written history. This early method of conveying an idea is, in intent,[xviii]substantially the same as the later hieroglyphic writing and historical painting of the Egyptians. The difference between them is merely one of development. Thus there is an indication in the art of Primitive Man of the two great departments of painting existent to-day.

1. DECORATIVE PAINTING.
2. EXPRESSIVE PAINTING.

Pure Decorative Painting is not usually expressive of ideas other than those of rhythmical line and harmonious color. It is not our subject. This volume treats of Expressive Painting; but in dealing with that it should be borne in mind that Expressive Painting has always a more or less decorative effect accompanying it, and that must be spoken of incidentally. We shall presently see the intermingling of both kinds of painting in the art of ancient Egypt—our first inquiry.

[1]

CHAPTER I.
EGYPTIAN PAINTING.

BOOKS RECOMMENDED: Brugsch, *History of Egypt under the Pharaohs*; Budge, *Dwellers on the Nile*; Duncker, *History of Antiquity; Egypt Exploration Fund Memoirs*; Ely, *Manual of Archæology*; Lepsius, *Denkmaler aus Aegypten und Aethiopen*; Maspero, *Life in Ancient Egypt and Assyria*; Maspero, *Guide du Visiteur au Musée de Boulaq*; Maspero, *Egyptian Archæology*; Perrot and Chipiez, *History of Art in Ancient Egypt*; Wilkinson, *Manners and Customs of the Ancient Egyptians*.

LAND AND PEOPLE: Egypt, as Herodotus has said, is "the gift of the Nile," one of the latest of the earth's geological formations, and yet one of the earliest countries to be settled and dominated by man. It consists now, as in the ancient days, of the valley of the Nile, bounded on the east by the Arabian mountains and on the west by the Libyan desert. Well-watered and fertile, it was doubtless at first a pastoral and agricultural country; then, by its riverine traffic, a commercial country, and finally, by conquest, a land enriched with the spoils of warfare.

Its earliest records show a strongly established monarchy. Dynasties of kings called Pharaohs succeeded one another by birth or conquest. The king made the laws, judged the people, declared war, and was monarch supreme. Next to him in rank came the priests, who were not only in the service of religion but in that of the state, as counsellors, secretaries, and the like. The common people, with true[2] Oriental lack of individuality, depending blindly on leaders, were little more than the servants of the upper classes.

FIG. 1.—HUNTING IN THE MARSHES. TOMB OF TI, SACCARAH.
(FROM PERROT AND CHIPIEZ.)
Please click here for a modern color image

The Egyptian religion existing in the earliest days was a worship of the personified elements of nature. Each element had its particular controlling god, worshipped as such. Later on in Egyptian history the number of gods was increased, and each city had its trinity of godlike protectors symbolized by the propylæa of the temples. Future life was a certainty, provided that the Ka, or spirit, did not fall a prey to Typhon, the God of Evil, during the long wait[3] in the tomb for the judgment-day. The belief that the spirit rested in the body until finally transported to the aaln fields (the Islands of the Blest, afterward adopted by the Greeks) was one reason for the careful preservation of the body by mummifying processes. Life itself was not more important than death. Hence the imposing ceremonies of the funeral and burial, the elaborate richness of the tomb and its wall paintings. Perhaps the first Egyptian art arose through religious observance, and certainly the first known to us was sepulchral.

ART MOTIVES: The centre of the Egyptian system was the monarch and his supposed relatives, the gods. They arrogated to themselves the chief thought of life, and the aim of the great bulk of the art was to glorify monarchy or deity. The massive buildings, still standing to-day in ruins, were built as the dwelling-places of kings or the sanctuaries of gods. The towers symbolized deity, the sculptures and paintings recited the functional duties of presiding spirits, or the Pharaoh's looks and acts. Almost everything about the public buildings in painting and sculpture was symbolic illustration, picture-written history—written with a chisel and brush, written large that all might read. There was no other safe way of preserving record. There were no books; the papyrus sheet, used extensively, was frail, and the Egyptians evidently wished their buildings, carvings, and paintings to last into eternity. So they wrought in and upon stone. The same hieroglyphic character of their papyrus writings appeared cut and colored on the palace walls, and above them and beside them the pictures ran as vignettes explanatory of the text. In a less ostentatious way the tombs perpetuated history in a similar manner, reciting the domestic scenes from the life of the individual, as the temples and palaces the religious and monarchical scenes.

In one form or another it was all record of Egyptian life, but this was not the only motive of their painting. The[4] temples and palaces, designed to shut out light and heat, were long squares of heavy stone, gloomy as the cave from which their plan may have originated. Carving and color were used to brighten and enliven the interior. The battles, the judgment scenes, the Pharaoh playing at draughts with his wives, the religious rites and ceremonies, were all given with brilliant arbitrary color, surrounded oftentimes by bordering bands of green, yellow, and blue. Color showed everywhere from floor to ceiling. Even the explanatory hieroglyphic texts ran in colors, lining the walls and winding around the cylinders of stone. The lotus capitals, the frieze and architrave, all glowed with bright hues, and often the roof ceiling was painted in blue and studded with golden stars.

FIG. 2.—PORTRAIT OF QUEEN TAIA.
(FROM PERROT AND CHIPIEZ.)

All this shows a decorative motive in Egyptian painting, and how constantly this was kept in view may be seen at times in the arrangement of the different scenes, the large ones being placed in the middle of the wall and the smaller ones going at the top and bottom, to act as a frieze and dado. There were, then, two leading motives for Egyptian painting; (1) History, monarchical, religious, or domestic; and (2) Decoration.

TECHNICAL METHODS: Man in the early stages of civilization comprehends objects more by line than by color[5] or light. The figure is not studied in itself, but in its sun-shadow or silhouette. The Egyptian hieroglyph represented objects by outlines or arbitrary marks and conveyed a simple meaning without circumlocution. The Egyptian painting was substantially an enlargement of the hieroglyph. There was no attempt to place objects in the setting which they hold in nature. Perspective and light-and-shade were disregarded. Objects, of whatever nature, were shown in flat profile. In the human figure the shoulders were square, the hips slight, the legs and arms long, the feet and hands flat. The head, legs, and arms were shown in profile, while the chest and eye were twisted to show the flat front view. There are only one or two full-faced figures among the remains of Egyptian painting. After the outline was drawn the enclosed space was filled in with plain color. In the absence of high light, or composed groups, prominence was given to an important figure, like that of the king, by making it much larger than the other figures. This may be seen in any of the battle-pieces of Rameses II., in which the monarch in his chariot is a giant where his followers are mere pygmies. In the absence of perspective, receding figures of men or of horses were given by multiplied outlines of legs, or heads, placed before, or after, or raised above one another. Flat water was represented by zigzag lines, placed as it were upon a map, one tree symbolized a forest, and one fortification a town.

These outline drawings were not realistic in any exact sense. The face was generally expressionless, the figure, evidently done from memory or pattern, did not reveal anatomical structure, but was nevertheless graceful, and in the representation of animals the sense of motion was often given with much truth. The color was usually an attempt at nature, though at times arbitrary or symbolic, as in the case of certain gods rendered with blue, yellow, or green skins. The backgrounds were always of flat color, arbitrary[6] in hue, and decorative only. The only composition was a balance by numbers, and the processional scenes rose tier upon tier above one another in long panels.

FIG. 3.—OFFERINGS TO THE DEAD, WALL PAINTING, EIGHTEENTH DYNASTY.
(FROM PERROT AND CHIPIEZ.)

Such work would seem almost ludicrous did we not keep in mind its reason for existence. It was, first, symbolic story-telling art, and secondly, architectural decoration. As a story-teller it was effective because of its simplicity and directness. As decoration, the repeated expressionless face and figure, the arbitrary color, the absence of perspective were not inappropriate then nor are they now. Egyptian painting never was free from the decorative motive. Wall[7] painting was little more than an adjunct of architecture, and probably grew out of sculpture. The early statues were colored, and on the wall the chisel, like the flint of Primitive Man, cut the outline of the figure. At first only this cut was filled with color, producing what has been called the koil-anaglyphic. In the final stage the line was made by drawing with chalk or coal on prepared stucco, and the color, mixed with gum-water (a kind of distemper), was applied to the whole enclosed space. Substantially the same method of painting was used upon other materials, such as wood, mummy cartonnage, papyrus; and in all its thousands of years of existence Egyptian painting never advanced upon or varied to any extent this one method of work.

HISTORIC PERIODS: Egyptian art may be traced back as far as the Third or Fourth Memphitic dynasty of kings. The date is uncertain, but it is somewhere near 3,500 B.C. The seat of empire, at that time, was located at Memphis in Lower Egypt, and it is among the remains of this

Memphitic Period that the earliest and best painting is found. In fact, all Egyptian art, literature, language, civilization, seem at their highest point of perfection in the period farthest removed from us. In that earliest age the finest portrait busts were cut, and the painting, found chiefly in the tombs and on the mummy-cases, was the attempted realistic with not a little of spirited individuality. The figure was rather short and squat, the face a little squarer than the conventional type afterward adopted, the action better, and the positions, attitudes, and gestures more truthful to local characteristics. The domestic scenes—hunting, fishing, tilling, grazing—were all shown in the one flat, planeless, shadowless method of representation, but with better drawing and color and more variety than appeared later on. Still, more or less conventional types were used, even in this early time, and continued to be used all through Egyptian history.[8]

FIG. 4.—VIGNETTE ON PAPYRUS, LOUVRE.
(FROM PERROT AND CHIPIEZ.)

The Memphitic Period comes down to the eleventh dynasty. In the fifteenth dynasty comes the invasion of the so-called Hyksos, or Shepherd Kings. Little is known of the Hyksos, and, in painting, the next stage is the

Theban Period, which, culminated in Thebes, in Upper Egypt, with Rameses II., of the nineteenth dynasty. Painting had then changed somewhat both in subject and character. The time was one of great temple and palace building, and, though the painting of *genre* subjects in tombs and sepulchres continued, the general body of art became more monumental and subservient to architecture. Painting was put to work on temple and palace-walls, depicting processional scenes, either religious or monarchical, and vast in extent. The figure, too, changed slightly. It became longer, slighter, with a pronounced nose, thick lips, and long eye. From constant repetition, rather than any set rule or canon, this figure grew conventional, and was re[9]produced as a type in a mechanical and unvarying manner for hundreds of years. It was, in fact, only a variation from the original Egyptian type seen in the tombs of the earliest dynasties. There was a great quantity of art produced during the Theban Period, and of a graceful, decorative character, but it was rather monotonous by repetition and filled with established mannerisms. The Egyptian really never was a free worker, never an artist expressing himself; but, for his day, a skilled mechanic following time-honored example. In the

Saitic Period the seat of empire was once more in Lower Egypt, and art had visibly declined with the waning power of the country. All spontaneity seemed to have passed out of it, it was repetition of repetition by poor workmen, and the simplicity and purity of the technic were corrupted by foreign influences. With the Alexandrian epoch Egyptian art came in contact with Greek methods, and grew imitative of the new art, to the detriment of its own native character. Eventually it was entirely lost in the art of the Greco-Roman world. It was never other than conventional, produced by a method almost as unvarying as that of the hieroglyphic writing, and in this very respect characteristic and reflective of the unchanging Orientals. Technically it had its shortcomings, but it conveyed the proper information to its beholders and was serviceable and graceful decoration for Egyptian days.

EXTANT PAINTINGS: The temples, palaces, and tombs of Egypt still reveal Egyptian painting in almost as perfect a state as when originally executed; the Ghizeh Museum has many fine examples; and there are numerous examples in the museums at Turin, Paris, Berlin, London, New York, and Boston. An interesting collection belongs to the New York Historical Society, and some of the latest "finds" of the Egypt Exploration Fund are in the Boston Museum.

[10]

CHAPTER II.
CHALDÆO-ASSYRIAN PAINTING.

BOOKS RECOMMENDED: Babelon, *Manual of Oriental Antiquities*; Botta, *Monument de Ninive*; Budge, *Babylonian Life and History*; Duncker, *History of Antiquity*; Layard, *Nineveh and its Remains*; Layard, *Discoveries Among Ruins of Nineveh and Babylon*; Lenormant,*Manual of the Ancient History of the East*; Loftus, *Travels in Chaldæa and Susiana*; Maspero, *Life in Ancient Egypt and Assyria*; Perrot and Chipiez, *History of Art in Chaldæa and Assyria*; Place, *Ninive et l'Assyrie*; Sayce, *Assyria: Its Palaces, Priests, and People*.

TIGRIS-EUPHRATES CIVILIZATION: In many respects the civilization along the Tigris-Euphrates was like that along the Nile. Both valleys were settled by primitive peoples, who grew rapidly by virtue of favorable climate and soil, and eventually developed into great nations headed by kings absolute in power. The king was the state in Egypt, and in Assyria the monarch was even more dominant and absolute. For the Pharaohs shared architecture, painting, and sculpture with the gods; but the Sargonids seem to have arrogated the most of these things to themselves alone.

Religion was perhaps as real in Assyria as in Egypt, but it was less apparent in art. Certain genii, called gods or demons, appear in the bas-reliefs, but it is not yet settled whether they represent gods or merely legendary heroes or monsters of fable. There was no great demonstration of religion by form and color, as in Egypt. The Assyrians[11] were Semites, and religion with them was more a matter of the spirit than the senses—an image in the mind rather than an image in metal or stone. The temple was not eloquent with the actions and deeds of the gods, and even the tomb, that fruitful source of art in Egypt, was in Chaldæa undecorated and in Assyria unknown. No one knows what the Assyrians did with their dead, unless they carried them back to the fatherland of the race, the Persian Gulf region, as the native tribes of Mesopotamia do to this day.

FIG. 5.—ENAMELLED BRICK. NIMROUD.
(FROM PERROT AND CHIPIEZ.)

ART MOTIVES: As in Egypt, there were two motives for art—illustration and decoration. Religion, as we have seen, hardly obtained at all. The king attracted the greatest attention. The countless bas-reliefs, cut on soft stone slabs, were pages from the history of the monarch in peace and war, in council, in the chase, or in processional rites. Beside him and around him his officers came in for a share of the background glory. Occasionally the common people had representations of their lives and their pursuits, but the main subject of all the valley art was the king and his doings. Sculpture and painting were largely illustrations accompanying a history written in the ever-present cuneiform characters.

But, while serving as history, like the picture-writings of the Egyptians, this illustration was likewise decoration, and was designed with that end in view. Rows upon rows of partly colored bas-reliefs were arranged like a dado along the palace-wall, and above them wall-paintings, or glazed tiles in patterns, carried out the color scheme. Almost all of the color has now disappeared, but it must have been[12]brilliant at one time, and was doubtless in harmony with the architecture. Both painting and sculpture were subordinate to and dependent upon architecture. Palace-building was the chief pursuit, and the other arts were called in mainly as adjuncts—ornamental records of the king who built.

FIG. 6.—ENAMELLED BRICK. KHORSABAD.
(FROM PERROT AND CHIPIEZ.)

THE TYPE, FORM, COLOR: There were only two distinct faces in Assyrian art—one with and one without a beard. Neither of them was a portrait except as attributes or inscriptions designated. The type was unendingly repeated. Women appeared in only one or two isolated cases, and even these are doubtful. The warrior, a strong, coarse-membered, heavily muscled creation, with a heavy, expressionless, Semitic face, appeared everywhere. The figure was placed in profile, with eye and bust twisted to show the front view, and the long feet projected one beyond the other, as in the Nile pictures. This was the Assyrian ideal of strength, dignity, and majesty, established probably in the early ages, and repeated for centuries with few characteristic variations. The figure was usually given in motion, walking, or riding, and had little of that grace seen in Egyptian painting, but in its place a great deal of rude[13] strength. In modelling, the human form was not so knowingly rendered as the animal. The long Eastern clothing probably prevented the close study of the figure. This failure in anatomical exactness was balanced in part by minute details in the dress and accessories, productive of a rich ornamental effect.

Hard stone was not found in the Mesopotamian regions. Temples were built of burnt brick, bas-reliefs were made upon alabaster slabs and heightened by coloring, and painting was largely upon tiles, with mineral paints, afterward glazed by fire. These glazed brick or tiles, with figured designs, were fixed upon the walls, arches, and archivolts by bitumen mortar, and made up the first mosaics of which we have record. There was a further painting upon plaster in distemper, of which some few traces remain. It did not differ in design from the bas-reliefs or the tile mosaics.

The subjects used were the Assyrian type, shown somewhat slighter in painting than in sculpture, animals, birds, and other objects; but they were obviously not attempts at nature. The color was arbitrary, not natural, and there was little perspective, light-and-shade, or relief. Heavy outline bands of color appeared about the object, and the prevailing hues were yellow and blue. There was perhaps less symbolism and more direct representation in Assyria than in Egypt. There was also more feeling for perspective and space, as shown in such objects as water and in the mountain landscapes of the late bas-reliefs; but, in the main, there was no advance upon Egypt. There was a difference which was not necessarily a development. Painting, as we know the art to-day, was not practised in Chaldæa-Assyria. It was never free from a servitude to architecture and sculpture; it was hampered by conventionalities; and the painter was more artisan than artist, having little freedom or individuality.[14]

FIG. 7.—WILD ASS. BAS-RELIEF, BRITISH MUSEUM.
(FROM PERROT AND CHIPIEZ.)

HISTORIC PERIODS: Chaldæa, of unknown antiquity, with Babylon its capital, is accounted the oldest nation in the Tigris-Euphrates valley, and, so far as is known, it was an original nation producing an original art. Its sculpture (especially in the Tello heads), and presumably its painting, were more realistic and individual than any other in the valley. Assyria coming later, and the heir of Chaldæa, was the

Second Empire: There are two distinct periods of this Second Empire, the first lasting from 1,400 B.C., down to about 900 B.C., and in art showing a great profusion of bas-reliefs. The second closed about 625 B.C., and in art produced much glazed-tile work and a more elaborate sculpture and painting. After this the Chaldæan provinces gained the ascendency again, and Babylon, under Nebuchadnezzar, became the first city of Asia. But the new Babylon did not last long. It fell before Cyrus and the Persians 536 B.C. Again, as in Egypt, the earliest art appears the[15] purest and the simplest, and the years of Chaldæo-Assyrian history known to us carry a record of change rather than of progress in art.

ART REMAINS: The most valuable collections of Chaldæo-Assyrian art are to be found in the Louvre and the British Museum. The other large museums of Europe have collections in this department, but all of them combined are little compared with the treasures that still lie buried in the mounds of the Tigris-Euphrates valley. Excavations have been made at Mugheir, Warka, Khorsabad, Kouyunjik, and elsewhere, but many difficulties have thus far rendered systematic work impossible. The complete history of Chaldæo-Assyria and its art has yet to be written.

PERSIAN PAINTING.

BOOKS RECOMMENDED: As before cited, Babelon, Duncker, Lenormant, Ely; Dieulafoy, *L'Art Antique de la Perse*; Flandin et Coste,*Voyage en Perse*; Justi, *Geschichte des alten Persiens*; Perrot and Chipiez, *History of Art in Persia*.

HISTORY AND ART MOTIVES: The Medes and Persians were the natural inheritors of Assyrian civilization, but they did not improve their birthright. The Medes soon lost their power. Cyrus conquered them, and established the powerful Persian monarchy upheld for two hundred years by Cambyses, Darius, and Xerxes. Substantially the same conditions surrounded the Persians as the Assyrians—that is, so far as art production was concerned. Their conceptions of life were similar, and their use of art was for historic illustration of kingly doings and ornamental embellishment of kingly palaces. Both sculpture and painting were accessories of architecture.

Of Median art nothing remains. The Persians left the record, but it was not wholly of their own invention, nor was it very extensive or brilliant. It had little originality about it, and was really only an echo of Assyria. The[16] sculptors and painters copied their Assyrian predecessors, repeating at Persepolis what had been better told at Nineveh.

FIG. 8.—LIONS' FRIEZE, SUSA.
(FROM PERROT AND CHIPIEZ.)

TYPES AND TECHNIC: The same subjects, types, and technical methods in bas-relief, tile, and painting on plaster were followed under Darius as under Shalmanezer. But the imitation was not so good as the original. The warrior, the winged monsters, the animals all lost something of their air of brutal defiance and their strength of modelling. Heroes still walked in procession along the bas-reliefs and glazed tiles, but the figure was smaller, more effeminate, the hair and beard were not so long, the drapery fell in slightly indicated folds at times, and there was a profusion of ornamental detail. Some of this detail and some modifications in the figure showed the influence of foreign nations other than the Greek; but, in the main, Persian art followed in the footsteps of Assyrian art. It was the last reflection of[17] Mesopotamian splendor. For with the conquest of Persia by Alexander the book of expressive art in that valley was closed, and, under Islam, it remains closed to this day.

ART REMAINS: Persian painting is something about which little is known because little remains. The Louvre contains some reconstructed friezes made in mosaics of stamped brick and square tile, showing figures of lions and a number of archers. The coloring is particularly rich, and may give some idea of Persian pigments. Aside from the chief museums of Europe the bulk of Persian art is still seen half-buried in the ruins of Persepolis and elsewhere.

PHŒNICIAN, CYPRIOTE, AND ASIA MINOR PAINTING.

BOOKS RECOMMENDED: As before cited, Babelon, Duncker, Ely, Girard, Lenormant; Cesnola, *Cyprus*; Cesnola, *Cypriote Antiquities in Metropolitan Museum of Art*; Kenrick, *Phœnicia*; Movers, *Die Phonizier*; Perrot and Chipiez, *History of Art in Phœnicia and Cyprus*; Perrot and Chipiez, *History of Art in Sardinia, Judea, Syria and Asia Minor*; Perrot and Chipiez, *History of Art in Phrygia, Lydia, etc.*; Renan, *Mission de Phénicie*.

THE TRADING NATIONS: The coast-lying nations of the Eastern Mediterranean were hardly original or creative nations in a large sense. They were at different times the conquered dependencies of Egypt, Assyria, Persia, Greece, and their lands were but bridges over which armies passed from east to west or from west to east. Located on the Mediterranean between the great civilizations of antiquity they naturally adapted themselves to circumstances, and became the middlemen, the brokers, traders, and carriers of the ancient world. Their lands were not favorable to agriculture, but their sea-coasts rendered commerce easy and lucrative. They made a kingdom of the sea, and their means of livelihood were gathered from it. There is no record that the Egyptians ever traversed the Mediterranean, the[18] Assyrians were not sailors, the Greeks had not yet arisen, and so probably Phœnicia and her neighbors had matters their own way. Colonies and trading stations were established at Cyprus, Carthage, Sardinia, the Greek islands, and the Greek mainland, and not only Eastern goods but Eastern ideas were thus carried to the West.

FIG. 9.—PAINTED HEAD FROM EDESSA.
(FROM PERROT AND CHIPIEZ.)

Politically, socially, and religiously these small middle nations were inconsequential. They simply adapted their politics or faith to the nation that for the time had them under its heel. What semi-original religion they possessed was an amalgamation of the religions of other nations, and their gods of bronze, terra-cotta, and enamel were irreverently sold in the market like any other produce.

ART MOTIVES AND METHODS: Building, carving, and painting were practised among the coastwise nations, but upon no such extensive scale as in either Egypt or Assyria. The mere fact that they were people of the sea rather than of the land precluded extensive or concentrated development. Politically Phœnicia was divided among five cities, and her artistic strength was distributed in a similar manner. Such art as was produced showed the religious and decorative motives, and in its spiritless materialistic make-up, the commercial motive. It was at the best a hybrid, mongrel art, borrowed from many sources and distributed to many[19] points of the compass. At one time it had a strong Assyrian cast, at another an Egyptian cast, and after Greece arose it accepted a retroactive influence from there.

It is impossible to characterize the Phœnician type, and even the Cypriote type, though more pronounced, varies so with the different influences that it has no very striking individuality. Technically both the Phœnician and Cypriote were fair workmen in bronze and stone, and doubtless taught many technical methods to the early Greeks, besides making known to them those deities afterward adopted under the names of Aphrodite, Adonis, and Heracles, and familiarizing them with the art forms of Egypt and Assyria.

FIG. 10.—CYPRIOTE VASE DECORATION.
(FROM PERROT AND CHIPIEZ.)

As for painting, there was undoubtedly figured decoration upon walls of stone and plaster, but there is not enough left to us from all the small nations like Phœnicia, Judea, Cyprus, and the kingdoms of Asia Minor, put together, to patch up a disjointed history. The first lands to meet the spoiler, their very ruins have perished. All that there is of painting comes to us in broken potteries and color traces on statuary. The remains of sculpture and architecture are of course better preserved. None of this intermediate art holds much rank by virtue of its inherent worth. It is[20] its influence upon the West—the ideas, subjects, and methods it imparted to the Greeks—that gives it importance in art history.

ART REMAINS: In painting chiefly the vases in the Metropolitan Museum, New York, the Louvre, British and Berlin Museums. These give a poor and incomplete idea of the painting in Asia Minor, Phœnicia and her colonies. The terra-cottas, figurines in bronze, and sculptures can be studied to more advantage. The best collection of Cypriote antiquities is in the Metropolitan Museum, New York. A new collection of Judaic art has been recently opened in the Louvre.

[21]

CHAPTER III.
GREEK PAINTING.

BOOKS RECOMMENDED: Baumeister, *Denkmäler des klassischen Altertums*—article "*Malerei*;" Birch, *History of Ancient Pottery*; Brunn,*Geschichte der griechischen Künstler*; Collignon, *Mythologie figurée de la Grèce*; Collignon, *Manuel d'Archaeologie Grecque*; Cros et Henry, *L'Encaustique et les autres procédés de Peinture chez les Anciens*; Girard, *La Peinture Antique*; Murray, *Handbook of Greek Archæology*; Overbeck, *Antiken Schriftquellen zur geschichte der bildenden Kunste bie den Griechen*; Perrot and Chipiez, *History of Art in Greece*; Woerman, *Die Landschaft in der Kunst der antiken Volker, see also books on Etruscan and Roman painting*.

GREECE AND THE GREEKS: The origin of the Greek race is not positively known. It is reasonably supposed that the early settlers in Greece came from the region of Asia Minor, either across the Hellespont or the sea, and populated the Greek islands and the mainland. When this was done has been matter of much conjecture. The early history is lost, but art remains show that in the period before Homer the Greeks were an established race with habits and customs distinctly individual. Egyptian and Asiatic influences are apparent in their art at this early time, but there is, nevertheless, the mark of a race peculiarly apart from all the races of the older world.

The development of the Greek people was probably helped by favorable climate and soil, by commerce and conquest, by republican institutions and political faith, by[22] freedom of mind and of body; but all these together are not sufficient to account for the keenness of intellect, the purity of taste, and the skill in accomplishment which showed in every branch of Greek life. The cause lies deeper in the fundamental make-up of the Greek mind, and its eternal aspiration toward mental, moral, and physical ideals. Perfect mind, perfect body, perfect conduct in this world were sought-for ideals. The Greeks aspired to completeness. The course of education and race development trained them physically as athletes and warriors, mentally as philosophers, law-makers, poets, artists, morally as heroes whose lives and actions emulated those of the gods, and were almost perfect for this world.

ART MOTIVES: Neither the monarchy nor the priesthood commanded the services of the artist in Greece, as in Assyria and Egypt. There was no monarch in an oriental sense, and the chosen leaders of the Greeks never, until the late days, arrogated art to themselves. It was something for all the people.

In religion there was a pantheon of gods established and worshipped from the earliest ages, but these gods were more like epitomes of Greek ideals than spiritual beings. They were the personified virtues of the Greeks, exemplars of perfect living; and in worshipping them the Greek was really worshipping order, conduct, repose, dignity, perfect life. The gods and heroes, as types of moral and physical qualities, were continually represented in an allegorical or legendary manner. Athene represented noble warfare, Zeus was majestic dignity and power, Aphrodite love, Phœbus song, Niké triumph, and all the lesser gods, nymphs, and fauns stood for beauties of nature or of life. The great bulk of Greek architecture, sculpture, and painting was put forth to honor these gods or heroes, and by so doing the artist repeated the national ideals and honored himself. The first motive of Greek art, then, was to praise[23] Hellas and the Hellenic view of life. In part it was a religious motive, but with little of that spiritual significance and belief which ruled in Egypt, and later on in Italy.

FIG. 11.—ATTIC GRAVE PAINTING.
(FROM BAUMEISTER.)

A second and ever-present motive in Greek painting was decoration. This appears in the tomb pottery of the earliest ages, and was carried on down to the latest times. Vase painting, wall painting, tablet and sculpture painting were all done with a decorative motive in view. Even the easel or panel pictures had some decorative effect about them, though they were primarily intended to convey ideas other than those of form and color.

SUBJECTS AND METHODS: The gods and heroes, their lives and adventures, formed the early subjects of Greek painting.[24] Certain themes taken from the "Iliad" and the "Odyssey" were as frequently shown as, afterward, the Annunciations in Italian painting. The traditional subjects, the Centaurs and Lapiths, the Amazon war, Theseus and Ariadne, Perseus and Andromeda, were frequently depicted. Humanity and actual Greek life came in for its share. Single figures, still-life, *genre*, caricature, all were shown, and as painting neared the Alexandrian age a semi-realistic portraiture came into vogue.

The materials employed by the Greeks and their methods of work are somewhat difficult to ascertain, because there are few Greek pictures, except those on the vases, left to us. From the confusing accounts of the ancient writers, the vases, some Greek slabs in Italy, and the Roman paintings imitative of the Greek, we may gain a general idea. The early Greek work was largely devoted to pottery and tomb decoration, in which much in manner and method was borrowed from Asia, Phœnicia, and Egypt. Later on, painting appeared in flat outline on stone or terra-cotta slabs, sometimes representing processional scenes, as in Egypt, and doubtless done in a hybrid fresco-work similar to the Egyptian method. Wall paintings were done in fresco and distemper, probably upon the walls themselves, and also upon panels afterward let into the wall. Encaustic painting (color mixed with wax upon the panel and fused with a hot spatula) came in with the Sikyonian school. It is possible that the oil medium and canvas were known, but not probable that either was ever used extensively.

There is no doubt about the Greeks being expert draughtsmen, though this does not appear until late in history. They knew the outlines well, and drew them with force and grace. That they modelled in strong relief is more questionable. Light-and-shade was certainly employed in the figure, but not in any modern way. Perspective in both figures and landscape was used; but the landscape was at first symbolic and[25] rarely got beyond a decorative background for the figure. Greek composition we know little about, but may infer that it was largely a series of balances, a symmetrical adjustment of objects to fill a given space with not very much freedom allowed to the artist. In atmosphere, sunlight, color, and those peculiarly sensuous charms that belong to painting, there is no reason to believe that the Greeks approached the moderns. Their interest was chiefly centred in the human figure. Landscape, with its many beauties, was reserved for modern hands to disclose. Color was used in abundance, without doubt, but it was probably limited to the leading hues, with little of that refinement or delicacy known in painting to-day.

ART HISTORY: For the history of Greek painting we have to rely upon the words of Aristotle, Plutarch, Pliny, Quintilian, Lucian, Cicero, Pausanias. Their accounts appear to be partly substantiated by the vase paintings, and such few slabs and Roman frescos as remain to us. There is no consecutive narrative. The story of painting originating from a girl seeing the wall-silhouette of her lover and filling it in with color, and the conjecture of painting having developed from embroidery work, have neither of them a foundation in fact. The earliest settlers of Greece probably learned painting from the Phœnicians, and employed it, after the Egyptian, Assyrian, and Phœnician manner, on pottery, terra-cotta slabs, and rude sculpture. It developed slower than sculpture perhaps; but were there anything of importance left to judge from, we should probably find that it developed in much the same manner as sculpture. Down to 500 B.C. there was little more than outline filled in with flat monochromatic paint and with a decorative effect similar, perhaps, to that of the vase paintings. After that date come the more important names of artists mentioned by the ancient writers. It is difficult to assign these artists to certain periods or schools, owing to the insufficient[26] knowledge we have about them. The following classifications and assignments may, therefore, in some instances, be questioned.

FIG. 12.—MUSE OF CORTONA, CORTONA MUSEUM.
Please click here for a modern color image

OLDER ATTIC SCHOOL: The first painter of rank was **Polygnotus** (fl. 475-455 B.C.), sometimes called the founder of Greek painting, because perhaps he was one of the first important painters in Greece proper. He seems to have been a good outline draughtsman, producing figures in profile, with little attempt at relief, perspective, or light-and-shade. His colors were local tones, but probably more like nature and more varied than anything in Egyptian painting. Landscapes, buildings, and the like, were given in a symbolic manner. Portraiture was a generalization, and in figure com[27]positions the names of the principal characters were written near them for purposes of identification. The most important works of Polygnotus were the wall paintings for the Assembly Room of the Knidians at Delphi. The subjects related to the Trojan War and the adventures of Ulysses.

Opposed to this flat, unrelieved style was the work of a follower, **Agatharchos** of Samos (fl. end of fifth century B.C.). He was a scene-painter, and by the necessities of his craft was led toward nature. Stage effect required a study of perspective, variation of light, and a knowledge of the laws of optics. The slight outline drawing of his predecessor was probably superseded by effective masses to create illusion. This was a distinct advance toward nature. **Apollodorus** (fl. end of fifth century B.C.) applied the principles of Agatharchos to figures. According to Plutarch, he was the first to discover variation in the shade of colors, and, according to Pliny, the first master to paint objects as they appeared in nature. He had the title of *skiagraphos* (shadow-painter), and possibly gave a semi-natural background with perspective. This was an improvement, but not a perfection. It is not likely that the backgrounds were other than conventional settings for the figure. Even these were not at once accepted by the painters of the period, but were turned to profit in the hands of the followers.

After the Peloponnesian Wars the art of painting seems to have flourished elsewhere than in Athens, owing to the Athenian loss of supremacy. Other schools sprang up in various districts, and one to call for considerable mention by the ancient writers was the

IONIAN SCHOOL, which in reality had existed from the sixth century. The painters of this school advanced upon the work of Apollodorus as regards realistic effect. **Zeuxis**, whose fame was at its height during the Peloponnesian Wars, seems to have regarded art as a matter of illusion, if one may judge by the stories told of his work.[28] The tale of his painting a bunch of grapes so like reality that the birds came to peck at them proves either that the painter's motive was deception, or that the narrator of the tale picked out the deceptive part of his picture for admiration. He painted many subjects, like Helen, Penelope, and many *genre* pieces on panel. Quintilian says he originated light-and-shade, an achievement credited by Plutarch to Apollodorus. It is probable that he advanced light-and-shade.

In illusion he seems to have been outdone by a rival, **Parrhasios** of Ephesus. Zeuxis deceived the birds with painted grapes, but Parrhasios deceived Zeuxis with a painted curtain. There must have been knowledge of color, modelling, and relief to have produced such an illusion, but the aim was petty and unworthy of the skill. There was evidently an advance technically, but some decline in the true spirit of art. Parrhasios finally suffered defeat at the hands of **Timanthes** of Kythnos, by a Contest between Ajax and Ulysses for the Arms of Achilles. Timanthes's famous work was the Sacrifice of Iphigenia, of which there is a supposed Pompeian copy.

SIKYONIAN SCHOOL: This school seems to have sprung up after the Peloponnesian Wars, and was perhaps founded by **Eupompos**, a contemporary of Parrhasios. His pupil **Pamphilos** brought the school to maturity. He apparently reacted from the deception motive of Zeuxis and Parrhasios, and taught academic methods of drawing, composing, and painting. He was also credited with bringing into use the encaustic method of painting, though it was probably known before his time. His pupil, **Pausias**, possessed some freedom of creation in *genre* and still-life subjects. Pliny says he had great technical skill, as shown in the foreshortening of a black ox by variations of the black tones, and he obtained some fame by a figure of Methè (Intoxication) drinking from a glass, the face being seen[29] through the glass. Again the motives seem trifling, but again advancing technical power is shown.

FIG. 13.—ODYSSEY LANDSCAPE, VATICAN.
(FROM WOLTMANN AND WOERMANN.)

THEBAN-ATTIC SCHOOL: This was the fourth school of Greek painting. **Nikomachus** (fl. about 360 B.C.), a facile painter, was at its head. His pupil,**Aristides**, painted pathetic scenes, and was perhaps as remarkable for teaching art to the celebrated **Euphranor** (fl. 360 B.C.) as for his own productions. Euphranor had great versatility in the arts, and in painting was renowned for his pictures of the Olympian gods at Athens. His successor, **Nikias** (fl. 340-300B.C.), was a contemporary of Praxiteles, the sculptor, and was possibly influenced by him in the painting of female figures. He was a technician of ability in composition, light-and-shade, and relief, and was praised for the roundness of his figures. He also did some tinting of sculpture, and is said to have tinted some of the works of Praxiteles.[30]

LATE PAINTERS: Contemporary with and following these last-named artists were some celebrated painters who really belong to the beginning of the Hellenistic Period (323 B.C.). At their head was **Apelles**, the painter of Philip and Alexander, and the climax of Greek painting. He painted many gods, heroes, and allegories, with much "gracefulness," as Pliny puts it. The Italian Botticelli, seventeen hundred years after him, tried to reproduce his celebrated Calumny, from Lucian's description of it. His chief works were his Aphrodite Anadyomene, carried to Rome by Augustus, and the portrait of Alexander with the Thunder-bolt. He was undoubtedly a superior man technically. **Protogenes** rivalled him, if we are to believe Petronius, by the foam on a dog's mouth and the wonder in the eye of a startled pheasant. **Aëtion**, the painter of Alexander's Marriage to Roxana, was not able to turn the aim of painting from this deceptive illusion. After Alexander, painting passed still further into the imitative and the theatrical, and when not grandiloquent was infinitely little over cobbler-shops and huckster-stalls. Landscape for purposes of decorative composition, and floor painting, done in mosaic, came in during the time of the Diadochi. There were no great names in the latter days, and such painters as still flourished passed on to Rome, there to produce copies of the works of their predecessors.

It is hard to reconcile the unworthy motive attributed to Greek painting by the ancient writers with the high aim of Greek sculpture. It is easier to think (and it is more probable) that the writers knew very little about art, and that they missed the spirit of Greek painting in admiring its insignificant details. That painting technically was at a high point of perfection as regards the figure, even the imitative Roman works indicate, and it can hardly be doubted that in spirit it was at one time equally strong.[31]

EXTANT REMAINS: There are few wall or panel pictures of Greek times in existence. Four slabs of stone in the Naples Museum, with red outline drawings of Theseus, Silenos, and some figures with masks, are probably Greek work from which the color has scaled. A number of Roman copies of Greek frescos and mosaics are in the Vatican, Capitoline, and Naples Museums. All these pieces show an imitation of late Hellenistic art—not the best period of Greek development.

Fig. 14.—AMPHORE, LOWER ITALY.

THE VASES: The history of Greek painting in its remains is traced with some accuracy in the decorative figures upon the vases. The first ware—dating before the seventh century B.C.—seems free from oriental influences in its designs. The vase is reddish, the decoration is in tiers, bands, or zig-zags, usually in black or brown, without the human figure. The second kind of ware dates from about the middle of the seventh century. It shows meander, wave, and other designs, and is called the "geometrical" style. Later on animals, rosettes, and vegetation appear that show Assyrian influence. The decoration is profuse and the rude human figure subordinate to it. The design is in black or dark-brown, on a cream-colored slip. The third kind of ware is the archaic or "strong" style. It dates from 500 B.C. to the Peloponnesian Wars, and is marked by black figures upon a yellow or red ground. White and purple are also used to define flesh, hair, and white objects. The figure is stiff, the action awkward, the composition is freer than before, but still conventional. The subjects are the gods, demi-gods, and heroes in scenes from their lives and adventures. The fourth kind of ware dates down into the Hellenistic age and shows red figures surrounded by a black ground. The figure, the drawing, the composition are better than at any other period and suggest a high excellence in other forms of Greek painting. After Alexander, vase painting seems to have shared the fate of wall and panel painting. There was a striving for effect, with ornateness and extravagance, and finally the art passed out entirely.

There was an establishment founded in Southern Italy which imitated the Greek and produced the Apulian ware, but the Romans gave little encouragement to vase painting, and about 65 B.C. it disappeared. Almost all the museums of the world have collections of Greek vases. The British, Berlin, and Paris collections are perhaps as complete as any.

[32]

ETRUSCAN AND ROMAN PAINTING.

BOOKS RECOMMENDED: See Bibliography of Greek Painting and also Dennis, *Cities and Cemeteries of Etruria*; Graul, *Die Portratgemalde aus den Grabstatten des Faiyum*; Helbig, *Die Wandgemalde Campaniens*; Helbig, *Untersuchungen uber die Campanische Wandmalerei*; Mau, *Geschichte der Decorativen Wandmalerei in Pompeii*; Martha, *L'Archéologie Étrusque et Romaine*.

ETRUSCAN PAINTING: Painting in Etruria has not a great deal of interest for us just here. It was largely decorative and sepulchral in motive, and was employed in the painting of tombs, and upon vases and other objects placed in the tombs. It had a native way of expressing itself, which at first was neither Greek nor Oriental, and yet a reminder of both. Technically it was not well done. Before 500 B.C. it was almost childish in the drawing. After that date the figures were better, though short and squat. Those on the vases usually show outline drawing filled in with dull browns and yellows. Finally there was a mingling of Etruscan with Greek elements, and an imitation of Greek methods. It was at best a hybrid art, but of some importance from an archæological point of view.

ROMAN PAINTING: Roman art is an appendix to the art history of Greece. It originated little in painting, and was content to perpetuate the traditions of Greece in an imitative way. What was worse, it copied the degeneracy of Greece by following the degenerate Hellenistic paintings. In motive and method it was substantially the same work as that of the Greeks under the Diadochi. The subjects, again, were often taken from Greek story, though there were Roman historical scenes, *genre* pieces, and many portraits.

FIG. 15.—RITUAL SCENE, PALATINE WALL PAINTING.
(FROM WOLTMANN AND WOERMANN.)

In the beginning of the Empire tablet or panel painting was rather abandoned in favor of mural decoration. That[33] is to say, figures or groups were painted in fresco on the wall and then surrounded by geometrical, floral, or architectural designs to give the effect of a panel let into the wall. Thus painting assumed a more decorative nature. Vitruvius says in effect that in the early days nature was followed in these wall paintings, but later on they became ornate and overdone, showing many unsupported architectural façades and impossible decorative framings. This can be traced in the Roman and Pompeian frescos. There were four kinds of these wall paintings. (1.) Those that covered all the walls of a room and did away with dado, frieze, and the like, such as figures with large landscape[34]backgrounds showing villas and trees. (2.) Small pictures separated or framed by pilasters. (3.) Panel pictures let into the wall or painted with that effect. (4.) Single figures with architectural backgrounds. The single figures were usually the best. They had grace of line and motion and all the truth to nature that decoration required. Some of the backgrounds were flat tints of red or black against which the figure was placed. In the larger pieces the com[35]position was rather rambling and disjointed, and the color harsh. In light-and-shade and relief they probably followed the Greek example.

FIG. 16.—PORTRAIT-HEAD.
(FROM FAYOUM, GRAF COL.)

ROMAN PAINTERS: During the first five centuries Rome was between the influences of Etruria and Greece. The first paintings in Rome of which there is record were done in the Temple of Ceres by the Greek artists of Lower Italy, **Gorgasos** and **Damophilos** (fl. 493 B.C.). They were doubtless somewhat like the vase paintings—profile work, without light, shade, or perspective. At the time and after Alexander Greek influence held sway. **Fabius Pictor** (fl. about 300 B.C.) is one of the celebrated names in historical painting, and later on **Pacuvius**, **Metrodorus**, and **Serapion** are mentioned. In the last century of the Republic,**Sopolis**, **Dionysius**, and **Antiochus Gabinius** excelled in portraiture. Ancient painting really ends for us with the destruction of Pompeii (79 A.D.), though after that there were interesting portraits produced, especially those found in the Fayoum (Egypt).[1]

[1]See Scribner's Magazine, vol. v., p. 219, New Series.

EXTANT REMAINS: The frescos that are left to us to-day are largely the work of mechanical decorators rather than creative artists. They are to be seen in Rome, in the Baths of Titus, the Vatican, Livia's Villa, Farnesina, Rospigliosi, and Barberini Palaces, Baths of Caracalla, Capitoline and Lateran Museums, in the houses of excavated Pompeii, and the Naples Museum. Besides these there are examples of Roman fresco and distemper in the Louvre and other European Museums. Examples of Etruscan painting are to be seen in the Vatican, Cortona, the Louvre, the British Museum and elsewhere.

[36]

CHAPTER IV.
ITALIAN PAINTING.
EARLY CHRISTIAN AND MEDIÆVAL PERIOD. 200-1250.

BOOKS RECOMMENDED: Bayet, *L'Art Byzantin*; Bennett, *Christian Archæology*; Bosio, *La Roma Sotterranea*; Burckhardt, *The Cicerone, an Art Guide to Painting in Italy, ed. by Crowe*; Crowe and Cavalcaselle, *New History of Painting in Italy*; De Rossi, *La Roma Sotterranea Cristiana*; De Rossi, *Bullettino di Archeologia Cristiana*; Didron, *Christian Iconography*; Eastlake (Kügler's), *Handbook of Painting—The Italian Schools*; Garrucci, *Storia dell' Arte Cristiana*; Gerspach, *La Mosaïque*; Lafenestre, *La Peinture Italienne*; Lanzi,*History of Painting in Italy*; Lecoy de la Marche, *Les Manuscrits et la Miniature*; Lindsay, *Sketches of the History of Christian Art*; Martigny, *Dictionnaire des Antiques Chrétiennes*; Pératé, *L'Archeologie Chretienne*; Reber, *History of Mediæval Art*; Rio, *Poetry of Christian Art*; Lethaby, *Medieval Art*; Smith and Cheetham, *Dictionary of Christian Antiquities*.

RISE OF CHRISTIANITY: Out of the decaying civilization of Rome sprang into life that remarkable growth known as Christianity. It was not welcomed by the Romans. It was scoffed at, scourged, persecuted, and, at one time, nearly exterminated. But its vitality was stronger than that of its persecutor, and when Rome declined, Christianity utilized the things that were Roman, while striving to live for ideas that were Christian.

FIG. 17.—CHAMBER IN CATACOMBS, SHOWING WALL DECORATION.

There was no revolt, no sudden change. The Christian idea made haste slowly, and at the start it was weighed down with many paganisms. The Christians themselves in[37] all save religious faith, were Romans, and inherited Roman tastes, manners, and methods. But the Roman world, with all its classicism and learning, was dying. The decline socially and intellectually was with the Christians as well as the Romans. There was good reason for it. The times were out of joint, and almost everything was disorganized, worn out, decadent. The military life of the Empire had begun to give way to the monastic and feudal life of the Church. Quarrels and wars between the powers kept life at fever heat. In the fifth century came the inpouring of the Goths and Huns, and with them the sacking and plunder[38] of the land. Misery and squalor, with intellectual blackness, succeeded. Art, science, literature, and learning degenerated to mere shadows of their former selves, and a semi-barbarism reigned for five centuries. During all this dark period Christian painting struggled on in a feeble way, seeking to express itself. It started Roman in form, method, and even, at times, in subject; it ended Christian, but not without a long period of gradual transition, during which it was influenced from many sources and underwent many changes.

ART MOTIVES: As in the ancient world, there were two principal motives for painting in early Christian times—religion and decoration. Religion was the chief motive, but Christianity was a very different religion from that of the Greeks and Romans. The Hellenistic faith was a worship of nature, a glorification of humanity, an exaltation of physical and moral perfections. It dealt with the material and the tangible, and Greek art appealed directly to the sensuous and earthly nature of mankind. The Hebraic faith or Christianity was just the opposite of this. It decried the human, the flesh, and the worldly. It would have nothing to do with the beauty of this earth. Its hopes were centred upon the life hereafter. The teaching of Christ was the humility and the abasement of the human in favor of the spiritual and the divine. Where Hellenism appealed to the senses, Hebraism appealed to the spirit. In art the fine athletic figure, or, for that matter, any figure, was an abomination. The early Church fathers opposed it. It was forbidden by the Mosaic decalogue and savored of idolatry.

But what should take its place in art? How could the new Christian ideas be expressed without form? Symbolism came in, but it was insufficient. A party in the Church rose up in favor of more direct representation. Art should be used as an engine of the Church to teach the Bible to[39] those who could not read. This argument held good, and notwithstanding the opposition of the Iconoclastic party painting grew in favor. It lent itself to teaching and came under ecclesiastical domination. As it left the nature of the classic world and loosened its grasp on things tangible it became feeble and decrepit in its form. While it grew in sentiment and religious fervor it lost in bodily vigor and technical ability.

FIG. 18.—CATACOMB FRESCO. CRYPT OF S. CECILIA. THIRD CENTURY.

For many centuries the religious motive held strong, and art was the servant of the Church. It taught the Bible truths, but it also embellished and adorned the interiors of the churches. All the frescos, mosaics, and altar-pieces had a decorative motive in their coloring and setting. The church building was a house of refuge for the oppressed, and it was made attractive not only in its lines and proportions but in its ornamentation. Hence the two motives of the early work—religious teaching and decoration.

SUBJECTS AND TECHNICAL METHODS: There was no distinct Judaic or Christian type used in the very early art. The painters took their models directly from the Roman frescos and marbles. It was the classic figure and the classic cos[40]tume, and those who produced the painting of the early period were the degenerate painters of the classic world. The figure was rather short and squat, coarse in the joints, hands, and feet, and almost expressionless in the face. Christian life at that time was passion-strung, but the faces in art do not show it, for the reason that the Roman frescos were the painter's model, not the people of the Christian community about him. There was nothing like a realistic presentation at this time. The type alone was given.

In the drawing it was not so good as that shown in the Roman and Pompeian frescos. There was a mechanism about its production, a copying by unskilled hands, a negligence or an ignorance of form that showed everywhere. The coloring, again, was a conventional scheme of flat tints in reddish-browns and bluish-greens, with heavy outline bands of brown. There was little perspective or background, and the figures in panels were separated by vines, leaves, or other ornamental division lines. Some relief was given to the figure by the brown outlines. Light-and-shade was not well rendered, and composition was formal. The great part of this early work was done in fresco after the Roman formula, and was executed on the walls of the Catacombs. Other forms of art showed in the gilded glasses, in manuscript illumination, and, later, in the mosaics.

Technically the work begins to decline from the beginning in proportion as painting was removed from the knowledge of the ancient world. About the fifth century the figure grew heavy and stiff A new type began to show itself. The Roman toga was exchanged for the long liturgical garment which hid the proportions of the body, the lines grew hard and dark, a golden nimbus appeared about the head, and the patriarchal in appearance came into art. The youthful Orphic face of Christ changed to a solemn visage, with large, round eyes, saint-like beard, and melancholy air. The classic qualities were fast disappearing.[41] Eastern types and elements were being introduced through Byzantium. Oriental ornamentation, gold embossing, rich color were doing away with form, perspective, light-and-shade, and background.

FIG. 19.—CHRIST AS GOOD SHEPHERD. MOSAIC, RAVENNA, FIFTH CENTURY.
Please click here for a modern color image

The color was rich and the mechanical workmanship fair for the time, but the figure had become paralytic. It shrouded itself in a sack-like brocaded gown, had no feet at times, and instead of standing on the ground hung in the air. Facial expression ran to contorted features, holiness became moroseness, and sadness sulkiness. The flesh was brown, the shadows green-tinted, giving an unhealthy look to the faces. Add to this the gold ground (a Persian inheritance), the gilded high lights, the absence of perspective, and the composing of groups so that the figures looked piled one upon another instead of receding, and we have the style of painting that prevailed in Byzantium and Italy from about the ninth to the thirteenth century. Nothing of a technical nature was in its favor except the rich coloring and the mechanical adroitness of the fitting.[42]

EARLY CHRISTIAN PAINTING: The earliest Christian painting appeared on the walls of the Catacombs in Rome. These were decorated with panels and within the panels were representations of trailing vines, leaves, fruits, flowers, with birds and little genii or cupids. It was painting similar to the Roman work, and had no Christian significance though in a Christian place. Not long after, however, the desire to express something of the faith began to show itself in a symbolic way. The cups and the vases became marked with the fish, because the Greek spelling of the word "icthus" gave the initials of the Christian confession of faith. The paintings of the shepherd bearing a sheep symbolized Christ and his flock; the anchor meant the Christian hope; the phœnix immortality; the ship the Church; the cock watchfulness, and so on. And at this time the decorations began to have a double meaning. The vine came to represent the "I am the vine" and the birds grew longer wings and became doves, symbolizing pure Christian souls.

It has been said this form of art came about through fear of persecution, that the Christians hid their ideas in symbols because open representation would be followed by violence and desecration. Such was hardly the case. The emperors persecuted the living, but the dead and their sepulchres were exempt from sacrilege by Roman law. They probably used the symbol because they feared the Roman figure and knew no other form to take its place. But symbolism did not supply the popular need; it was impossible to originate an entirely new figure; so the painters went back and borrowed the old Roman form. Christ appeared as a beardless youth in Phrygian costume, the Virgin Mary was a Roman matron, and the Apostles looked like Roman senators wearing the toga.

Classic story was also borrowed to illustrate Bible truth. Hermes carrying the sheep was the Good Shepherd, Psyche discovering Cupid was the curiosity of Eve, Ulysses clos[43]ing his ears to the Sirens was the Christian resisting the tempter. The pagan Orpheus charming the animals of the wood was finally adopted as a symbol, or perhaps an ideal likeness of Christ. Then followed more direct representation in classic form and manner, the Old Testament prefiguring and emphasizing the New. Jonah appeared cast into the sea and cast by the whale on dry land again as a symbol of the New Testament resurrection, and also as a representation of the actual occurrence. Moses striking the rock symbolized life eternal, and David slaying Goliath was Christ victorious.

FIG. 20.—CHRIST AND SAINTS. FRESCO. S. GENEROSA, SEVENTH CENTURY (?).

The chronology of the Catacombs painting is very much mixed, but it is quite certain there was degeneracy from the start. The cause was neglect of form, neglect of art as art, mechanical copying instead of nature study, and finally, the predominance of the religious idea over the forms of nature. With Constantine Christianity was recognized as the national religion. Christian art came out of the Catacombs and began to show itself in illuminations, mosaics, and church decorations. Notwithstanding it was now free from restraint it did not improve. Church traditions prevailed,[44] sentiment bordered upon sentimentality, and the technic of painting passed from bad to worse.

The decline continued during the sixth and seventh centuries, owing somewhat perhaps to the influence of Byzantium and the introduction into Italy of Eastern types and elements. In the eighth century the Iconoclastic controversy broke out again in fury with the edict of Leo the Isaurian. This controversy was a renewal of the old quarrel in the Church about the use of pictures and images. Some wished them for instruction in the Word; others decried them as leading to idolatry. It was a long quarrel of over a hundred years' duration, and a deadly one for art. When it ended, the artists were ordered to follow the traditions, not to make any new creations, and not to model any figure in the round. The nature element in art was quite dead at that time, and the order resulted only in diverting the course of painting toward the unrestricted miniatures and manuscripts. The native Italian art was crushed for a time by this new ecclesiastical burden. It did not entirely disappear, but it gave way to the stronger, though equally restricted art that had been encroaching upon it for a long time—the art of Byzantium.

BYZANTINE PAINTING: Constantinople was rebuilt and rechristened by Constantine, a Christian emperor, in the year 328 A.D. It became a stronghold of Christian traditions, manners, customs, art. But it was not quite the same civilization as that of Rome and the West. It was bordered on the south and east by oriental influences, and much of Eastern thought, method, and glamour found its way into the Christian community. The artists fought this influence, stickling a long time for the severer classicism of ancient Greece. For when Rome fell the traditions of the Old World centred around Constantinople. But classic form was ever being encroached upon by oriental richness of material and color. The struggle was a long but hopeless one. As in[45] Italy, form failed century by century. When, in the eighth century, the Iconoclastic controversy cut away the little Greek existing in it, the oriental ornament was about all that remained.

FIG. 21.—EZEKIEL BEFORE THE LORD. MS. ILLUMINATION. PARIS, NINTH CENTURY.

There was no chance for painting to rise under the prevailing conditions. Free artistic creation was denied the artist. An advocate of painting at the Second Nicene Council declared that: "It is not the invention of the painter that creates the picture, but an inviolable law of the Catholic Church. It is not the painter but the holy fathers who have to invent and dictate. To them manifestly belongs the composition, to the painter only the execution." Painting was in a strait-jacket. It had to follow precedent and copy what had gone before in old Byzantine patterns. Both in Italy and in Byzantium the creative artist had passed away in favor of the skilled artisan—the repeater of time-honored forms or colors. The workmanship was good for the time, and the coloring and ornamental borders made a rich setting, but the real life of art had gone. A long period of heavy, morose, almost formless art, eloquent of mediæval darkness and ignorance, followed.

It is strange that such an art should be adopted by[46] foreign nations, and yet it was. Its bloody crucifixions and morbid madonnas were well fitted to the dark view of life held during the Middle Ages, and its influence was wide-spread and of long duration. It affected French and German art, it ruled at the North, and in the East it lives even to this day. That it strongly affected Italy is a very apparent fact. Just when it first began to show its influence there is matter of dispute. It probably gained a foothold at Ravenna in the sixth century, when that province became a part of the empire of Justinian. Later it permeated Rome, Sicily, and Naples at the south, and Venice at the north. With the decline of the early Christian art of Italy this richer, and in many ways more acceptable, Byzantine art came in, and, with Italian modifications, usurped the field. It did not literally crush out the native Italian art, but practically it superseded it, or held it in check, from the ninth to the twelfth century. After that the corrupted Italian art once more came to the front.

EARLY CHRISTIAN AND BYZANTINE REMAINS: The best examples of Early Christian painting are still to be seen in the Catacombs at Rome. Mosaics in the early churches of Rome, Ravenna, Naples, Venice, Constantinople. Sculptures, ivories, and glasses in the Lateran, Ravenna, and Vatican museums. Illuminations in Vatican and Paris libraries. Almost all the museums of Europe, those of the Vatican and Naples particularly, have some examples of Byzantine work. The older altar-pieces of the early Italian churches date back to the mediæval period and show Byzantine influence. The altar-pieces of the Greek and Russian churches show the same influence even in modern work.

CHAPTER V.
ITALIAN PAINTING.
GOTHIC PERIOD. 1250-1400.

BOOKS RECOMMENDED: As before, Burckhardt, Crowe and Cavalcaselle, Eastlake, Lafenestre, Lanzi, Lindsay, Reber; also Burton,*Catalogue of Pictures in the National Gallery, London (unabridged edition)*; Cartier, *Vie de Fra Angelico*; Förster, *Leben und Werke des Fra Angelico*; Habich, *Vade Mecum pour la Peinture Italienne des Anciens Maîtres*; Lacroix, *Les Arts au Moyen-Age et à la Époque de la Renaissance*; Mantz, *Les Chefs-d'œuvre de la Peinture Italienne*; Morelli, *Italian Masters in German Galleries*; Morelli, *Italian Masters, Critical Studies in their Works*; Rumohr, *Italienische Forschungen*; Selincourt, *Giotto*; Stillman, *Old Italian Masters*; Vasari,*Lives of the Most Eminent Painters*; consult also General Bibliography (p. xv).

SIGNS OF THE AWAKENING: It would seem at first as though nothing but self-destruction could come to that struggling, praying, throat-cutting population that terrorized Italy during the Mediæval Period. The people were ignorant, the rulers treacherous, the passions strong, and yet out of the Dark Ages came light. In the thirteenth century the light grew brighter, but the internal dissensions did not cease. The Hohenstaufen power was broken, the imperial rule in Italy was crushed. Pope and emperor no longer warred each other, but the cries of "Guelf" and "Ghibelline" had not died out.

Throughout the entire Romanesque and Gothic periods (1000-1400) Italy was torn by political wars, though the[48] free cities, through their leagues of protection and their commerce, were prosperous. A commercial rivalry sprang up among the cities. Trade with the East, manufactures, banking, all flourished; and even the philosophies, with law, science, and literature, began to be studied. The spirit of learning showed itself in the founding of schools and universities. Dante, Petrarch, and Boccaccio, reflecting respectively religion, classic learning, and the inclination toward nature, lived and gave indication of the trend of thought. Finally the arts, architecture, sculpture, painting, began to stir and take upon themselves new appearances.

SUBJECTS AND METHODS: In painting, though there were some portraits and allegorical scenes produced during the Gothic period, the chief theme was Bible story. The Church was the patron, and art was only the servant, as it had been from the beginning. It was the instructor and consoler of the faithful, a means whereby the Church made converts, and an adornment of wall and altar. It had not entirely escaped from symbolism. It was still the portrayal of things for what they meant, rather than for what they looked. There was no such thing then as art for art's sake. It was art for religion's sake.

The demand for painting increased, and its subjects multiplied with the establishment at this time of the two powerful orders of Dominican and Franciscan monks. The first exacted from the painters more learned and instructive work; the second wished for the crucifixions, the martyrdoms, the dramatic deaths, wherewith to move people by emotional appeal. To offset this the ultra-religious character of painting was encroached upon somewhat by the growth of the painters' guilds, and art production largely passing into the hands of laymen. In consequence painting produced many themes, but, as yet, only after the Byzantine style. The painter was more of a workman than an artist. The Church had more use for his fingers than for[49] his creative ability. It was his business to transcribe what had gone before. This he did, but not without signs here and there of uneasiness and discontent with the pattern. There was an inclination toward something truer to nature, but, as yet, no great realization of it. The study of nature came in very slowly, and painting was not positive in statement until the time of Giotto and Lorenzetti.

FIG. 22.—GIOTTO, FLIGHT INTO EGYPT. ARENA CHAP. PADUA.
Please click here for a modern color image

The best paintings during the Gothic period were executed upon the walls of the churches in fresco. The prepared color was laid on wet plaster, and allowed to soak in. The small altar and panel pictures were painted in distemper, the gold ground and many Byzantine features being retained by most of the painters, though discarded by some few.[50]

CHANGES IN THE TYPE, ETC.: The advance of Italian art in the Gothic age was an advance through the development of the imposed Byzantine pattern. It was not a revolt or a starting out anew on a wholly original path. When people began to stir intellectually the artists found that the old Byzantine model did not look like nature. They began, not by rejecting it, but by improving it, giving it slight movements here and there, turning the head, throwing out a hand, or shifting the folds of drapery. The Eastern type was still seen in the long pathetic face, oblique eyes, green flesh tints, stiff robes, thin fingers, and absence of feet; but the painters now began to modify and enliven it. More realistic Italian faces were introduced, architectural and landscape backgrounds encroached upon the Byzantine gold grounds, even portraiture was taken up.

This looks very much like realism, but we must not lay too much stress upon it. The painters were taking notes of natural appearances. It showed in features like the hands, feet, and drapery; but the anatomy of the body had not yet been studied, and there is no reason to believe their study of the face was more than casual, nor their portraits more than records from memory.

No one painter began this movement. The whole artistic region of Italy was at that time ready for the advance. That all the painters moved at about the same pace, and continued to move at that pace down to the fifteenth century, that they all based themselves upon Byzantine teaching, and that they all had a similar style of working is proved by the great difficulty in attributing their existing pictures to certain masters, or even certain schools. There are plenty of pictures in Italy to-day that might be attributed to either Florence or Sienna, Giotto or Lorenzetti, or some other master; because though each master and each school had slight peculiarities, yet they all had a common origin in the art traditions of the time.[51]

FIG. 23.—ORCAGNA, PARADISE (DETAIL). S. M. NOVELLA, FLORENCE.

FLORENTINE SCHOOL: Cimabue (1240?-1302?) seems the most notable instance in early times of a Byzantine-educated painter who improved upon the traditions. He has been called the father of Italian painting, but Italian painting had no father. Cimabue was simply a man of more originality and ability than his contemporaries, and departed further from the art teachings of the time without decidedly opposing them. He retained the Byzantine pattern, but loosened the lines of drapery somewhat, turned the head to one side, infused the figure with a little appearance of life. His contemporaries elsewhere in Italy were doing the same thing, and none of them was any more than a link in the progressive chain.[52]

Cimabue's pupil, **Giotto** (1266?-1337), was a great improver on all his predecessors because he was a man of extraordinary genius. He would have been great in any time, and yet he was not great enough to throw off wholly the Byzantine traditions. He tried to do it. He studied nature in a general way, changed the type of face somewhat by making the jaw squarer, and gave it expression and nobility. To the figure he gave more motion, dramatic gesture, life. The drapery was cast in broader, simpler masses, with some regard for line, and the form and movement of the body were somewhat emphasized through it. In methods Giotto was more knowing, but not essentially different from his contemporaries; his subjects were from the common stock of religious story; but his imaginative force and invention were his own. Bound by the conventionalities of his time he could still create a work of nobility and power. He came too early for the highest achievement. He had genius, feeling, fancy, almost everything except accurate knowledge of the laws of nature and art. His art was the best of its time, but it still lacked, nor did that of his immediate followers go much beyond it technically.

Taddeo Gaddi (1300?-1366?) was Giotto's chief pupil, a painter of much feeling, but lacking in the large elements of construction and in the dramatic force of his master. **Agnolo Gaddi** (1333?-1396?), **Antonio Veneziano** (1312?-1388?), **Giovanni da Milano** (fl. 1366), **Andrea da Firenze** (fl. 1377), were all followers of the Giotto methods, and were so similar in their styles that their works are often confused and erroneously attributed. **Giottino** (1324?-1357?) was a supposed imitator of Giotto, of whom little is known. **Orcagna** (1329?-1376?) still further advanced the Giottesque type and method. He gathered up and united in himself all the art teachings of his time. In working out problems of form and in delicacy and charm of expression he went beyond his predecessors. He was[53] a many-sided genius, knowing not only in a matter of natural appearance, but in color problems, in perspective, shadows, and light. His art was further along toward the Renaissance than that of any other Giottesque. He almost changed the character of painting, and yet did not live near enough to the fifteenth century to accomplish it completely. **Spinello Aretino** (1332?-1410?) was the last of the great Giotto followers. He carried out the teachings of the school in technical features, such as composition, drawing, and relief by color rather than by light, but he lacked the creative power of Giotto. In fact, none of the Giottesque can be said to have improved upon the master, taking him as a whole. Toward the beginning of the fifteenth century the school rather declined.

SIENNESE SCHOOL: The art teachings and traditions of the past seemed deeper rooted at Sienna than at Florence. Nor was there so much attempt to shake them off as at Florence. Giotto broke the immobility of the Byzantine model by showing the draped figure in action. So also did the Siennese to some extent, but they cared more for the expression of the spiritual than the beauty of the natural. The Florentines were robust, resolute, even a little coarse at times; the Siennese were more refined and sentimental. Their fancy ran to sweetness of face rather than to bodily vigor. Again, their art was more ornate, richer in costume, color, and detail than Florentine art; but it was also more finical and narrow in scope.

FIG. 24.—A. LORENZETTI. PEACE (DETAIL). TOWN-HALL, SIENNA.

There was little advance upon Byzantinism in the work of **Guido da Sienna** (fl. 1275). Even **Duccio** (1260?——?), the real founder of the Siennese school, retained Byzantine[54] methods and adopted the school subjects, but he perfected details of form, such as the hands and feet, and while retaining the long Byzantine face, gave it a melancholy tenderness of expression. He possessed no dramatic force, but had a refined workmanship for his time—a workmanship perhaps better, all told, than that of his Florentine contemporary, Cimabue. **Simone di Martino** (1283?-1344?) changed the type somewhat by rounding the form. His drawing was not always correct, but in color he was good and in detail exact and minute. He probably profited somewhat by the example of Giotto.

The Siennese who came the nearest to Giotto's excellence were the brothers **Ambrogio** (fl. 1342) and **Pietro** (fl. 1350) **Lorenzetti**. There is little known about them except that they worked together in a similar manner. The most of their work has perished, but what remains shows an intellectual grasp equal to any of the age. The Sienna frescos by Ambrogio Lorenzetti are strong in facial character, and some of the figures, like that of the white-robed Peace, are beautiful in their flow of line. **Lippo Memmi** (?-1356), **Bartolo di Fredi** (1330-1410), and **Taddeo di Bartolo** (1362-1422), were other painters of the school. The late men rather carried detail to excess, and the school grew conventional instead of advancing.

TRANSITION PAINTERS: Several painters, **Starnina** (1354-1413), **Gentile da Fabriano** (1360?-1440?), **Fra Angelico** (1387-1455), have been put down in art history as the makers of the transition from Gothic to Renaissance painting. They hardly deserve the title. There was no transition. The development went on, and these painters, coming late in the fourteenth century and living into the fifteenth, simply showed the changing style, the advance in the study of nature and the technic of art. Starnina's work gave strong evidence of the study of form, but it was no such work as Masaccio's. There is always a little of the past in[55] the present, and these painters showed traces of Byzantinism in details of the face and figure, in coloring, and in gold embossing.

Gentile had all that nicety of finish and richness of detail and color characteristic of the Siennese. Being closer to the Renaissance than his predecessors he was more of a nature student. He was the first man to show the effect of sunlight in landscape, the first one to put a gold sun in the sky. He never, however, outgrew Gothic methods and really belongs in the fourteenth century. This is true of Fra Angelico. Though he lived far into the Early Renaissance he did not change his style and manner of work in conformity with the work of others about him. He was the last inheritor of the Giottesque traditions. Religious sentiment was the strong feature of his art. He was behind Giotto and Lorenzetti in power and in imagination, and behind Orcagna as a painter. He knew little of light, shade, perspective, and color, and in characterization was feeble, except in some late work. One face or type answered him for all classes of people—a sweet, fair face, full of divine tenderness. His art had enough nature in it to express his meanings, but little more. He was pre-eminently a devout painter, and really the last of the great religionists in painting.

FIG. 25.—FRA ANGELICO. ANGEL (DETAIL). UFFIZI.

The other regions of Italy had not at this time developed schools of painting of sufficient consequence to mention.[56]

PRINCIPAL WORKS: FLORENTINES—**Cimabue**, Madonnas S. M. Novella and Acad. Florence, frescos Upper Church of Assisi (?); **Giotto**, frescos Upper and Lower churches Assisi, best work Arena chapel Padua, Bardi and Peruzzi chapels S. Croce, injured frescos Bargello Florence; **Taddeo Gaddi**, frescos entrance wall Baroncelli chapel S. Croce, Spanish chapel S. M. Novella (designed by Gaddi (?)); **Agnolo Gaddi** frescos in choir S. Croce, S. Jacopo tra Fossi Florence, panel pictures Florence Acad.; **Giovanni da Milano**, Bewailing of Christ Florence Acad., Virgin enthroned Prato Gal., altar-piece Uffizi Gal., frescos S. Croce Florence; **Antonio Veneziano**, frescos in ceiling of Spanish chapel, S. M. Novella, Campo Santo Pisa; **Orcagna**, altar-piece Last Judgment and Paradise Strozzi chapel S. M. Novella, S. Zenobio Duomo, Saints Medici chapel S. Croce, Descent of Holy Spirit Badia Florence, altar-piece Nat. Gal. Lon.; **Spinello Aretino**, Life of St. Benedict S. Miniato al Monte near Florence, Annunciation Convent degl' Innocenti Arezzo, frescos Campo Santo Pisa, Coronation Florence Acad., Barbarossa frescos Palazzo Publico Sienna; **Andrea da Firenze**, Church Militant, Calvary, Crucifixion Spanish chapel, Upper series of Life of S. Raniera Campo Santo Pisa.

SIENNESE—**Guido da Sienna**, Madonna S. Domenico Sienna; **Duccio**, panels Duomo and Acad. Sienna, Madonna Nat. Gal. Lon.; **Simone di Martino**, frescos Palazzo Pubblico, Sienna, altar-piece and panels Seminario Vescovile, Pisa Gal., altar-piece and Madonna Opera del Duomo Orvieto; **Lippo Memmi**, frescos Palazzo del Podesta S. Gemignano, Annunciation Uffizi Florence; **Bartolo di Fredi**, altar-pieces Acad. Sienna, S. Francesco Montalcino; **Taddeo di Bartolo**, Palazzo Pubblico Sienna, Duomo, S. Gemignano, S. Francesco Pisa; **Ambrogio**

Lorenzetti, frescos Palazzo Pubblico Sienna, Triumph of Death (with Pietro Lorenzetti) Campo Santo Pisa, St. Francis frescos Lower Church Assisi, S. Francesco and S. Agostino Sienna, Annunciation Sienna Acad., Presentation Florence Acad.; **Pietro Lorenzetti**, Virgin S. Ansano, altar-pieces Duomo Sienna, Parish Church of Arezzo (worked with his brother Ambrogio).

TRANSITION PAINTERS: Starnina, frescos Duomo Prato (completed by pupil); **Gentile da Fabriano**, Adoration Florence Acad., Coronation Brera Milan, Madonna Duomo Orvieto; **Fra Angelico**, Coronation and many small panels Uffizi, many pieces Life of Christ Florence Acad., other pieces S. Marco Florence, Last Judgment Duomo, Orvieto.

[57]
CHAPTER VI.
ITALIAN PAINTING.
EARLY RENAISSANCE. 1400-1500.

BOOKS RECOMMENDED: As before, Burckhardt, Crowe and Cavalcaselle, Eastlake, Lafenestre, Lanzi, Habich, Lacroix, Mantz, Morelli, Burton, Rumohr, Stillman, Vasari; also Crowe and Cavalcaselle, *History of Painting in North Italy*; Berenson, *Florentine Painters of Renaissance*; Berenson, *Venetian Painters of Renaissance*; Berenson, *Central Italian Painters of Renaissance*; *Study and Criticism of Italian Art*; Boschini, *La Carta del Navegar*; Calvi, *Memorie della Vita ed opere di Francesco Raibolini*; Cibo, *Niccolo Alunno e la scuola Umbra*; Citadella, *Notizie relative a Ferrara*; Cruttwell, *Verrocchio*; Cruttwell, *Pollaiuolo*; Morelli, Anonimo, *Notizie*; Mezzanotte, *Commentario della Vita di Pietro Vanucci*; Mundler, *Essai d'une Analyse critique de la Notice des tableaux Italiens au Louvre*; Muntz, *Les Précurseurs de la Renaissance*; Muntz, *La Renaissance en Italie et en France*; Patch, *Life of Masaccio*; Hill, Pisanello, *Publications of the Arundel Society*; Richter, *Italian Art in National Gallery, London*; Ridolfi, *Le Meraviglie dell' Arte*; Rosini, *Storia della Pittura Italiana*; Schnaase, *Geschichte der bildenden Kunste*; Symonds, *Renaissance in Italy—the Fine Arts*; Vischer, *Lucas Signorelli und die Italienische Renaissance*; Waagen, *Art Treasures*; Waagen, *Andrea Mantegna und Luca Signorelli* (in *Raumer's Taschenbuch*, (1850)); Zanetti, *Della Pittura Veneziana*.

THE ITALIAN MIND: There is no way of explaining the Italian fondness for form and color other than by considering the necessities of the people and the artistic character of the Italian mind. Art in all its phases was not only an adornment but a necessity of Christian civilization. The Church taught people by sculpture, mosaic, miniature, and fresco. It was an object-teaching, a grasping of ideas by[58] forms seen in the mind, not a presenting of abstract ideas as in literature. Printing was not known. There were few manuscripts, and the majority of people could not read. Ideas came to them for centuries through form and color, until at last the Italian mind took on a plastic and pictorial character. It saw things in symbolic figures, and when the Renaissance came and art took the lead as one of its strongest expressions, painting was but the color-thought and form-language of the people.

FIG. 26.—FRA FILIPPO. MADONNA. UFFIZI.
Please click here for a modern color image

And these people, by reason of their peculiar education, were an exacting people, knowing what was good and demanding it from the artists. Every Italian was, in a way, an art critic, because every church in Italy was an art school. The artists may have led the people, but the people spurred on the artists, and so the Italian mind went on developing and unfolding until at last it produced the great art of the Renaissance.

THE AWAKENING: The Italian civilization of the fourteenth century was made up of many impulses and inclinations, none of them very strongly defined. There was a feeling about in the dark, a groping toward the light, but the lead[59]ers stumbled often on the road. There was good reason for it. The knowledge of the ancient world lay buried under the ruins of Rome. The Italians had to learn it all over again, almost without a precedent, almost without a preceptor. With the fifteenth century the horizon began to brighten. The Early Renaissance was begun. It was not a revolt, a reaction, or a starting out on a new path. It was a development of the Gothic period; and the three inclinations of the Gothic period—religion, the desire for classic knowledge, and the study of nature—were carried into the art of the time with greater realization.

The inference must not be made that because nature and the antique came to be studied in Early Renaissance times that therefore religion was neglected. It was not. It still held strong, and though with the Renaissance there came about a strange mingling of crime and corruption, æstheticism and immorality, yet the Church was never abandoned for an hour. When enlightenment came, people began to doubt the spiritual power of the Papacy. They did not cringe to it so servilely as before. Religion was not violently embraced as in the Middle Ages, but there was no revolt. The Church held the power and was still the patron of art. The painter's subjects extended over nature, the antique, the fable, allegory, history, portraiture; but the religious subject was not neglected. Fully three-quarters of all the fifteenth-century painting was done for the Church, at her command, and for her purposes.

But art was not so wholly pietistic as in the Gothic age. The study of nature and the antique materialized painting somewhat. The outside world drew the painter's eyes, and the beauty of the religious subject and its sentiment were somewhat slurred for the beauty of natural appearances. There was some loss of religious power, but religion had much to lose. In the fifteenth century it was still dominant.[60]

FIG. 27.—BOTTICELLI. CORONATION OF MADONNA. UFFIZI.
Please click here for a modern color image

KNOWLEDGE OF THE ANTIQUE AND NATURE: The revival of antique learning came about in real earnest during this period. The scholars set themselves the task of restoring the polite learning of ancient Greece, studying coins and marbles, collecting manuscripts, founding libraries and schools of philosophy. The wealthy nobles, Palla Strozzi, the Albizzi, the Medici, and the Dukes of Urbino, encouraged it. In 1440 the Greek was taught in five cities. Immediately afterward, with Constantinople falling into the hands of the Turks, came an influx of Greek scholars into Italy. Then followed the invention of printing and the age of discovery on land and sea. Not the antique alone but the natural were being pried into by the spirit of inquiry. Botany, geology, astronomy, chemistry, medicine, anatomy, law, lit[61]erature—nothing seemed to escape the keen eye of the time. Knowledge was being accumulated from every source, and the arts were all reflecting it.

The influence of the newly discovered classic marbles upon painting was not so great as is usually supposed. The painters studied them, but did not imitate them. Occasionally in such men as Botticelli and Mantegna we see a following of sculpturesque example—a taking of details and even of whole figures—but the general effect of the antique marbles was to impress the painters with the idea that nature was at the bottom of it all. They turned to the earth not only to study form and feature, but to learn perspective, light, shadow, color—in short, the technical features of art. True, religion was the chief subject, but nature and the antique were used to give it setting. All the fifteenth-century painting shows nature study, force, character, sincerity; but it does not show elegance, grace, or the full complement of color. The Early Renaissance was the promise of great things; the High Renaissance was the fulfilment.

FLORENTINE SCHOOL: The Florentines were draughtsmen more than colorists. The chief medium was fresco on the walls of buildings, and architectural necessities often dictated the form of compositions. Distemper in easel pictures was likewise used, and oil-painting, though known, was not extensively employed until the last quarter of the century. In technical knowledge and intellectual grasp Florence was at this time the leader and drew to her many artists from neighboring schools. **Masaccio** (1401?-1428?) was the first great nature student of the Early Renaissance, though his master, **Masolino** (1383-1447), had given proof positive of severe nature study in bits of modelling, in drapery, and in portrait heads. Masaccio, however, seems the first to have gone into it thoroughly and to have grasped nature as a whole. His mastery of form, his plastic composition, his free, broad folds of drapery, and his[62] knowledge of light and perspective, all placed him in the front rank of fifteenth-century painters. Though an exact student he was not a literalist. He had a large artistic sense, a breadth of view, and a comprehension of nature as a mass that Michael Angelo and Raphael did not disdain to follow. He was not a pietist, and there was no great religious feeling in his work. Dignified truthful appearance was his creed, and in this he was possibly influenced by Donatello the sculptor.

FIG. 28.—GHIRLANDAJO. THE VISITATION. LOUVRE.
Please click here for a modern color image

He came early in the century and died early, but his contemporaries did not continue the advance from where he carried it. There was wavering all along the line. Some from lack of genius could not equal him, others took[63] up nature with indecision, and others clung fondly to the gold-embossed ornaments and gilded halos of the past. **Paolo Uccello** (1397?-1475), **Andrea Castagno** (1390-1457), **Benozzo Gozzoli** (1420?-1497?), **Baldovinetti** (1427-1499), **Antonio del Pollajuolo**(1426-1498), **Cosimo Rosselli** (1439-1507), can hardly be looked upon as improvements upon the young leader. The first real successor of Masaccio was his contemporary, and possibly his pupil, the monk **Fra Filippo Lippi** (1406-1469). He was a master of color and light-and-shade for his time, though in composition and command of line he did not reach up to Masaccio. He was among the first of the painters to take the individual faces of those about him as models for his sacred characters, and clothe them in contemporary costume. Piety is not very pronounced in any of his works, though he is not without imagination and feeling, and there is in his women a charm of sweetness. His tendency was to materialize the sacred characters.

With **Filippino** (1457?-1504), **Botticelli** (1446-1510), and **Ghirlandajo** (1449-1494) we find a degree of imagination, culture, and independence not surpassed by any of the Early Florentines. Filippino modelled his art upon that of his father, Fra Filippo, and was influenced by Botticelli. He was the weakest of the trio, without being by any means a weak man. On the contrary, he was an artist of fine ability, much charm and tenderness, and considerable style, but not a great deal of original force, though occasionally doing forceful things. Purity in his type and graceful sentiment in pose and feature seem more characteristic of his work. Botticelli, even, was not so remarkable for his strength as for his culture, and an individual way of looking at things. He was a pupil of Fra Filippo, a man imbued with the religious feeling of Dante and Savonarola, a learned student of the antique and one of the first to take subjects from it, a severe nature student, and a painter of much[64] technical skill. Religion, classicism, and nature all met in his work, but the mingling was not perfect. Religious feeling and melancholy warped it. His willowy figures, delicate and refined in drawing, are more passionate than powerful, more individual than comprehensive, but they are nevertheless very attractive in their tenderness and grace.

Without being so original or so attractive an artist as Botticelli, his contemporary, Ghirlandajo, was a stronger one. His strength came more from assimilation than from invention. He combined in his work all the art learning of his time. He drew well, handled drapery simply and beautifully, was a good composer, and, for Florence, a good colorist. In addition, his temperament was robust, his style dignified, even grand, and his execution wonderfully free. He was the most important of the fifteenth-century technicians, without having any peculiar distinction or originality, and in spite of being rather prosaic at times.

FIG. 29.—FRANCESCA. DUKE OF URBINO. UFFIZI.
Please click here for a modern color image

Verrocchio (1435-1488) was more of a sculptor than a painter, but in his studio were three celebrated pupils—Perugino, Leonardo da Vinci, and Lorenzo di Credi—who were half-way between the Early and the High Renaissance. Only one of them, Leonardo, can be classed among the[65] High Renaissance men. Perugino belongs to the Umbrian school, and **Lorenzo di Credi** (1450-1537), though Florentine, never outgrew the fifteenth century. He was a pure painter, with much feeling, but weak at times. His drawing was good, but his painting lacked force, and he was too pallid in flesh color. There is much detail, study, and considerable grace about his work, but little of strength. **Piero di Cosimo** (1462-1521) was fond of mythological and classical studies, was somewhat fantastic in composition, pleasant in color, and rather distinguished in landscape backgrounds. His work strikes one as eccentric, and eccentricity was the strong characteristic of the man.

UMBRIAN AND PERUGIAN SCHOOLS: At the beginning of the fifteenth century the old Siennese school founded by Duccio and the Lorenzetti was in a state of decline. It had been remarkable for intense sentiment, and just what effect this sentiment of the old Siennese school had upon the painters of the neighboring Umbrian school of the early fifteenth century is a matter of speculation with historians. It must have had some, though the early painters, like **Ottaviano Nelli**, do not show it. That which afterward became known as the Umbrian sentiment probably first appeared in the work of **Niccolò da Foligno** (1430?-1502), who was probably a pupil of Benozzo Gozzoli, who was, in turn, a pupil of Fra Angelico. That would indicate Florentine influence, but there were many influences at work in this upper-valley country. Sentiment had been prevalent enough all through Central Italian painting during the Gothic age—more so at Sienna than elsewhere. With the Renaissance Florence rather forsook sentiment for precision of forms and equilibrium of groups; but the Umbrian towns being more provincial, held fast to their sentiment, their detail, and their gold ornamentation. Their influence upon Florence was slight, but the influence of Florence upon them was considerable. The larger city drew the provincials its way to[66] learn the new methods. The result was a group of Umbro-Florentine painters, combining some up-country sentiment with Florentine technic. Gentile da Fabriano, Niccolo da Foligno,**Bonfiglio** (1425?-1496?), and **Fiorenzo di Lorenzo** (1444?-1520) were of this mixed character.

FIG. 30.—SIGNORELLI. THE CURSE (DETAIL). ORVIETO.

The most positive in methods among the early men was **Piero della Francesca** (1420?-1492). Umbrian born, but Florentine trained, he became more scientific than sentimental, and excelled as a craftsman. He knew drawing, perspective, atmosphere, light-and-shade in a way that rather foreshadowed Leonardo da Vinci. From working in the Umbrian country his influence upon his fellow-Umbrians was large. It showed directly in **Signorelli** (1441?-1523), whose master he was, and whose style he[67] probably formed. Signorelli was Umbrian born, like Piero, but there was not much of the Umbrian sentiment about him. He was a draughtsman and threw his strength in line, producing athletic, square-shouldered figures in violent action, with complicated foreshortenings quite astonishing. The most daring man of his time, he was a master in anatomy, composition, motion. There was nothing select about his type, and nothing charming about his painting. His color was hot and coarse, his lights lurid, his shadows brick red. He was, however, a master-draughtsman, and a man of large conceptions and great strength.**Melozzo da Forli** (1438-1494), of whom little is known, was another pupil of Piero, and **Giovanni Santi** (1435?-1494), the father of Raphael, was probably influenced by both of these last named.

The true descent of the Umbrian sentiment was through Foligno and Bonfiglio to **Perugino** (1446-1524). Signorelli and Perugino seem opposed to each other in their art. The first was the forerunner of Michael Angelo, the second was the master of Raphael; and the difference between Michael Angelo and Raphael was, in a less varied degree, the difference between Signorelli and Perugino. The one showed Florentine line, the other Umbrian sentiment and color. It is in Perugino that we find the old religious feeling. Fervor, tenderness, and devotion, with soft eyes, delicate features, and pathetic looks characterized his art. The figure was slight, graceful, and in pose sentimentally inclined to one side. The head was almost affectedly placed on the shoulders, and the round olive face was full of wistful tenderness. This Perugino type, used in all his paintings, is well described by Taine as a "body belonging to the Renaissance containing a soul that belonged to the Middle Ages." The sentiment was more purely human, however, than in such a painter, for instance, as Fra Angelico. Religion still held with Perugino and the Umbrians, but even[68] with them it was becoming materialized by the beauty of the world about them.

FIG. 31.—PERUGINO. MADONNA, SAINTS, AND ANGELS. LOUVRE.
Please click here for a modern color image

As a technician Perugino was excellent. There was no dramatic fire and fury about him. The composition was simple, with graceful figures in repose. The coloring was rich, and there were many brilliant effects obtained by the use of oils. He was among the first of his school to use that medium. His friend and fellow-worker,**Pinturricchio** (1454-1513), did not use oils, but was a superior man in fresco. In type and sentiment he was rather like Perugino, in composition a little extravagant and huddled, in landscape backgrounds quite original and inventive. He never was a serious rival of Perugino, though a more varied and interesting painter. Perugino's best pupil, after Raphael,[69] was **Lo Spagna** (?-1530?), who followed his master's style until the High Renaissance, when he became a follower of Raphael.

SCHOOLS OF FERRARA AND BOLOGNA: The painters of Ferrara, in the fifteenth century, seemed to have relied upon Padua for their teaching. The best of the early men was **Cosimo Tura** (1430-1495), who showed the Paduan influence of Squarcione in anatomical insistences, coarse joints, infinite detail, and fantastic ornamentation. He was probably the founder of the school in which **Francesco Cossa** (fl. 1435-1480), a *naif* and strong, if somewhat morbid painter,**Ercole di Giulio Grandi** (fl. 1465-1535), and **Lorenzo Costa** (1460?-1535) were the principal masters. Cossa and Grandi, it seems, afterward removed to Bologna, and it was probably their move that induced Lorenzo Costa to follow them. In that way the Ferrarese school became somewhat complicated with the Bolognese school, and is confused in its history to this day. Costa was not unlikely the real founder, or, at the least, the strongest influencer of the Bolognese school. He was a painter of a rugged, manly type, afterward tempered by Southern influences to softness and sentiment. This was the result of Paduan methods meeting at Bologna with Umbrian sentiment.

The Perugino type and influence had found its way to Bologna, and showed in the work of **Francia** (1450-1518), a contemporary and fellow-worker with Costa. Though trained as a goldsmith, and learning painting in a different school, Francia, as regards his sentiment, belongs in the same category with Perugino. Even his subjects, types, and treatment were, at times, more Umbrian than Bolognese. He was not so profound in feeling as Perugino, but at times he appeared loftier in conception. His color was usually rich, his drawing a little sharp at first, as showing the goldsmith's hand, the surfaces smooth, the detail elaborate. Later on, his work had a Raphaelesque tinge, show[70]ing perhaps the influence of that rising master. It is probable that Francia at first was influenced by Costa's methods, and it is quite certain that he in turn influenced Costa in the matter of refined drawing and sentiment, though Costa always adhered to a certain detail and ornament coming from the north, and a landscape background that is peculiar to himself, and yet reminds one of Pinturricchio's landscapes. These two men, Francia and Costa, were the Perugino and Pinturricchio of the Ferrara-Bolognese school, and the most important painters in that school.

FIG. 32.—SCHOOL OF FRANCIA. MADONNA AND CHILD. LOUVRE.

THE LOMBARD SCHOOL: The designation of the Lombard school is rather a vague one in the history of painting, and is used by historians to cover a number of isolated schools[71] or men in the Lombardy region. In the fifteenth century these schools counted for little either in men or in works. The principal activity was about Milan, which drew painters from

Brescia, Vincenza, and elsewhere to form what is known as the Milanese school. **Vincenzo Foppa** (fl. 1455-1492), of Brescia, and afterward at Milan, was probably the founder of this Milanese school. His painting is of rather a harsh, exacting nature, and points to the influence of Padua, at which place he perhaps got his early art training. **Borgognone** (1450-1523) is set down as his pupil, a painter of much sentiment and spiritual feeling. The school was afterward greatly influenced by the example of Leonardo da Vinci, as will be shown further on.

PRINCIPAL WORKS: FLORENTINES—**Masaccio**, frescos in Brancacci Chapel Carmine Florence (the series completed by Filippino);**Masolino**, frescos Church and Baptistery Castiglione d' Olona; **Paolo Uccello**, frescos S. M. Novella, equestrian portrait Duomo Florence, battle-pieces in Louvre and Nat. Gal. Lon.; **Andrea Castagno**, heroes and sibyls Uffizi, altar-piece Acad. Florence, equestrian portrait Duomo Florence; **Benozzo Gozzoli**, Francesco Montefalco, Magi Ricardi palace Florence, frescos Campo Santo Pisa;**Baldovinetti**, Portico of the Annunziata Florence, altar-pieces Uffizi; **Antonio Pollajuolo**, Hercules Uffizi, St. Sebastian Pitti and Nat. Gal. Lon.; **Cosimo Rosselli**, frescos S. Ambrogio Florence, Sistine Chapel Rome, Madonna Uffizi; **Fra Filippo**, frescos Cathedral Prato, altar-pieces Florence Acad., Uffizi, Pitti and Berlin Gals., Nat. Gal. Lon.; **Filippino**, frescos Carmine Florence, Caraffa Chapel Minerva Rome, S. M. Novella and Acad. Florence, S. Domenico Bologna, easel pictures in Pitti, Uffizi, Nat. Gal. Lon., Berlin Mus., Old Pinacothek Munich; **Botticelli**, frescos Sistine Chapel Rome, Spring and Coronation Florence Acad., Venus, Calumny, Madonnas Uffizi, Pitti, Nat. Gal. Lon., Louvre, etc.; **Ghirlandajo**, frescos Sistine Chapel Rome, S. Trinità Florence, S. M. Novella, Palazzo Vecchio, altar-pieces Uffizi and Acad. Florence, Visitation Louvre; **Verrocchio**, Baptism of Christ Acad. Florence; **Lorenzo di Credi**, Nativity Acad. Florence, Madonnas Louvre and Nat. Gal. Lon., Holy Family Borghese Gal. Rome; **Piero di Cosimo**, Perseus and Andromeda Uffizi, Procris Nat. Gal. Lon., Venus and Mars Berlin Gal.

UMBRIANS—**Ottaviano Nelli**, altar-piece S. M. Nuovo Gubbio, St. [72]Augustine legends S. Agostino Gubbio; **Niccolò da Foligno**, altar-piece S. Niccolò Foligno; **Bonfigli**, frescos Palazzo Communale, altar-pieces Acad. Perugia; **Fiorenzo di Lorenzo**, many pictures Acad. Perugia, Madonna Berlin Gal.; **Piero della Francesca**, frescos Communitá and Hospital Borgo San Sepolcro, San Francesco Arezzo, Chapel of the Relicts Rimini, portraits Uffizi, pictures Nat. Gal. Lon.; **Signorelli**, frescos Cathedral Orvieto, Sistine Rome, Palazzo Petrucci Sienna, altar-pieces Arezzo, Cortona, Perugia, pictures Pitti, Uffizi, Berlin, Louvre, Nat. Gal. Lon.; **Melozzo da Forli**, angels St. Peter's Rome, frescos Vatican, pictures Berlin and Nat. Gal. Lon.; **Giovanni Santi**, Annunciation Milan, Pieta Urbino, Madonnas Berlin, Nat. Gal. Lon., S. Croce Fano; **Perugino**, frescos Sistine Rome, Crucifixion S. M. Maddalena Florence, Sala del Cambio Perugia, altar-pieces Pitti, Fano, Cremona, many pictures in European galleries; **Pinturricchio**, frescos S. M. del Popolo, Appartamento Borgo Vatican, Bufolini Chapel Aracoeli Rome, Duomo Library Sienna, altar-pieces Perugia and Sienna Acads., Pitti, Louvre; **Lo Spagna**, Madonna Lower Church Assisi, frescos at Spoleto, Turin, Perugia, Assisi.

FERRARESE AND BOLOGNESE—**Cosimo Tura**, altar-pieces Berlin Mus., Bergamo, Museo Correr Venice, Nat. Gal. Lon.; **Francesco Cossa**, altar-pieces S. Petronio and Acad. Bologna, Dresden Gal.; Grandi, St. George Corsini Pal. Rome, several canvases Constabili Collection Ferrara; **Lorenzo Costa**, frescos S. Giacomo Maggiore, altar-pieces S. Petronio, S. Giovanni in Monte and Acad. Bologna, also Louvre, Berlin, and Nat. Gal. Lon.; **Francia**, altar-pieces S. Giacomo Maggiore, S. Martino Maggiore, and many altar-pieces in Acad. Bologna, Annunciation Brera Milan, Rose Garden Munich, Pieta Nat. Gal. Lon., Scappi Portrait Uffizi, Baptism Dresden.

LOMBARDS—**Foppa**, altar-pieces S. Maria di Castello Savona, Borromeo Col. Milan, Carmine Brescia, panels Brera Milan; **Borgognone**, altar-pieces Certosa of Pavia, Church of Melegnano, S. Ambrogio, Ambrosian Lib., Brera Milan, Nat. Gal. Lon.

[73]
CHAPTER VII.
ITALIAN PAINTING.
EARLY RENAISSANCE—1400-1500—CONTINUED.

BOOKS RECOMMENDED: Those on Italian art before mentioned; also consult the General Bibliography (page xv.)

PADUAN SCHOOL: It was at Padua in the north that the influence of the classic marbles made itself strongly apparent. Umbria remained true to the religious sentiment, Florence engaged itself largely with nature study and technical problems, introducing here and there draperies and poses that showed knowledge of ancient sculpture, but at Padua much of the classic in drapery, figures, and architecture seems to have been taken directly from the rediscovered antique or the modern bronze.

The early men of the school were hardly great enough to call for mention. During the fourteenth century there was some Giotto influence felt—that painter having been at Padua working in the Arena Chapel. Later on there was a slight influence from Gentile da Fabriano and his fellow-worker Vittore Pisano, of Verona. But these influences seem to have died out and the real direction of the school in the early fifteenth century was given by **Francesco Squarcione** (1394-1474). He was an enlightened man, a student, a collector and an admirer of ancient sculpture, and though no great painter himself he taught an anatomical statuesque art, based on ancient marbles and nature, to many pupils.[74]

Squarcione's work has perished, but his teaching was reflected in the work of his great pupil **Andrea Mantegna** (1431-1506). Yet Mantegna never received the full complement of his knowledge from Squarcione. He was of an observing nature and probably studied Paolo Uccello and Fra Filippo, some of whose works were then in Paduan edifices. He gained color knowledge from the Venetian Bellinis, who lived at Padua at one time and who were connected with Mantegna by marriage. But the sculpturesque side of his art came from Squarcione, from a study of the antique, and from a deeper study of Donatello, whose bronzes to this day are to be seen within and without the Paduan Duomo of S. Antonio.

FIG. 33.—MANTEGNA. GONZAGA FAMILY GROUP (DETAIL). MANTUA.

The sculpturesque is characteristic of Mantegna's work. His people are hard, rigid at times, immovable human beings, not so much turned to stone as turned to bronze—the bronze of Donatello. There is little sense of motion[75] about them. The figure is sharp and harsh, the drapery, evidently studied from sculpture, is "liney," and the archæology is often more scientific than artistic. Mantegna was not, however, entirely devoted to the sculpturesque. He was one of the severest nature students of the Early Renaissance, knew about nature, and carried it out in more exacting detail than was perhaps well for his art. In addition he was a master of light-and-shade, understood composition, space, color, atmosphere, and was as scientific in perspective as Piero della Francesca. There is stiffness in his figures but nevertheless great truth and character. The forms are noble, even grand, and for invention and imagination they were never, in his time, carried further or higher. He was little of a sentimentalist or an emotionalist, not much of a brush man or a colorist, but as a draughtsman, a creator of noble forms, a man of power, he stood second to none in the century.

Of Squarcione's other pupils **Pizzolo** (fl. 1470) was the most promising, but died early. **Marco Zoppo** (1440-1498) seems to have followed the Paduan formula of hardness, dryness, and exacting detail. He was possibly influenced by Cosimo Tura, and in turn influenced somewhat the Ferrara-Bolognese school. Mantegna, however, was the greatest of the school, and his influence was far-reaching. It affected the school of Venice in matters of drawing, beside influencing the Lombard and Veronese schools in their beginnings.

SCHOOLS OF VERONA AND VICENZA: Artistically Verona belonged with the Venetian provinces, because it was largely an echo of Venice except at the very start. **Vittore Pisano** (1380-1456), called Pisanello, was the earliest painter of note, but he was not distinctly Veronese in his art. He was medallist and painter both, worked with Gentile da Fabriano in the Ducal Palace at Venice and elsewhere, and his art seems to have an affinity with that of his companion.[76]

Liberale da Verona (1451-1536?) was at first a miniaturist, but afterward developed a larger style based on a following of Mantegna's work, with some Venetian influences showing in the coloring and backgrounds. **Francesco Bonsignori** (1455-1519) was of the Verona school, but established himself later at Mantua and was under the Mantegna influence. His style at first was rather severe, but he afterward developed much ability in portraiture, historical work, animals, and architectural features. **Francesco Caroto** (1470-1546), a pupil of Liberale, really belongs to the next century—the High Renaissance—but his early works show his education in Veronese and Paduan methods.

FIG. 34.—B. VIVARINI. MADONNA AND CHILD. TURIN.

In the school of Vicenza the only master of much note[77] in this Early Renaissance time was **Bartolommeo Montagna** (1450?-1523), a painter in both oil and fresco of much severity and at times grandeur of style. In drawing he was influenced by Mantegna, in composition and coloring he showed a study of Giovanni Bellini and Carpaccio.

VENETIAN LIFE AND ART: The conditions of art production in Venice during the Early Renaissance were quite different from those in Florence or Umbria. By the disposition of her people Venice was not a learned or devout city. Religion, though the chief subject, was not the chief spirit of Venetian art. Christianity was accepted by the Venetians, but with no fevered enthusiasm. The Church was strong enough there to defy the Papacy at one time, and yet religion with the people was perhaps more of a civic function or a duty than a spiritual worship. It was sincere in its way, and the early painters painted its subjects with honesty, but the Venetians were much too proud and worldly minded to take anything very seriously except their own splendor and their own power.

Again, the Venetians were not humanists or students of the revived classic. They housed manuscripts, harbored exiled humanists, received the influx of Greek scholars after the fall of Constantinople, and later the celebrated Aldine press was established in Venice; but, for all that, classic learning was not the fancy of the Venetians. They made no quarrel over the relative merits of Plato and Aristotle, dug up no classic marbles, had no revival of learning in a Florentine sense. They were merchant princes, winning wealth by commerce and expending it lavishly in beautifying their island home. Not to attain great learning, but to revel in great splendor, seems to have been their aim. Life in the sovereign city of the sea was a worthy existence in itself. And her geographical and political position aided her prosperity. Unlike Florence she was not torn by contending princes within and foreign foes without—at least not to her[78] harm. She had her wars, but they were generally on distant seas. Popery, Paganism, Despotism, all the convulsions of Renaissance life threatened but harmed her not. Free and independent, her kingdom was the sea, and her livelihood commerce, not agriculture.

The worldly spirit of the Venetian people brought about a worldly and luxurious art. Nothing in the disposition or education of the Venetians called for the severe or the intellectual. The demand was for rich decoration that would please the senses without stimulating the intellect or firing the imagination to any great extent. Line and form were not so well suited to them as color—the most sensuous of all mediums. Color prevailed through Venetian art from the very beginning, and was its distinctive characteristic.

FIG. 35.—GIOVANNI BELLINI. MADONNA OF SS. GEORGE AND PAUL. VENICE ACAD.

Where this love of color came from is matter of specula[79]tion. Some say out of Venetian skies and waters, and, doubtless, these had something to do with the Venetian color-sense; but Venice in its color was also an example of the effect of commerce on art. She was a trader with the East from her infancy—not Constantinople and the Byzantine East alone, but back of these the old Mohammedan East, which for a thousand years has cast its art in colors rather than in forms. It was Eastern ornament in mosaics, stuffs, porcelains, variegated marbles, brought by ship to Venice and located in S. Marco, in Murano, and in Torcello, that first gave the color-impulse to the Venetians. If Florence was the heir of Rome and its austere classicism, Venice was the heir of Constantinople and its color-charm. The two great color spots in Italy at this day are Venice and Ravenna, commercial footholds of the Byzantines in Mediæval and Renaissance days. It may be concluded without error that Venice derived her color-sense and much of her luxurious and material view of life from the East.

THE EARLY VENETIAN PAINTERS: Painting began at Venice with the fabrication of mosaics and ornamental altar-pieces of rich gold stucco-work. The "Greek manner"—that is, the Byzantine—was practised early in the fifteenth century by **Jacobello del Fiore** and **Semitecolo**, but it did not last long. Instead of lingering for a hundred years, as at Florence, it died a natural death in the first half of the fifteenth century. Gentile da Fabriano, who was at Venice about 1420, painting in the Ducal Palace with Pisano as his assistant, may have brought this about. He taught there in Venice, was the master of Jacopo Bellini, and if not the teacher then the influencer of the Vivarinis of Murano. There were two of the Vivarinis in the early times, so far as can be made out, **Antonio Vivarini** (?-1470) and **Bartolommeo Vivarini** (fl. 1450-1499), who worked with **Johannes Alemannus**, a painter of supposed German birth and training. They all signed themselves from Murano (an outlying Ve[80]netian island), where they were producing church altars and ornaments with some Paduan influence showing in their work. They made up the Muranese school, though this school was not strongly marked apart either in characteristics or subjects from the Venetian school, of which it was, in fact, a part.

FIG. 36.—CARPACCIO. PRESENTATION (DETAIL). VENICE ACAD.
Please click here for a modern color image

Bartolommeo was the best of the group, and contended long time in rivalry with the Bellinis at Venice, but toward 1470 he fell away and died comparatively forgotten. **Luigi Vivarini** (fl. 1461-1503) was the latest of this family, and with his death the history of the Muranese merges into the Venetian school proper, except as it continues to appear in some pupils and followers. Of these latter **Carlo Crivelli** (1430?[81]1493?) was the only one of much mark. He apparently gathered his art from many sources—ornament and color from the Vivarini, a lean and withered type from the early Paduans under Squarcione, architecture from Mantegna, and a rather repulsive sentiment from the same school. His faces were contorted and sulky, his hands and feet stringy, his drawing rather bad; but he had a transparent color, beautiful ornamentation and not a little tragic power.

Venetian art practically dates from the Bellinis. They did not begin where the Vivarini left off. The two families of painters seem to have started about the same time, worked along together from like inspirations, and in somewhat of a similar manner as regards the early men. **Jacopo Bellini** (1400?-1464?) was the pupil of Gentile da Fabriano, and a painter of considerable rank. His son, **Gentile Bellini** (1426?-1507), was likewise a painter of ability, and an extremely interesting one on account of his Venetian subjects painted with much open-air effect and knowledge of light and atmosphere. The younger son, **Giovanni Bellini** (1428?-1516), was the greatest of the family and the true founder of the Venetian school.

About the middle of the fifteenth century the Bellini family lived at Padua and came in contact with the classic-realistic art of Mantegna. In fact, Mantegna married Giovanni Bellini's sister, and there was a mingling of family as well as of art. There was an influence upon Mantegna of Venetian color, and upon the Bellinis of Paduan line. The latter showed in Giovanni Bellini's early work, which was rather hard, angular in drapery, and anatomical in the joints, hands, and feet; but as the century drew to a close this melted away into the growing splendor of Venetian color. Giovanni Bellini lived into the sixteenth century, but never quite attained the rank of a High Renaissance painter. He had religious feeling, earnestness, honesty, simplicity, character, force, knowledge; but not the full[82] complement of brilliancy and painter's power. He went beyond all his contemporaries in technical strength and color-harmony, and was in fact the epoch-making man of early Venice. Some of his pictures, like the S. Zaccaria Madonna, will compare favorably with any work of any age, and his landscape backgrounds (see the St. Peter Martyr in the National Gallery, London) were rather wonderful for the period in which they were produced.

Of Bellini's contemporaries and followers there were many, and as a school there was a similarity of style, subject, and color-treatment carrying through them all, with individual peculiarities in each painter. After Giovanni Bellini comes **Carpaccio** (?-1522?), a younger contemporary, about whose history little is known. He worked with Gentile Bellini, and was undoubtedly influenced by Giovanni Bellini. In subject he was more romantic and chivalric than religious, though painting a number of altar-pieces. The legend was his delight, and his great success, as the St. Ursula and St. George pictures in Venice still indicate. He was remarkable for his knowledge of architecture, costumes, and Oriental settings, put forth in a realistic way, with much invention and technical ability in the handling of landscape, perspective, light, and color. There is a truthfulness of appearance—an out-of-doors feeling—about his work that is quite captivating. In addition, the spirit of his art was earnestness, honesty, and sincerity, and even the awkward bits of drawing which occasionally appeared in his work served to add to the general naive effect of the whole.

FIG. 37.—ANTONELLO DA MESSINA. UNKNOWN MAN. LOUVRE.

Cima da Conegliano (1460?-1517?) was probably a pupil of Giovanni Bellini, with some Carpaccio influence about him. He was the best of the immediate followers, none of whom came up to the master. They were trammelled somewhat by being educated in distemper work, and then midway in their careers changing to the oil medium, that[83] medium having been introduced into Venice by Antonello da Messina in 1473. Cima's subjects were largely half-length madonnas, given with strong qualities of light-and-shade and color. He was not a great originator, though a man of ability. **Catena** (?-1531) had a wide reputation in his day, but it came more from a smooth finish and pretty accessories than from creative power. He imitated Bellini's style so well that a number of his pictures pass for works by the master even to this day. Later he followed Giorgione and Carpaccio. A man possessed of knowledge, he seemed to have no original propelling purpose behind him. That was largely the make-up of the other men of the school, **Basaiti** (1490-1521?), **Previtali** (1470?-1525?), **Bissolo** (1464[84]1528),**Rondinelli** (1440?-1500?), **Diana** (?-1500?), **Mansueti** (fl. 1500).

Antonello da Messina (1444?-1493), though Sicilian born, is properly classed with the Venetian school. He obtained a knowledge of Flemish methods probably from Flemish painters or pictures in Italy (he never was a pupil of Jan van Eyck, as Vasari relates, and probably never saw Flanders), and introduced the use of oil as a medium in the Venetian school. His early work was Flemish in character, and was very accurate and minute. His late work showed the influence of the Bellinis. His counter-influence upon Venetian portraiture has never been quite justly estimated. That fine, exact, yet powerful work, of which the Doge Loredano by Bellini, in the National Gallery, London, is a type, was perhaps brought about by an amalgamation of Flemish and Venetian methods, and Antonello was perhaps the means of bringing it about. He was an excellent, if precise, portrait-painter.

PRINCIPAL WORKS: PADUANS—**Andrea Mantegna**, Eremitani Padua, Madonna of S. Xeno Verona, St. Sebastian Vienna Mus., St. George Venice Acad., Camera di Sposi Castello di Corte Mantua, Madonna and Allegories Louvre, Scipio Summer Autumn Nat. Gal.

Lon.; **Pizzoli** (with Mantegna), Eremitani Padua; **Marco Zoppo** frescos Casa Colonna Bologna, Madonna Berlin Gal.

VERONESE AND VICENTINE PAINTERS—**Vittore Pisano**, St. Anthony and George Nat. Gal. Lon., St. George S. Anastasia Verona; **Liberale da Verona**, miniatures Duomo Sienna, St. Sebastian Brera Milan, Madonna Berlin Mus., other works Duomo and Gal. Verona;**Bonsignori**, S. Bernardino and Gal. Verona, Mantua, and Nat. Gal. Lon.; **Caroto**, In S. Tommaso, S. Giorgio, S. Caterina and Gal. Verona, Dresden and Frankfort Gals.; **Montagna**, Madonnas Brera, Venice Acad., Bergamo, Berlin, Nat. Gal. Lon., Louvre.

VENETIANS—**Jacobello del Fiore** and **Semitecolo**, all attributions doubtful; **Antonio Vivarini** and **Johannes Alemannus**, together altar-pieces Venice Acad., S. Zaccaria Venice; Antonio alone, Adoration of Kings Berlin Gal.; **Bartolommeo Vivarini**, Madonna Bologna Gal. (with Antonio), altar-pieces SS. Giovanni e Paolo, Frari, Venice; **Luigi [85]Vivarini**, Madonna Berlin Gal., Frari and Acad. Venice;**Carlo Crivelli**, Madonnas and altar-pieces Brera, Nat. Gal. Lon., Lateran, Berlin Gals.; **Jacopo Bellini**, Crucifixion Verona Gal., Sketch-book Brit. Mus.; **Gentile Bellini**, Organ Doors S. Marco, Procession and Miracle of Cross Acad. Venice, St. Mark Brera; **Giovanni Bellini**, many pictures in European galleries, Acad., Frari, S. Zaccaria SS. Giovanni e Paolo Venice; **Carpaccio**, Presentation and Ursula pictures Acad., St. George and St. Jerome S. Giorgio da Schiavone Venice, St. Stephen Berlin Gal.; **Cima**, altar-pieces S. Maria dell Orte, S. Giovanni in Bragora, Acad. Venice, Louvre, Berlin, Dresden, Munich, Vienna, and other galleries; **Catena**, Altar-pieces S. Simeone, S. M. Mater Domini, SS. Giovanni e Paolo, Acad. Venice, Dresden, and in Nat. Gal. Lon. (the Warrior and Horse attributed to "School of Bellini"); **Basaiti**, Venice Acad. Nat. Gal. Lon., Vienna, and Berlin Gals.; **Previtali**, altar-pieces S. Spirito Bergamo, Brera, Berlin, and Dresden Gals., Nat. Gal. Lon., Venice Acad.; **Bissolo**, Resurrection Berlin Gal., S. Caterina Venice Acad.; **Rondinelli**, two pictures Palazzo Doria Rome, Holy Family (No. 6) Louvre (attributed to Giovanni Bellini); **Diana**, Altar-pieces Venice Acad.; **Mansueti**, large pictures Venice Acad.; **Antonella da Messina**, Portraits Louvre, Berlin and Nat. Gal. Lon., Crucifixion Antwerp Mus.

[86]

CHAPTER VIII.
ITALIAN PAINTING.
THE HIGH RENAISSANCE—1500-1600.

BOOKS RECOMMENDED: Those on Italian art before mentioned, and also, Berenson, *Lorenzo Lotto*; Clement, *Michel Ange, L. da Vinci, Raphael*; Crowe and Cavalcaselle, *Titian*; same authors, *Raphael*; Grimm, *Michael Angelo*; Gronau, *Titian*; Holroyd, *Michael Angelo*; Meyer, *Correggio*; Moore, *Correggio*; Muntz, *Leonardo da Vinci*; Passavant, *Raphael*; Pater, *Studies in History of Renaissance*; Phillips,*Titian*; Reumont, *Andrea del Sarto*; Ricci, *Correggio*; Richter, *Leonardo di Vinci*; Ridolfi, *Vita di Paolo Cagliari Veronese*; Springer,*Rafael und Michel Angelo*; Symonds, *Michael Angelo*; Taine, *Italy—Florence and Venice*.

THE HIGHEST DEVELOPMENT: The word "Renaissance" has a broader meaning than its strict etymology would imply. It was a "new birth," but something more than the revival of Greek learning and the study of nature entered into it. It was the grand consummation of Italian intelligence in many departments—the arrival at maturity of the Christian trained mind tempered by the philosophy of Greece, and the knowledge of the actual world. Fully aroused at last, the Italian intellect became inquisitive, inventive, scientific, skeptical—yes, treacherous, immoral, polluted. It questioned all things, doubted where it pleased, saturated itself with crime, corruption, and sensuality, yet bowed at the shrine of the beautiful and knelt at the altar of Christianity. It is an illustration of the contradictions that may exist when the intellectual, the religious,[87] and the moral are brought together, with the intellectual in predominance.

FIG. 38.—FRA BARTOLOMMEO. DESCENT FROM CROSS. PITTI.
Please click here for a modern color image

And that keen Renaissance intellect made swift progress. It remodelled the philosophy of Greece, and used its literature as a mould for its own. It developed Roman law and introduced modern science. The world without and the world within were rediscovered. Land and sea, starry sky and planetary system, were fixed upon the chart. Man himself, the animals, the planets, organic and inorganic life, the small things of the earth gave up their secrets. Inventions utilized all classes of products, commerce flourished, free cities were builded, universities arose, learning spread itself on the pages of newly invented books of print, and, perhaps, greatest of all, the arts arose on strong wings of life to the very highest altitude.[88]

For the moral side of the Renaissance intellect it had its tastes and refinements, as shown in its high quality of art; but it also had its polluting and degrading features, as shown in its political and social life. Religion was visibly weakening though the ecclesiastical still held strong.

People were forgetting the faith of the early days, and taking up with the material things about them. They were glorifying the human and exalting the natural. The story of Greece was being repeated in Italy. And out of this new worship came jewels of rarity and beauty, but out of it also came faithlessness, corruption, vice.

Strictly speaking, the Renaissance had been accomplished before the year 1500, but so great was its impetus that, in the arts at least, it extended half-way through the sixteenth century. Then it began to fail through exhaustion.

MOTIVES AND METHODS: The religious subject still held with the painters, but this subject in High-Renaissance days did not carry with it the religious feeling as in Gothic days. Art had grown to be something else than a teacher of the Bible. In the painter's hands it had come to mean beauty for its own sake—a picture beautiful for its form and color, regardless of its theme. This was the teaching of antique art, and the study of nature but increased the belief. A new love had arisen in the outer and visible world, and when the Church called for altar-pieces the painters painted their new love, christened it with a religious title, and handed it forth in the name of the old. Thus art began to free itself from Church domination and to live as an independent beauty. The general motive, then, of painting during the High Renaissance, though apparently religious from the subject, and in many cases still religious in feeling, was largely to show the beauty of form or color, in which religion, the antique, and the natural came in as modifying elements.

In technical methods, though extensive work was still[89] done in fresco, especially at Florence and Rome, yet the bulk of High-Renaissance painting was in oils upon panel and canvas. At Venice even the decorative wall paintings were upon canvas, afterward inserted in wall or ceiling.

FIG. 39.—ANDREA DEL SARTO. MADONNA OF ST. FRANCIS. UFFIZI.
Please click here for a modern color image

THE FLORENTINES AND ROMANS: There was a severity and austerity about the Florentine art, even at its climax. It was never too sensuous and luxurious, but rather exact and intellectual. The Florentines were fond of lustreless fresco, architectural composition, towering or sweeping lines, rather sharp color as compared with the Venetians, and theological, classical, even literary and allegorical subjects. Probably this was largely due to the classic bias of the painters and the intellectual and social influences of Florence and Rome. Line and composition were means of[90] expressing abstract thought better than color, though some of the Florentines employed both line and color knowingly.

This was the case with **Fra Bartolommeo** (1475-1517), a monk of San Marco, who was a transition painter from the fifteenth to the sixteenth century. He was a religionist, a follower of Savonarola, and a man of soul who thought to do work of a religious character and feeling; but he was also a fine painter, excelling in composition, drawing, drapery, color. The painter's element in his work, its material and earthly beauty, rather detracted from its spiritual significance. He opposed the sensuous and the nude, and yet about the only nude he ever painted—a St. Sebastian for San Marco—had so much of the earthly about it that people forgot the suffering saint in admiring the fine body, and the picture had to be removed from the convent. In such ways religion in art was gradually undermined, not alone by naturalism and classicism but by art itself. Painting brought into life by religion no sooner reached maturity than it led people away from religion by pointing out sensuous beauties in the type rather than religious beauties in the symbol.

Fra Bartolommeo was among the last of the pietists in art. He had no great imagination, but some feeling and a fine color-sense for Florence. Naturally he was influenced somewhat by the great ones about him, learning perspective from Raphael, grandeur from Michael Angelo, and contours from Leonardo da Vinci. He worked in collaboration with **Albertinelli** (1474-1515), a skilled artist and a fellow-pupil with Bartolommeo in the workshop of Cosimo Rosselli. Their work is so much alike that it is often difficult to distinguish the painters apart. Albertinelli was not so devout as his companion, but he painted the religious subject with feeling, as his Visitation in the Uffizi indicates. Among the followers of Bartolommeo and Albertinelli were **Fra Paolino** (1490[91]1547), **Bugiardini** (1475-1554), **Granacci** (1477-1543), who showed many influences, and **Ridolfo Ghirlandajo** (1483-1561).

FIG. 40.—MICHAEL ANGELO. ATHLETE. SISTINE, ROME.

Andrea del Sarto (1486-1531) was a Florentine pure and simple—a painter for the Church producing many madonnas and altar-pieces, and yet possessed of little religious feeling or depth. He was a painter more than a pietist, and was called by his townsmen "the faultless painter." So he was as regards the technical features of his art. He was the best brushman and colorist of the Florentine school. Dealing largely with the material side his craftsmanship was excellent and his pictures exuberant with life and color, but his madonnas and saints were decidedly of the earth—handsome Florentine models garbed as sacred characters—well[92]-

drawn and easily painted, with little devotional feeling about them. He was influenced by other painters to some extent. Masaccio, Ghirlandajo, and Michael Angelo were his models in drawing; Leonardo and Bartolommeo in contours; while in warmth of color, brush-work, atmospheric and landscape effects he was quite by himself. He had a large number of pupils and followers, but most of them deserted him later on to follow Michael Angelo. **Pontormo** (1493-1558) and **Franciabigio**(1482-1525) were among the best of them.

Michael Angelo (1474-1564) has been called the "Prophet of the Renaissance," and perhaps deserves the title, since he was more of the Old Testament than the New—more of the austere and imperious than the loving or the forgiving. There was no sentimental feature about his art. His conception was intellectual, highly imaginative, mysterious, at times disordered and turbulent in its strength. He came the nearest to the sublime of any painter in history through the sole attribute of power. He had no tenderness nor any winning charm. He did not win, but rather commanded. Everything he saw or felt was studied for the strength that was in it. Religion, Old-Testament history, the antique, humanity, all turned in his hands into symbolic forms of power, put forth apparently in the white heat of passion, and at times in defiance of every rule and tradition of art. Personal feeling was very apparent in his work, and in this he was as far removed as possible from the Greeks, and nearer to what one would call to-day a romanticist. There was little of the objective about him. He was not an imitator of facts but a creator of forms and ideas. His art was a reflection of himself—a self-sufficient man, positive, creative, standing alone, a law unto himself.

Technically he was more of a sculptor than a painter. He said so himself when Julius commanded him to paint the Sistine ceiling, and he told the truth. He was a magnificent draughtsman, and drew magnificent sculpturesque figures on[93] the Sistine vault. That was about all his achievement with the brush. In color, light, air, perspective—in all those features peculiar to the painter—he was behind his contemporaries. Composition he knew a great deal about, and in drawing he had the most positive, far-reaching command of line of any painter of any time. It was in drawing that he showed his power. Even this is severe and harsh at times, and then again filled with a grace that is majestic and in scope universal, as witness the Creation of Adam in the Sistine.

FIG. 41.—RAPHAEL. LA BELLE JARDINIÈRE. LOUVRE.
Please click here for a modern color image

He came out of Florence, a pupil of Ghirlandajo, with a school feeling for line, stimulated by the frescos of Masaccio and Signorelli. At an early age he declared himself, and hewed a path of his own through art, sweeping along with him many of the slighter painters of his age. Long-lived he saw his contemporaries die about him and Humanism end in bloodshed with the coming of the Jesuits; but alone, gloomy, resolute, steadfast to his belief, he held his way, the last great representative of Florentine art, the first great representative of individualism in art. With him and after him came many followers who strove to imitate his "terrible style," but they did not succeed any too well.[94]

The most of these followers find classification under the Mannerists of the Decadence. Of those who were immediate pupils of Michael Angelo, or carried out his designs, **Daniele da Volterra**(1509-1566) was one of the most satisfactory. His chief work, the Descent from the Cross, was considered by Poussin as one of the three great pictures of the world. It is sometimes said to have been designed by Michael Angelo, but that is only a conjecture. It has much action and life in it, but is somewhat affected in pose and gesture, and Volterra's work generally was deficient in real energy of conception and execution. **Marcello Venusti** (1515-1585?) painted directly from Michael Angelo's designs in a delicate and precise way, probably imbibed from his master, Perino del Vaga, and from association with Venetians like **Sebastiano del Piombo** (1485-1547). This last-named painter was born in Venice and trained under Bellini and Giorgione, inheriting the color and light-and-shade qualities of the Venetians; but later on he went to Rome and came under the influence of Michael Angelo and Raphael. He tried, under Michael Angelo's inspiration it is said, to unite the Florentine grandeur of line with the Venetian coloring, and thus outdo Raphael. It was not wholly successful, though resulting in an excellent quality of art. As a portrait-painter he was above reproach. His early works were rather free in impasto, the late ones smooth and shiny, in imitation of Raphael.

Raphael Sanzio (1483-1520) was more Greek in method than any of the great Renaissance painters. In subject he was not more classic than others of his time; he painted all subjects. In thought he was not particularly classic; he was chiefly intellectual, with a leaning toward the sensuous that was half-pagan. It was in method and expression more than elsewhere that he showed the Greek spirit. He aimed at the ideal and the universal, independent, so far as possible, of the individual, and sought by a union of all[95] elements to produce perfect harmony. The Harmonist of the Renaissance is his title. And this harmony extended to a blending of thought, form, and expression, heightening or modifying every element until they ran together with such rhythm that it could not be seen where one left off and another began. He was the very opposite of Michael Angelo. The art of the latter was an expression of individual power and was purely subjective. Raphael's art was largely a unity of objective beauties, with the personal element as much in abeyance as was possible for his time.

His education was a cultivation of every grace of mind and hand. He assimilated freely whatever he found to be good in the art about him. A pupil of Perugino originally, he levied upon features of excellence in Masaccio, Fra Bartolommeo, Leonardo, Michael Angelo. From the first he got tenderness, from the second drawing, from the third color and composition, from the fourth charm, from the fifth force. Like an eclectic Greek he drew from all sources, and then blended and united these features in a peculiar style of his own and stamped them with his peculiar Raphaelesque stamp.

In subject Raphael was religious and mythological, but he was imbued with neither of these so far as the initial spirit was concerned. He looked at all subjects in a calm, intellectual, artistic way. Even the celebrated Sistine Madonna is more intellectual than pietistic, a Christian Minerva ruling rather than helping to save the world. The same spirit ruled him in classic and theological themes. He did not feel them keenly or execute them passionately—at least there is no indication of it in his work. The doing so would have destroyed unity, symmetry, repose. The theme was ever held in check by a regard for proportion and rhythm. To keep all artistic elements in perfect equilibrium, allowing no one to predominate, seemed the mainspring of his action, and in[96] doing this he created that harmony which his admirers sometimes refer to as pure beauty.

For his period and school he was rather remarkable technically. He excelled in everything except brush-work, which was never brought to maturity in either Florence or Rome. Even in color he was fine for Florence, though not equal to the Venetians. In composition, modelling, line, even in texture painting (see his portraits) he was a man of accomplishment; while in grace, purity, serenity, loftiness he was the Florentine leader easily first.

FIG. 42.—GIULIO ROMANO. APOLLO AND MUSES. PITTI.
Please click here for a modern color image

The influence of Raphael's example was largely felt throughout Central Italy, and even at the north, resulting in many imitators and followers, who tried to produce Raphaelesque effects. Their efforts were usually successful in precipitating charm into sweetness and sentiment into sentimentality. **Francesco Penni**(1488?-1528) seems to have been content to work under Raphael with some ability. **Giulio Romano** (1492-1546) was the strongest of the pupils, and became the founder and leader of the Roman school, which had considerable influence upon the painters of the Decadence. He adopted the classic subject and tried to adopt Raphael's style, but he was not completely[97] successful. Raphael's refinement in Giulio's hands became exaggerated coarseness. He was a good draughtsman, but rather hot as a colorist, and a composer of violent, restless, and, at times, contorted groups. He was a prolific painter, but his work tended toward the baroque style, and had a bad influence on the succeeding schools.

Primaticcio (1504-1570) was one of his followers, and had much to do with the founding of the school of Fontainebleau in France. **Giovanni da Udine** (1487-1564), a Venetian trained painter, became a follower of Raphael, his only originality showing in decorative designs. **Perino del Vaga** (1500-1547) was of the same cast of mind. **Andrea Sabbatini** (1480?-1545) carried Raphael's types and methods to the south of Italy, and some artists at Bologna, and in Umbria, like **Innocenza da Imola** (1494-1550?), and **Timoteo di Viti** (1467-1523), adopted the Raphael type and method to the detriment of what native talent they may have possessed, though about Timoteo there is some doubt whether he adopted Raphael's type, or Raphael his type.

PRINCIPAL WORKS: FLORENTINES—**Fra Bartolommeo**, Descent from the Cross Salvator Mundi St. Mark Pitti, Madonnas and Prophets Uffizi, other pictures Florence Acad., Louvre, Vienna Gal.; **Albertinelli**, Visitation Uffizi, Christ Magdalene Madonna Louvre, Trinity Madonna Florence Acad., Annunciation Munich Gal.; **Fra Paolino**, works at San Spirito Sienna, S. Domenico and S. Paolo Pistoia, Madonna Florence Acad.; **Bugiardini**, Madonna Uffizi, St. Catherine S. M. Novella Florence, Nativity Berlin, St. Catherine Bologna Gal.; **Granacci**, altar-pieces Uffizi, Pitti, Acad. Florence, Berlin and Munich Gals.; **Ridolfo Ghirlandajo**, S. Zenobio pictures Uffizi, also Louvre and Berlin Gal.; **Andrea del Sarto**, many pictures in Uffizi and Pitti, Louvre, Berlin, Dresden, Madrid, Nat. Gal. Lon., frescos S. Annunziata and the Scalzo Florence; **Pontormo**, frescos Annunziata Florence, Visitation and Madonna Louvre, portrait Berlin Gal., Supper at Emmaus Florence Acad.; **Franciabigio**, frescos courts of the Servi and Scalzo Florence, Bathsheba Dresden Gal., many portraits in Louvre, Pitti, Berlin Gal.; **Michael Angelo**, frescos Sistine Rome, Holy Family Uffizi;**Daniele da Volterra**, [98]frescos Hist. of Cross Trinità de' Monti Rome, Innocents Uffizi; **Venusti**, frescos Castel San Angelo, S. Spirito Rome, Annunciation St. John Lateran Rome; **Sebastiano del**

Piombo, Lazarus Nat. Gal. Lon., Pietà Viterbo, Fornarina Uffizi (ascribed to Raphael) Fornarina and Christ Bearing Cross Berlin and Dresden Gals., Agatha Pitti, Visitation Louvre, portrait Doria Gal. Rome;**Raphael**, Marriage of Virgin Brera, Madonna and Vision of Knight Nat. Gal. Lon., Madonnas St. Michael and St. George Louvre, many Madonnas and portraits in Uffizi, Pitti, Munich, Vienna, St. Petersburgh, Madrid Gals., Sistine Madonna Dresden, chief frescos Vatican Rome.

ROMANS: **Giulio Romano**, frescos Sala di Constantino Vatican Rome (with Francesco Penni after Raphael), Palazzo del Tè Mantua, St. Stephen, S. Stefano Genoa, Holy Family Dresden Gal., other works in Louvre, Nat. Gal. Lon., Pitti, Uffizi; **Primaticcio**, works attributed to him doubtful—Scipio Louvre, Lady at Toilet and Venus Musée de Cluny; **Giovanni da Udine**, decorations, arabesques and grotesques in Vatican Loggia; **Perino del Vaga**, Hist. of Joshua and David Vatican (with Raphael), frescos Trinità de' Monti and Castel S. Angelo Rome, Creation of Eve S. Marcello Rome; **Sabbatini**, Adoration Naples Mus., altar-pieces in Naples and Salerno churches;**Innocenza da Imola**, works in Bologna, Berlin and Munich Gals.; **Timoteo di Viti**, Church of the Pace Rome (after Raphael), madonnas and Magdalene Brera, Acad. of St. Luke Rome, Bologna Gal., S. Domenico Urbino, Gubbio Cathedral.

[99]
CHAPTER IX.
ITALIAN PAINTING.
THE HIGH RENAISSANCE, 1500-1600.—CONTINUED.

BOOKS RECOMMENDED: The works on Italian art before mentioned and consult also the General Bibliography (p. xv.)

LEONARDO DA VINCI AND THE MILANESE: The third person in the great Florentine trinity of painters was **Leonardo da Vinci** (1452-1519), the other two being Michael Angelo and Raphael. He greatly influenced the school of Milan, and has usually been classed with the Milanese, yet he was educated in Florence, in the workshop of Verrocchio, and was so universal in thought and methods that he hardly belongs to any school.

He has been named a realist, an idealist, a magician, a wizard, a dreamer, and finally a scientist, by different writers, yet he was none of these things while being all of them—a full-rounded, universal man, learned in many departments and excelling in whatever he undertook. He had the scientific and experimental way of looking at things. That is perhaps to be regretted, since it resulted in his experimenting with everything and completing little of anything. His different tastes and pursuits pulled him different ways, and his knowledge made him sceptical of his own powers. He pondered and thought how to reach up higher, how to penetrate deeper, how to realize more comprehensively, and in the end he gave up in despair. He could not fulfil his ideal of the head of Christ nor the head of Mona Lisa, and after[100] years of labor he left them unfinished. The problem of human life, the spirit, the world engrossed him, and all his creations seem impregnated with the psychological, the mystical, the unattainable, the hidden.

FIG. 43.—LEONARDO DA VINCI. MONA LISA. LOUVRE.
Please click here for a modern color image

He was no religionist, though painting the religious subject with feeling; he was not in any sense a classicist, nor had he any care for the antique marbles, which he considered a study of nature at second-hand. He was more in love with physical life without being an enthusiast over it. His regard for contours, rhythm of line, blend of light with shade, study of atmosphere, perspective, trees, animals, humanity, show that though he examined nature scientifically, he pictured it æsthetically. In his types there is much[101] sweetness of soul, charm of disposition, dignity of mien, even grandeur and majesty of presence. His people we would like to know better. They are full of life, intelligence, sympathy; they have fascination of manner, winsomeness of mood, grace of bearing. We see this in his best-known work—the Mona Lisa of the Louvre. It has much allurement of personal presence, with a depth and abundance of soul altogether charming.

Technically, Leonardo was not a handler of the brush superior in any way to his Florentine contemporaries. He knew all the methods and mediums of the time, and did much to establish oil-painting among the Florentines, but he was never a painter like Titian, or even Correggio or Andrea del Sarto. A splendid draughtsman, a man of invention, imagination, grace, elegance, and power, he nevertheless carried more by mental penetration and æsthetic sense than by his technical skill. He was one of the great men of the Renaissance, and deservedly holds a place in the front rank.

Though Leonardo's accomplishment seems slight because of the little that is left to us, yet he had a great following not only among the Florentines but at Milan, where Vincenza Foppa had started a school in the Early Renaissance time. Leonardo was there for fourteen years, and his artistic personality influenced many painters to adopt his type and methods. **Bernardino Luini** (1475?-1532?) was the most prominent of the disciples. He cultivated Leonardo's sentiment, style, subjects, and composition in his middle period, but later on developed independence and originality. He came at a period of art when that earnestness of characterization which marked the early men was giving way to gracefulness of recitation, and that was the chief feature of his art. For that matter gracefulness and pathetic sweetness of mood, with purity of line and warmth of color characterized all the Milanese painters.

FIG. 44.—LUINI. DAUGHTER OF HERODIAS WITH HEAD OF JOHN THE BAPTIST. UFFIZI.

Please click here for a modern color image

The more prominent lights of the school were **Salaino**[102] (fl. 1495-1518), of whose work nothing authentic exists, **Boltraffio** (1467-1516), a painter of limitations but of much refinement and purity, and **Marco da Oggiono** (1470?-1530) a close follower of Leonardo. **Solario** (1458?-1515?) probably became acquainted early with the Flemish mode of working practised by Antonello da Messina, but he afterward came under Leonardo's spell at Milan. He was a careful, refined painter, possessed of feeling and tenderness, producing pictures with enamelled surfaces and much detail. **Gianpietrino** (fl. 1520-1540) and **Cesare da Sesto** (1477-1523?) were also of the Milanese school, the latter afterward falling under the Raphael influence. **Gaudenzio Ferrara** (1481?-1547?), an exceptionally brilliant colorist and a painter of much dis[103]tinction, was under Leonardo's influence at one time, and with the teachings of that master he mingled a little of Raphael in the type of face. He was an uneven painter, often excessive in sentiment, but at his best one of the most charming of the northern painters.

SODOMA AND THE SIENNESE: Sienna, alive in the fourteenth century to all that was stirring in art, in the fifteenth century was in complete eclipse, no painters of consequence emanating from there or being established there. In the sixteenth century there was a revival of art because of a northern painter settling there and building up a new school. This painter was **Sodoma** (1477?-1549). He was one of the best pupils of Leonardo da Vinci, a master of the human figure, handling it with much grace and charm of expression, but not so successful with groups or studied compositions, wherein he was inclined to huddle and over-crowd space. He was afterward led off by the brilliant success of Raphael, and adopted something of that master's style. His best work was done in fresco, though he did some easel pictures that have darkened very much through time. He was a friend of Raphael, and his portrait appears beside Raphael's in the latter painter's celebrated School of Athens. The pupils and followers of the Siennese School were not men of great strength. **Pacchiarotta** (1474-1540?), **Girolamo della Pacchia** (1477-1535), **Peruzzi** (1481-1536), a half-Lombard half-Umbrian painter of ability, and **Beccafumi** (1486-1551) were the principal lights. The influence of the school was slight.

FIG. 45.—SODOMA. ECSTASY OF ST. CATHERINE. SIENNA.

FERRARA AND BOLOGNESE SCHOOLS: The painters of these schools during the sixteenth century have usually been classed among the followers and imitators of Raphael, but not without some injustice. The influence of Raphael was great throughout Central Italy, and the Ferrarese and Bolognese felt it, but not to the extinction of their native thought and methods. Moreover, there was some influence in color coming from the Venetian school, but again not to[104] the entire extinction of Ferrarese individuality. **Dosso Dossi** (1479?-1541), at Ferrara, a pupil of Lorenzo Costa, was the chief painter of the time, and he showed more of Giorgione in color and light-and-shade than anyone else, yet he never abandoned the yellows, greens, and reds peculiar to Ferrara, and both he and Garofolo were strikingly original in their background landscapes. **Garofolo** (1481-1559) was a pupil of Panetti and Costa, who made several visits to Rome and there fell in love with Raphael's work, which showed in a fondness for the sweep and flow of line, in the type of face adopted, and in the calmness of his many easel pictures. He was not so dramatic a painter as Dosso, and in addition he had certain mannerisms or earmarks, such as sootiness in[105] his flesh tints and brightness in his yellows and greens, with dulness in his reds. He was always Ferrarese in his landscapes and in the main characteristics of his technic. **Mazzolino** (1478?-1528?) was another of the school, probably a pupil of Panetti. He was an elaborate painter, fond of architectural backgrounds and glowing colors enlivened with gold in the high lights. **Bagnacavallo** (1484-1542) was a pupil of Francia at Bologna, but with much of Dosso and Ferrara about him. He, in common with Imola, already mentioned, was indebted to the art of Raphael.

CORREGGIO AT PARMA: In **Correggio** (1494?-1534) all the Boccaccio nature of the Renaissance came to the surface. It was indicated in Andrea del Sarto—this nature-worship—but Correggio was the consummation. He was the Faun of the Renaissance, the painter with whom the beauty of the human as distinguished from the religious and the classic showed at its very strongest. Free animal spirits, laughing madonnas, raving nymphs, excited children of the wood, and angels of the sky pass and repass through his pictures in an atmosphere of pure sensuousness. They appeal to us not religiously, not historically, not intellectually, but sensuously and artistically through their rhythmic lines, their palpitating flesh, their beauty of color, and in the light and atmosphere that surround them. He was less of a religionist than Andrea del Sarto. Religion in art was losing ground in his day, and the liberality and worldliness of its teachers appeared clearly enough in the decorations of the Convent of St. Paul at Parma, where Correggio was allowed to paint mythological Dianas and Cupids in the place of saints and madonnas. True enough, he painted the religious subject very often, but with the same spirit of life and joyousness as profane subjects.

FIG. 46—CORREGGIO. MARRIAGE OF ST. CATHERINE AND CHRIST. LOUVRE.
Please click here for a modern color image

The classic subject seemed more appropriate to his spirit, and yet he knew and probably cared less about it than the religious subject. His Dianas and Ledas are only[106] so in name. They have little of the Hellenic spirit about them, and for the sterner, heroic phases of classicism—the lofty, the grand—Correggio never essayed them. The things of this earth and the sweetness thereof seemed ever his aim. Women and children were beautiful to him in the same way that flowers and trees and skies and sunsets were beautiful. They were revelations of grace, charm, tenderness, light, shade, color. Simply to exist and be glad in the sunlight was sweetness to Correggio. He would have no Sibylesque mystery, no prophetic austerity, no solemnity, no great intellectuality. He was no leader of a tragic chorus. The dramatic, the forceful, the powerful, were [107]foreign to his mood. He was a singer of lyrics and pastorals, a lover of the material beauty about him, and it is because he passed by the pietistic, the classic, the literary, and showed the beauty of physical life as an art motive that he is called the Faun of the Renaissance. The appellation is not inappropriate.

How or why he came to take this course would be hard to determine. It was reflective of the times; but Correggio, so far as history tells us, had little to do with the movements and people of his age. He was born and lived and died near Parma, and is sometimes classed among the Bologna-Ferrara painters, but the reasons for the classification are not too strong. His education, masters, and influences are all shadowy and indefinite. He seems, from his drawing and composition, to have known something of Mantegna at Mantua; from his coloring something of Dosso and Garofolo, especially in his straw-yellows; from his early types and faces something of Costa and Francia, and his contours and light-and-shade indicate a knowledge of Leonardo's work. But there is no positive certainty that he saw the work of any of these men.

His drawing was faulty at times, but not obtrusively so; his color and brush-work rich, vivacious, spirited; his light brilliant, warm, penetrating; his contours melting, graceful; his atmosphere omnipresent, enveloping. In composition he rather pushed aside line in favor of light and color. It was his technical peculiarity that he centralized his light and surrounded it by darks as a foil. And in this very feature he was one of the first men in Renaissance Italy to paint a picture for the purpose of weaving a scheme of lights and darks through a tapestry of rich colors. That is art for art's sake, and that, as will be seen further on, was the picture motive of the great Venetians.

Correggio's immediate pupils and followers, like those of Raphael and Andrea del Sarto, did him small honor. As was usually the case in Renaissance art-history they[108] caught at the method and lost the spirit of the master. His son, **Pomponio Allegri** (1521-1593?), was a painter of some mark without being in the front rank.**Michelangelo Anselmi** (1491-1554?), though not a pupil, was an indifferent imitator of Correggio. **Parmigianino** (1504-1540), a mannered painter of some brilliancy, and of excellence in portraits, was perhaps the best of the immediate followers. It was not until after Correggio's death, and with the painters of the Decadence, that his work was seriously taken up and followed.

PRINCIPAL WORKS: MILANESE—**Leonardo da Vinci**, Last Supper S. M. delle Grazie Milan (in ruins), Mona Lisa, Madonna with St. Anne (badly damaged) Louvre, Adoration (unfinished) Uffizi, Angel at left in Verrocchio's Baptism Florence Acad.; **Luini**, frescos Monastero Maggiore, 71 fragments in Brera Milan, Church of the Pilgrims Sarrona, S. M. degli Angeli Lugano, altar-pieces Duomo Como, Ambrosian Library Milan, Brera, Uffizi, Louvre, Madrid, St. Petersburgh, and other galleries; **Beltraffio**, Madonna Louvre, Barbara Berlin Gal., Madonna Nat. Gal. Lon., fresco Convent of S. Onofrio Rome (ascribed to Da Vinci); **Marco da Oggiono**, Archangels and other works Brera, Holy Family Madonna Louvre; **Solario**, Ecce Homo Repose Poldi-Pezzoli Gal. Milan, Holy Family Brera, Madonna Portrait Louvre, Portraits Nat. Gal. Lon., Assumption Certosa of Pavia; **Giampietrino**, Magdalene Brera, Madonna S. Sepolcro Milan, Magdalene and Catherine Berlin Gal.; **Cesare da Sesto**, Madonna Brera, Magi

Naples Mus.; **Gaudenzio Ferrara**, frescos Church of Pilgrims Saronna, other pictures in Brera, Turin Gal., S. Gaudenzio Novara, S. Celso Milan.

SIENNESE—**Sodoma**, frescos Convent of St. Anne near Pienza, Benedictine Convent of Mont' Oliveto Maggiore, Alexander and Roxana Villa Farnesina Rome, S. Bernardino Palazzo Pubblico, S. Domenico Sienna, pictures Uffizi, Brera, Munich, Vienna Gals.;**Pacchiarotto**, Ascension Visitation Sienna Gal.; **Girolamo del Pacchia**, frescos (3) S. Bernardino, altar-pieces S. Spirito and Sienna Acad., Munich and Nat. Gal. Lon.; **Peruzzi**, fresco Fontegiuste Sienna, S. Onofrio, S. M. della Pace Rome; **Beccafumi**, St. Catherine Saints Sienna Acad., frescos S. Bernardino Hospital and S. Martino Sienna, Palazzo Doria Rome, Pitti, Berlin, Munich Gals.

FERRARESE AND BOLOGNESE—**Dosso Dossi**, many works Ferrara [109]Modena Gals., Duomo S. Pietro Modena, Brera, Borghese, Doria, Berlin, Dresden, Vienna, Gals.; **Garofolo**, many works Ferrara churches and Gal., Borghese, Campigdoglio, Louvre, Berlin, Dresden, Munich, Nat. Gal. Lon.; **Mazzolino**, Ferrara, Berlin, Dresden, Louvre, Doria, Borghese, Pitti, Uffizi, and Nat. Gal. Lon.; **Bagnacavallo**, Misericordia and Gal. Bologna, Louvre, Berlin, Dresden Gals.

PARMESE—**Correggio**, frescos Convent of S. Paolo, S. Giovanni Evangelista, Duomo Parma, altar-pieces Dresden (4), Parma Gals., Louvre, mythological pictures Antiope Louvre, Danae Borghese, Leda Jupiter and Io Berlin, Venus Mercury and Cupid Nat. Gal. Lon., Ganymede Vienna Gal.; **Pomponio Allegri**, frescos Capella del Popolo Parma; **Anselmi**, frescos S. Giovanni Evangelista, altar-pieces Madonna della Steccata, Duomo, Gal. Parma, Louvre; **Parmigianino**, frescos Moses Steccata, S. Giovanni Parma, altar-pieces Santa Margherita, Bologna Gal., Madonna Pitti, portraits Uffizi, Vienna, Naples Mus., other works Dresden, Vienna, and Nat. Gal. Lon.

[110]

CHAPTER X.
ITALIAN PAINTING.
THE HIGH RENAISSANCE. 1500-1600. (*Continued.*)

BOOKS RECOMMENDED: The works on Italian art before mentioned and also consult General Bibliography, (page xv.).

THE VENETIAN SCHOOL: It was at Venice and with the Venetian painters of the sixteenth century that a new art-motive was finally and fully adopted. This art-motive was not religion. For though the religious subject was still largely used, the religious or pietistic belief was not with the Venetians any more than with Correggio. It was not a classic, antique, realistic, or naturalistic motive. The Venetians were interested in all phases of nature, and they were students of nature, but not students of truth for truth's sake.

What they sought, primarily, was the light and shade on a nude shoulder, the delicate contours of a form, the flow and fall of silk or brocade, the richness of a robe, a scheme of color or of light, the character of a face, the majesty of a figure. They were seeking effects of line, light, color—mere sensuous and pictorial effects, in which religion and classicism played secondary parts. They believed in art for art's sake; that painting was a creation, not an illustration; that it should exist by its pictorial beauties, not by its subject or story. No matter what their subjects, they invariably painted them so as to show the beauties they prized the highest. The Venetian conception was less[111] austere, grand, intellectual, than pictorial, sensuous, concerning the beautiful as it appealed to the eye. And this was not a slight or unworthy conception. True it dealt with the fulness of material life, but regarded as it was by the Venetians—a thing full-rounded, complete, harmonious, splendid—it became a great ideal of existence.

FIG. 47.—GIORGIONE(?). ORDEAL OF MOSES. UFFIZI.
Please click here for a modern color image

In technical expression color was the note of all the school, with hardly an exception. This in itself would seem to imply a lightness of spirit, for color is somehow associated in the popular mind with decorative gayety; but nothing could be further removed from the Venetian school than triviality. Color was taken up with the greatest seriousness, and handled in such masses and with such[112] dignified power that while it pleased it also awed the spectator. Without having quite the severity of line, some of the Venetian chromatic schemes rise in sublimity almost to the Sistine modellings of Michael Angelo. We do not feel this so much in Giovanni Bellini, fine in color as he was. He came too early for the full splendor, but he left many pupils who completed what he had inaugurated.

THE GREAT VENETIANS: The most positive in influence upon his contemporaries of all the great Venetians was **Giorgione** (1477?-1511). He died young, and what few pictures by him are left to us have been so torn to pieces by historical criticism that at times one begins to doubt if there ever was such a painter. His different styles have been confused, and his pictures in consequence thereof attributed to followers instead of to the master. Painters change their styles, but seldom their original bent of mind. With Giorgione there was a lyric feeling as shown in music. The voluptuous swell of line, the melting tone of color, the sharp dash of light, the undercurrent of atmosphere, all mingled for him into radiant melody. He sought pure pictorial beauty and found it in everything of nature. He had little grasp of the purely intellectual, and the religious was something he dealt with in no strong devotional way. The fête, the concert, the fable, the legend, with a landscape setting, made a stronger appeal to him. More of a recorder than a thinker he was not the less a leader showing the way into that new Arcadian grove of pleasure whose inhabitants thought not of creeds and faiths and histories and literatures, but were content to lead the life that was sweet in its glow and warmth of color, its light, its shadows, its bending trees, and arching skies. A strong full-blooded race, sober-minded, dignified, rationally happy with their lot, Giorgione portrayed them with an art infinite in variety and consummate in skill. Their least features under his brush seemed to glow like jewels. The[113] sheen of armor and rich robe, a bare forearm, a nude back, or loosened hair—mere morsels of color and light—all took on a new beauty. Even landscape with him became more significant. His master, Bellini, had been realistic enough in the details of trees and hills, but Giorgione grasped the meaning of landscape as an entirety, and rendered it with poetic breadth.

Technically he adopted the oil medium brought to Venice by Antonello da Messina, introducing scumbling and glazing to obtain brilliancy and depth of color. Of light-and-shade he was a master, and in atmosphere excellent. He, in common with all the Venetians, is sometimes said to be lacking in drawing, but that is the result of a misunderstanding. The Venetians never cared to accent line, choosing rather to model in masses of light and shadow and color. Giorgione was a superior man with the brush, but not quite up to his contemporary Titian.

FIG. 48.—TITIAN. VENUS EQUIPPING CUPID. BORGHESE PAL., ROME.
Please click here for a modern color image

That is not surprising, for **Titian** (1477-1576) was the[114] painter easily first in the whole range of Italian art. He was the first man in the history of painting to handle a brush with freedom, vigor, and gusto. And Titian's brush-work was probably the least part of his genius. Calm in mood, dignified, and often majestic in conception, learned beyond all others in his craft, he mingled thought, feeling, color, brush-work into one grand and glowing whole. He emphasized nothing, yet elevated everything. In pure intellectual thought he was not so strong as Raphael. He never sought to make painting a vehicle for theological, literary, or classical ideas. His tale was largely of humanity under a religious or classical name, but a noble, majestic humanity. In his art dignified senators, stern doges, and solemn ecclesiastics mingle with open-eyed madonnas, winning Ariadnes, and youthful Bacchuses. Men and women they are truly, but the very noblest of the Italian race, the mountain race of the Cadore country—proud, active, glowing with life; the sea race of Venice—worldly wise, full of character, luxurious in power.

In himself he was an epitome of all the excellences of painting. He was everything, the sum of Venetian skill, the crowning genius of Renaissance art. He had force, power, invention, imagination, point of view; he had the infinite knowledge of nature and the infinite mastery of art. In addition, Fortune smiled upon him as upon a favorite child. Trained in mind and hand he lived for ninety-nine years and worked unceasingly up to a few months of his death. His genius was great and his accomplishment equally so. He was celebrated and independent at thirty-five, though before that he showed something of the influence of Giorgione. After the death of Giorgione and his master, Bellini, Titian was the leader in Venice to the end of his long life, and though having few scholars of importance his influence was spread through all North Italian painting.[115]

Taking him for all in all, perhaps it is not too much to say that he was the greatest painter known to history. If it were possible to describe that greatness in one word, that word would be "universality." He saw and painted that which was universal in its truth. The local and particular, the small and the accidental, were passed over for those great truths which belong to all the world of life. In this respect he was a veritable Shakespeare, with all the calmness and repose of one who overlooked the world from a lofty height.

FIG. 49.—TINTORETTO. MERCURY AND GRACES. DUCAL PAL., VENICE.
Please click here for a modern color image

The restfulness and easy strength of Titian were not characteristics of his follower **Tintoretto** (1518-1592). He[116] was violent, headlong, impulsive, more impetuous than Michael Angelo, and in some respects a strong reminder of him. He had not Michael Angelo's austerity, and there was more clash and tumult and fire about him, but he had a command of line like the Florentine, and a way of hurling things, as seen in the Fall of the Damned, that reminds one of the Last Judgment of the Sistine. It was his aim to combine the line of Michael Angelo and the color of Titian; but without reaching up to either of his models he produced a powerful amalgam of his own.

He was one of the very great artists of the world, and the most rapid workman in the whole Renaissance period. There are to-day, after centuries of decay, fire, theft, and repainting, yards upon yards of Tintoretto's canvases rotting upon the walls of the Venetian churches. He produced an enormous amount of work, and, what is to be regretted, much of it was contract work or experimental sketching. This has given his art a rather bad name, but judged by his best works in the Ducal Palace and the Academy at Venice, he will not be found lacking. Even in his masterpiece (The Miracle of the Slave) he is "Il Furioso," as they used to call him; but his thunderbolt style is held in check by wonderful grace, strength of modelling, superb contrasts of light with shade, and a coloring of flesh and robes not unworthy of the very greatest. He was a man who worked in the white heat of passion, with much imagination and invention. As a technician he sought difficulties rather than avoided them. There is some antagonism between form and color, but Tintoretto tried to reconcile them. The result was sometimes clashing, but no one could have done better with them than he did. He was a fine draughtsman, a good colorist, and a master of light. As a brushman he was a superior man, but not equal to Titian.

Paolo Veronese (1528-1588), the fourth great Venetian,[117] did not follow the line direction set by Tintoretto, but carried out the original color-leaning of the school. He came a little later than Tintoretto, and his art was a reflection of the advancing Renaissance, wherein simplicity was destined to lose itself in complexity, grandeur, and display. Paolo came on the very crest of the Renaissance wave, when art, risen to its greatest height, was gleaming in that transparent splendor that precedes the fall.

FIG. 50.—P. VERONESE. VENICE ENTHRONED. DUCAL PAL., VENICE.
Please click here for a modern color image

The great bulk of his work had a large decorative motive behind it. Almost all of the late Venetian work was of that character. Hence it was brilliant in color, elaborate in subject, and grand in scale. Splendid robes, hangings, furniture, architecture, jewels, armor, appeared everywhere, and not in flat, lustreless hues, but with that brilliancy which they possess in nature. Drapery gave way to clothing, and texture-painting was introduced even in the largest canvases. Scenes from Scripture and legend turned into grand pageants of Venetian glory, and the facial expression of the characters rather passed out in favor of telling masses of color to be seen at a distance upon wall[118] or ceiling. It was pomp and glory carried to the highest pitch, but with all seriousness of mood and truthfulness in art. It was beyond Titian in variety, richness, ornament, facility; but it was perhaps below Titian in sentiment, sobriety, and depth of insight. Titian, with all his sensuous beauty, did appeal to the higher intelligence, while Paolo and his companions appealed more positively to the eye by luxurious color-setting and magnificence of invention. The decadence came after Paolo, but not with him. His art was the most gorgeous of the Venetian school, and by many is ranked the highest of all, but perhaps it is better to say it was the height. Those who came after brought about the decline by striving to imitate his splendor, and thereby falling into extravagance.

These are the four great Venetians—the men of first rank. Beside them and around them were many other painters, placed in the second rank, who in any other time or city would have held first place. **Palma il Vecchio** (1480?-1528) was so excellent in many ways that it seems unjust to speak of him as a secondary painter. He was not, however, a great original mind, though in many respects a perfect painter. He was influenced by Bellini at first, and then by Giorgione. In subject there was nothing dramatic about him, and he carries chiefly by his portrayal of quiet, dignified, and beautiful Venetians under the names of saints and holy families. The St. Barbara is an example of this, and one of the most majestic figures in all painting.

FIG. 51.—LOTTO. THREE AGES. PITTI.
Please click here for a modern color image

Palma's friend and fellow-worker, **Lorenzo Lotto** (1480?-1556?) came from the school of the Bellini, and at different times was under the influence of several Venetian painters—Palma, Giorgione, Titian—without obliterating a sensitive individuality of his own. He was a somewhat mannered but very charming painter, and in portraits can hardly be classed below Titian. **Rocco Marconi** (fl. 1505-1520) was another Bellini-educated painter, showing the influence of[119] Palma and even of Paris Bordone. In color and landscape he was excellent. **Pordenone** (1483-1540) rather followed after Giorgione, and unsuccessfully competed with Titian. He was inclined to exaggeration in dramatic composition, but was a painter of undeniable power. **Cariani** (1480-1541) was another Giorgione follower.**Bonifazio Pitati** probably came from a Veronese family. He showed the influence of Palma, and was rather deficient in drawing, though exceedingly brilliant and rich in coloring. This latter may be said for **Paris Bordone** (1495-1570), a painter of Titian's school, gorgeous in color, but often lacking in truth of form. His portraits are very fine. Another painter family, the Bassani—there were six of them, of whom **Jacopo Bassano** (1510-1592)[120] and his son **Francesco Bassano**(1550-1591), were the most noted—formed themselves after Venetian masters, and were rather remarkable for violent contrasts of light and dark, *genre* treatment of sacred subjects, and still-life and animal painting.

PAINTING IN VENETIAN TERRITORIES: Venetian painting was not confined to Venice, but extended through all the Venetian territories in Renaissance times, and those who lived away from the city were, in their art, decidedly Venetian, though possessing local characteristics.

At Brescia **Savoldo** (1480?-1548), a rather superficial painter, fond of weird lights and sheeny draperies, and **Romanino** (1485?-1566), a follower of Giorgione, good in composition but unequal and careless in execution, were the earliest of the High Renaissance men. **Moretto** (1498?-1555) was the strongest and most original, a man of individuality and power, remarkable technically for his delicacy and unity of color under a veil of "silvery tone." In composition he was dignified and noble, and in brush-work simple and direct. One of the great painters of the time, he seemed to stand more apart from Venetian influence than any other on Venetian territory. He left one remarkable pupil, **Moroni** (fl. 1549-1578) whose portraits are to-day the gems of several galleries, and greatly admired for their modern spirit and treatment.

At Verona **Caroto** and **Girolamo dai Libri** (1474-1555), though living into the sixteenth century were more allied to the art of the fifteenth century. **Torbido**(1486?-1546?) was a vacillating painter, influenced by Liberale da Verona, Giorgione, Bonifazio Veronese, and later, even by Giulio Romano. **Cavazzola** (1486-1522) was more original, and a man of talent. There were numbers of other painters scattered all through the Venetian provinces at this time, but they were not of the first, or even the second rank, and hence call for no mention here.[121]

PRINCIPAL WORKS: Giorgione, Fête Rustique Louvre, Sleeping Venus Dresden, altar-piece Castelfranco, Ordeal of Moses Judgment of Solomon Knight of Malta Uffizi; **Titian**, Sacred and Profane Love Borghese, Tribute Money Dresden, Annunciation S. Rocco, Pesaro Madonna Frari Venice, Entombment Man with Glove Louvre, Bacchus Nat. Gal. Lon., Charles V. Madrid, Danæ Naples, many other works in almost every European gallery; **Tintoretto**, many works in Venetian churches, Salute SS. Giovanni e Paolo S. Maria dell' Orto Scuola and Church of S. Rocco Ducal Palace Venice Acad. (best work Miracle of Slave); **Paolo Veronese**, many Pictures in S. Sebastiano Ducal Palace Academy Venice, Pitti, Uffizi, Brera, Capitoline and Borghese Galleries Rome, Turin, Dresden, Vienna, Louvre, Nat. Gal. Lon.; **Palma il Vecchio**, Jacob and Rachel Three Sisters Dresden, Barbara S. M. Formosa Venice, other altar-pieces Venice Acad., Colonna Palace Rome, Brera, Naples Mus., Vienna, Nat. Gal. Lon.; **Lotto**, Three Ages Pitti, Portraits Brera, Nat. Gal. Lon., altar-pieces SS. Giovanni e Paolo Venice and churches at Bergamo, Treviso, Recanti, also Uffizi, Vienna, Madrid Gals.;**Marconi**, Descent Venice Acad., altar-pieces S. Giorgio Maggiore SS. Giovanni e Paolo Venice; **Pordenone**, S. Lorenzo Madonna Venice Acad., Salome Doria St. George Quirinale Rome, other works Madrid, Dresden, St. Petersburg, Nat. Gal. Lon.; **Bonifazio**, St. John, St. Joseph, etc. Ambrosian Library Milan (attributed to Giorgione), Holy Family Colonna Pal. Rome, Ducal Pal., Pitti, Dresden Gals.; Supper at Emmaus Brera, other works Venice Acad.; **Paris Bordone**, Fisherman and Doge, Venice Acad., Madonna Casa Tadini Lovere, portraits in Uffizi, Pitti, Louvre, Munich, Vienna, Nat. Gal. Lon., Brignola Pal. Genoa; **Jacopo Bassano**, altar-pieces in Bassano churches, also Ducal Pal. Venice, Nat. Gal. Lon., Uffizi, Naples Mus.; **Francesco Bassano**, large pictures Ducal Pal., St. Catherine Pitti, Sabines Turin, Adoration and Christ in Temple Dresden, Adoration and Last Supper Madrid; **Savoldo**, altar-pieces Brera, S. Niccolò Treviso, Uffizi, Turin Gal., S. Giobbe Venice, Nat. Gal. Lon.; **Romanino**, altar-pieces S. Francesco Brescia, Berlin Gal., S. Giovanni Evangelista Brescia, Duomo Cremona, Padua, and Nat. Gal. Lon.; **Moretto**, altar-pieces Brera, Staedel Mus., S. M. della Pieta Venice, Vienna, Berlin, Louvre, Pitti, Nat. Gal. Lon.; **Moroni**, portraits Bergamo Gal., Uffizi, Nat. Gal. Lon., Berlin, Dresden, Madrid; **Girolamo dai Libri**, Madonna Berlin, Conception S. Paolo Verona, Virgin Verona Gal., S. Giorgio Maggiore Verona, Nat. Gal. Lon.; **Torbido**, frescos Duomo, altar-pieces S. Zeno and S. Eufemia Verona; **Cavazzola**, altar-pieces, Verona Gal. and Nat. Gal. Lon.

[122]

CHAPTER XI.
ITALIAN PAINTING.
THE DECADENCE AND MODERN WORK. 1600-1894.

BOOKS RECOMMENDED: As before, also General Bibliography, (page xv.); Calvi, *Notizie della vita e delle opere di Gio. Francesco Barbiera*; Malvasia, *Felsina Pittrice*; Sir Joshua Reynolds, *Discourses*; Symonds, *Renaissance in Italy—The Catholic Reaction*; Willard,*Modern Italian Art*.

THE DECLINE: An art movement in history seems like a wave that rises to a height, then breaks, falls, and parts of it are caught up from beneath to help form the strength of a new advance. In Italy Christianity was the propelling force of the wave. In the Early Renaissance, the antique, and the study of nature came in as additions. At Venice in the High Renaissance the art-for-art's-sake motive made the crest of light and color. The highest point was reached then, and there was nothing that could follow but the breaking and the scattering of the wave. This took place in Central Italy after 1540, in Venice after 1590.

Art had typified in form, thought, and expression everything of which the Italian race was capable. It had perfected all the graces and elegancies of line and color, and adorned them with a superlative splendor. There was nothing more to do. The idea was completed, the motive power had served its purpose, and that store of race-impulse which seems necessary to the making of every great art was exhausted. For the men that came after Michael Angelo and[123] Tintoretto there was nothing. All that they could do was to repeat what others had said, or to recombine the old thoughts and forms. This led inevitably to imitation, over-refinement of style, and conscious study of beauty, resulting in mannerism and affectation. Such qualities marked the art of those painters who came in the latter part of the sixteenth century and the first of the seventeenth. They were unfortunate men in the time of their birth. No painter could have been great in the seventeenth century of Italy. Art lay prone upon its face under Jesuit rule, and the late men were left upon the barren sands by the receding wave of the Renaissance.

FIG. 52.—BRONZINO. CHRIST IN LIMBO. UFFIZI.

ART MOTIVES AND SUBJECTS: As before, the chief subject of the art of the Decadence was religion, with many heads and busts of the Madonna, though nature and the classic still played their parts. After the Reformation at the North the Church in Italy started the Counter-Reformation. One of the chief means employed by this Catholic reaction was the embellishment of church worship, and painting on a large scale, on panel rather than in fresco, was demanded for decorative purposes. But the religious motive had passed out, though its subject was retained, and[124] the pictorial motive had reached its climax at Venice. The faith of the one and the taste and skill of the other were not attainable by the late men, and, while consciously striving to achieve them, they fell into exaggerated sentiment and technical weakness. It seems perfectly apparent in their works that they had nothing of their own to say, and that they were trying to say over again what Michael Angelo, Correggio, and Titian had said before them much better. There were earnest men and good painters among them, but they could produce only the empty form of art. The spirit had fled.

THE MANNERISTS: Immediately after the High Renaissance leaders of Florence and Rome came the imitators and exaggerators of their styles. They produced large, crowded compositions, with a hasty facility of the brush and striking effects of light. Seeking the grand they overshot the temperate. Their elegance was affected, their sentiment forced, their brilliancy superficial glitter. When they thought to be ideal they lost themselves in incomprehensible allegories; when they thought to be real they grew prosaic in detail. These men are known in art history as the Mannerists, and the men whose works they imitated were chiefly Raphael, Michael Angelo, and Correggio. There were many of them, and some of them have already been spoken of as the followers of Michael Angelo.

Agnolo Bronzino (1502?-1572) was a pupil of Pontormo, and an imitator of Michael Angelo, painting in rather heavy colors with a thin brush. His characters were large, but never quite free from weakness, except in portraiture, where he appeared at his best. **Vasari** (1511-1574)—the same Vasari who wrote the lives of the painters—had versatility and facility, but his superficial imitations of Michael Angelo were too grandiose in conception and too palpably false in modelling. **Salviati** (1510-1563) was a friend of Vasari, a painter of about the same cast of mind and[125] hand as Vasari, and **Federigo Zucchero** (1543-1609) belongs with him in producing things muscularly big but intellectually small. **Baroccio** (1528-1612), though classed among the Mannerists as an imitator of Correggio and Raphael, was really one of the strong men of the late times. There was affectation and sentimentality about his work, a prettiness of face, rosy flesh tints, and a general lightness of color, but he was a superior brushman, a good colorist, and, at times, a man of earnestness and power.

FIG. 53.—BAROCCIO. ANNUNCIATION.
Please click here for a modern color image

THE ECLECTICS: After the Mannerists came the Eclectics of Bologna, led by the **Caracci**, who, about 1585, sought to "revive" art. They started out to correct the faults of the Mannerists, and yet their own art was based more on the art of their great predecessors than on nature. They thought to make a union of Renaissance excellences by combining Michael Angelo's line, Titian's color, Correggio's light-and-shade and Raphael's symmetry and grace. The attempt was praiseworthy for the time, but hardly successful. They caught the lines and lights and colors of the great men, but they overlooked the fact that the excellence of the imitated lay largely in[126] their inimitable individualities, which could not be combined. The Eclectic work was done with intelligence, but their system was against them and their baroque age was against them. Midway in their career the Caracci themselves modified their eclecticism and placed more reliance upon nature. But their pupils paid little heed to the modification.

There were five of the Caracci, but three of them—**Ludovico** (1555-1619), **Agostino** (1557-1602), and **Annibale** (1560-1609)—led the school, and of these Annibale was the most distinguished. They had many pupils, and their influence was widely spread over Italy. In Sir Joshua Reynolds's day they were ranked with Raphael, but at the present time criticism places them where they belong—painters of the Decadence with little originality or spontaneity in their art, though much technical skill. **Domenichino** (1581-1641) was the strongest of the pupils. His St. Jerome was rated by Poussin as one of the three great paintings of the world, but it never deserved such rank. It is powerfully composed, but poor in coloring and handling. The painter had great repute in his time, and was one of the best of the seventeenth century men. **Guido Reni** (1575-1642) was a painter of many gifts and accomplishments, combined with many weaknesses. His works are well composed and painted, but excessive in sentiment and overdone in pathos. **Albani** (1578-1660) ran to elegance and a porcelain-like prettiness. **Guercino** (1591-1666) was originally of the Eclectic School at Bologna, but later took up with the methods of the Naturalists at Naples. He was a painter of far more than the average ability. **Sassoferrato** (1605-1685) and **Carlo Dolci** (1616-1686) were so super-saturated with sentimentality that often their skill as painters is overlooked or forgotten. In spirit they were about the weakest of the century. There were other eclectic schools started throughout Italy—at Milan, Cremona,[127] Ferrara—but they produced little worth recording. At Rome certain painters like **Cristofano Allori** (1577-1621), an exceptionally strong man for the time, **Berrettini** (1596-1669), and **Maratta** (1625-1713), manufactured a facile kind of painting from what was attractive in the various schools, but it was never other than meretricious work.

FIG. 54.—ANNIBALE CARACCI. ENTOMBMENT OF CHRIST. LOUVRE.

THE NATURALISTS: Contemporary with the Eclectics sprang up the Neapolitan school of the Naturalists, led by **Caravaggio** (1569-1609) and his pupils. These schools opposed each other, and yet influenced each other. Especially was this true with the later men, who took what was best in both schools. The Naturalists were, perhaps, more firmly based upon nature than the Bolognese Eclectics.[128] Their aim was to take nature as they found it, and yet, in conformity with the extravagance of the age, they depicted extravagant nature. Caravaggio thought to represent sacred scenes more truthfully by taking his models from the harsh street life about him and giving types of saints and apostles from Neapolitan brawlers and bandits. It was a brutal, coarse representation, rather fierce in mood and impetuous in action, yet not without a good deal of tragic power. His subjects were rather dismal or morose, but there was knowledge in the drawing of them, some good color and brush-work and a peculiar darkness of shadow masses (originally gained from Giorgione), that stood as an ear-mark of his whole school. From the continuous use of black shadows the school got the name of the "Darklings," by which they are still known. **Giordano** (1632-1705), a painter of prodigious facility and invention, **Salvator Rosa** (1615-1673), best known as one of the early painters of landscape, and **Ribera**, a Spanish painter, were the principal pupils.

THE LATE VENETIANS: The Decadence at Venice, like the Renaissance, came later than at Florence, but after the death of Tintoretto mannerisms and the imitation of the great men did away with originality. There was still much color left, and fine ceiling decorations were done, but the nobility and calm splendor of Titian's days had passed. **Palma il Giovine** (1544-1628) with a hasty brush produced imitations of Tintoretto with some grace and force, and in remarkable quantity. He and Tintoretto were the most rapid and productive painters of the century; but Palma's was not good in spirit, though quite dashing in technic.**Padovanino** (1590-1650) was more of a Titian follower, but, like all the other painters of the time, he was proficient with the brush and lacking in the stronger mental elements. The last great Italian painter was **Tiepolo** (1696-1770), and he was really great[129] beyond his age. With an art founded on Paolo Veronese, he produced decorative ceilings and panels of high quality, with wonderful invention, a limpid brush, and a light flaky color peculiarly appropriate to the walls of churches and palaces. He was, especially in easel pictures, a brilliant, vivacious brushman, full of dash and spirit, tempered by a large knowledge of what was true and pictorial. Some of his best pictures are still in Venice, and modern painters are unstinted in their praise of them. He left a son, **Domenico Tiepolo** (1726-1795), who followed his methods. In the late days of Venetian painting, **Canaletto** (1697-1768) and **Guardi** (1712-1793) achieved reputation by painting Venetian canals and architecture with much color effect.

FIG. 55.—CARAVAGGIO. THE CARD PLAYERS. DRESDEN.

NINETEENTH-CENTURY PAINTING IN ITALY: There is little in the art of Italy during the present century that shows a positive national spirit. It has been leaning on the rest of Europe for many years, and the best that the living[130] painters show is largely an echo of Dusseldorf, Munich, or Paris. The revived classicism of David in France affected nineteenth-century painting in Italy somewhat. Then it was swayed by Cornelius and Overbeck from Germany. **Morelli**(1826-[2]) shows this latter influence, though one of the most important of the living men.[3] In the 1860's Mariano Fortuny, a Spaniard at Rome, led the younger element in the glittering and the sparkling, and this style mingled with much that is more strikingly Parisian than Italian, may be found in the works of painters like**Michetti**, **De Nittis** (1846-1884), **Favretto**, **Tito**, **Nono**, **Simonetti**, and others.

[2]Died, 1901.

[3]See *Scribner's Magazine*, Neapolitan Art, Dec., 1890, Feb., 1891.

Of recent days the impressionistic view of light and color has had its influence; but the Italian work at its best is below that of France. **Segantini**[4] was one of the most promising of the younger men in subjects that have an archaic air about them. **Boldini**, though Italian born and originally following Fortuny's example, is really more Parisian than anything else. He is an artist of much power and technical strength in *genre* subjects and portraits. The newer men are **Fragiocomo**,**Fattori**, **Mancini**, **Marchetti**.

[4]Died, 1899.

PRINCIPAL WORKS: MANNERISTS—**Agnolo Bronzino**, Christ in Limbo and many portraits in Uffizi and Nat. Gal. Lon.; **Vasari**, many pictures in galleries at Arezzo, Bologna, Berlin, Munich, Louvre, Madrid; **Salviati**, Charity Christ Uffizi, Patience Pitti, St. Thomas Louvre, Love and Psyche Berlin; **Federigo Zucchero**, Duomo Florence, Ducal Palace Venice, Allegories Uffizi, Calumny Hampton Court; **Baroccio**, Pardon of St. Francis Urbino, Annunciation Loreto, several pictures in Uffizi, Nat. Gal. Lon., Louvre, Dresden Gal.

ECLECTICS—**Ludovico Caracci**, Cathedral frescos Bologna, thirteen pictures Bologna Gal.; **Agostino Caracci**, frescos (with Annibale) Farnese Pal. Rome, altar-pieces Bologna Gal.; **Annibale Carracci**, frescos (with Agostino) Farnese Pal. Rome, other pictures Bologna Gal., Uffizi, Naples Mus., Dresden, Berlin, Louvre, Nat. Gal. Lon.; **Domenichino**, St. Jerome Vatican, S. Pietro in Vincoli, Diana Borghese, Bologna, Pitti, Louvre, Nat. Gal. Lon.; **Guido Reni**, frescos Aurora Rospigliosi Pal. Rome, many pictures Bologna, Borghese Gal., Pitti, Uffizi, Brera, Naples, [131]Louvre, and other galleries of Europe; **Albani**, **Guercino**, **Sassoferrato**, and **Carlo Dolci**, works in almost every European gallery, especially Bologna; **Cristofano Allori**, Judith Pitti, also pictures in Uffizi; **Berrettini** and **Maratta**, many examples in Italian galleries, also Louvre.

NATURALISTS—**Caravaggio**, Entombment Vatican, many other works in Pitti, Uffizi, Naples, Louvre, Dresden, St. Petersburg; **Giordano**, Judgment of Paris Berlin, many pictures in Dresden and Italian galleries; **Salvator Rosa**, best marine in Pitti, other works Uffizi, Brera, Naples, Madrid galleries and Colonna, Corsini, Doria, Chigi Palaces Rome.

LATE VENETIANS—**Palma il Giovine**, Ducal Palace Venice, Cassel, Dresden, Munich, Madrid, Naples, Vienna galleries; **Padovanino**, Marriage in Cana Kneeling Angel and other works Venice Acad., Carmina Venice, also galleries of Louvre, Uffizi, Borghese, Dresden, London; **Tiepolo**, large fresco Villa Pisani Stra, Palazzo Labia Scuola Carmina, Venice, Villa Valmarana, and at Wurtzburg, easel pictures Venice Acad., Louvre, Berlin, Madrid; **Canaletto** and **Guardi**, many pictures in European galleries.

MODERN ITALIANS[5]—**Morelli**, Madonna Royal chap. Castiglione, Assumption Royal chap. Naples; **Michetti**, The Vow Nat. Gal. Rome;**De Nittis**, Place du Carrousel Luxembourg Paris; **Boldini**, Gossips Met. Mus. New York.

[5]Only works in public places are given. Those in private hands change too often for record here. For detailed list of works see Champlin and Perkins, *Cyclopedia of Painters and Paintings*.

[132]

CHAPTER XII.
FRENCH PAINTING.
SIXTEENTH, SEVENTEENTH, AND EIGHTEENTH-CENTURY PAINTING.

BOOKS RECOMMENDED: Amorini, *Vita del celebre pittore Francesco Primaticcio*; Berger, *Histoire de l'École Française de Peinture au XVIIme Siècle*; Bland, *Les Peintres des fêtes galantes, Watteau, Boucher, et al.*; Curmer, *L'Œuvre de Jean Fouquet*; Delaborde, *Études sur les Beaux Arts en France et en Italie*; Didot, *Études sur Jean Cousin*; Dimier, *French Painting in XVI Century*; Dumont, *Antoine Watteau*; Dussieux, *Nouvelles Recherches sur la Vie de E. Lesueur*; Genevay, *Le Style Louis XIV., Charles Le Brun*; Goncourt, *L'Art du XVIIIme Siècle*; Guibel, *Éloge de Nicolas Poussin*; Guiffrey, *La Famille de Jean*

Cousin; Laborde, *La Renaissance des Arts à la Cour de France*; Lagrange, J. *Vernet et la Peinture au XVIIIme Siècle*; Lecoy de la Marche, *Le Roi René*; Mantz, *François Boucher*; Michiels,*Études sur l'Art Flamand dans l'est et le midi de la France*; Muntz, *La Renaissance en Italie et en France*; Palustre, *La Renaissance en France*; Pattison, *Renaissance of Art in France*; Pattison, *Claude Lorrain*; Poillon, *Nicolas Poussin*; Stranahan, *History of French Painting*.

EARLY FRENCH ART: Painting in France did not, as in Italy, spring directly from Christianity, though it dealt with the religious subject. From the beginning a decorative motive—the strong feature of French art—appears as the chief motive of painting. This showed itself largely in church ornament, garments, tapestries, miniatures, and illuminations. Mural paintings were produced during the fifth century, probably in imitation of Italian or Roman example.[133] Under Charlemagne, in the eighth century, Byzantine influences were at work. In the eleventh, twelfth, and thirteenth centuries much stained-glass work appeared, and also many missal paintings and furniture decorations.

Fig. 56.—POUSSIN. ET IN ARCADIA EGO. LOUVRE.
Please click here for a modern color image

In the fifteenth century **René of Anjou** (1408-1480), king and painter, gave an impetus to art which he perhaps originally received from Italy. His work showed some Italian influence mingled with a great deal of Flemish precision, and corresponded for France to the early Renaissance work of Italy, though by no means so advanced. Contemporary with René was **Jean Fouquet** (1415?-1480?) an illuminator and portrait-painter, one of the earliest in French history. He was an artist of some original characteristics and produced an art detailed and exact in its realism. **Jean Péreal** (?-1528?) and **Jean Bourdichon** (1457?-1521?) with Fouquet's pupils and sons, formed a school at Tours which afterward came to[134] show some Italian influence. The native workmen at Paris—they sprang up from illuminators to painters in all probability—showed more of the Flemish influence. Neither of the schools of the fifteenth century reflected much life or thought, but what there was of it was native to the soil, though their methods were influenced from without.

SIXTEENTH-CENTURY PAINTING: During this century Francis I., at Fontainebleau, seems to have encouraged two schools of painting, one the native French and the other an imported Italian, which afterward took to itself the name of the "School of Fontainebleau." Of the native artists the **Clouets** were the most conspicuous. They were of Flemish origin, and followed Flemish methods both in technic and mediums. There were four of them, of whom **Jean** (1485?-1541?) and **François** (1500?-1572?) were the most noteworthy. They painted many portraits, and François' work, bearing some resemblance to that of Holbein, it has been doubtfully said that he was a pupil of that painter. All of their work was remarkable for detail and closely followed facts.

The Italian importation came about largely through the travels of Francis I. in Italy. He invited to Fontainebleau Leonardo da Vinci, Andrea del Sarto, Il Rosso, Primaticcio, and Niccolò dell' Abbate. These painters rather superseded and greatly influenced the French painters. The result was an Italianized school of French art which ruled in France for many years. Primaticcio was probably the greatest of the influencers, remaining as he did for thirty years in France. The native painters, **Jean Cousin** (1500?-1589) and **Toussaint du Breuil** (1561-1602) followed his style, and in the next century the painters were even more servile imitators of Italy—imitating not the best models either, but the Mannerists, the Eclectics, and the Roman painters of the Decadence.

FIG. 57.—CLAUDE LORRAIN. FLIGHT INTO EGYPT. DRESDEN.
Please click here for a modern color image

SEVENTEENTH-CENTURY PAINTING: This was a century of great development and production in France, the time of[135] the founding of the French Academy of Painting and Sculpture, and the formation of many picture collections. In the first part of the century the Flemish and native tendencies existed, but they were overawed, outnumbered by the Italian. Not even Rubens's painting for Marie de' Medici, in the palace of the Luxembourg, could stem the tide of Italy. The French painters flocked to Rome to study the art of their great predecessors and were led astray by the flashy elegance of the late Italians. Among the earliest of this century was **Fréminet** (1567-1619). He was first taught by his father and Jean Cousin, but afterward spent fifteen years in Italy studying Parmigianino and Michael Angelo. His work had something of the Mannerist style about it and was overwrought and exaggerated. In[136] shadows he seemed to have borrowed from Caravaggio. **Vouet** (1590-1649) was a student in Italy of Veronese's painting and afterward of Guido Reni and Caravaggio. He was a mediocre artist, but had a great vogue in France and left many celebrated pupils.

By all odds the best painter of this time was **Nicolas Poussin** (1593-1665). He lived almost all of his life in Italy, and might be put down as an Italian of the Decadence. He was well versed in classical archæology, and had much of the classic taste and feeling prevalent at that time in the Roman school of Giulio Romano. His work showed great intelligence and had an elevated grandiloquent style about it that was impressive. It reflected nothing French, and had little more root in present human sympathy than any of the other painting of the time, but it was better done. The drawing was correct if severe, the composition agreeable if formal, the coloring variegated if violent. Many of his pictures have now changed for the worse in coloring owing to the dissipation of surface pigments. He was the founder of the classic and academic in French art, and in influence was the most important man of the century. He was especially strong in the heroic landscape, and in this branch helped form the style of his brother-in-law, **Gaspard (Dughet) Poussin** (1613-1675).

The landscape painter of the period, however, was **Claude Lorrain** (1600-1682). He differed from Poussin in making his pictures depend more strictly upon landscape than upon figures. With both painters, the trees, mountains, valleys, buildings, figures, were of the grand classic variety. Hills and plains, sylvan groves, flowing streams, peopled harbors, Ionic and Corinthian temples, Roman aqueducts, mythological groups, were the materials used, and the object of their use was to show the ideal dwelling-place of man—the former Garden of the Gods. Panoramic and slightly theatrical at times, Claude's work was not without its poetic side,[137]shrewd knowledge, and skilful execution. He was a leader in landscape, the man who first painted real golden sunlight and shed its light upon earth. There is a soft summer's-day drowsiness, a golden haze of atmosphere, a feeling of composure and restfulness about his pictures that are attractive. Like Poussin he depended much upon long sweeping lines in composition, and upon effects of linear perspective.

FIG. 58—WATTEAU. GILLES. LOUVRE.
Please click here for a modern color image

COURT PAINTING: When Louis XIV. came to the throne painting took on a decided character, but it was hardly national or race character. The popular idea, if the people had an idea, did not obtain. There was no motive springing from the French except an inclination to follow Italy;[138] and in Italy all the great art-motives were dead. In method the French painters followed the late Italians, and imitated an imitation; in matter they bowed to the dictates of the court and reflected the king's mock-heroic spirit. Echoing the fashion of the day, painting became pompous, theatrical, grandiloquent—a mass of vapid vanity utterly lacking in sincerity and truth. **Lebrun** (1619-1690), painter in ordinary to the king, directed substantially all the painting of the reign. He aimed at pleasing royalty with flattering allusions to Cæsarism and extravagant personifications of the king as a classic conqueror. His art had neither truth, nor genius, nor great skill, and so sought to startle by subject or size. Enormous canvases of Alexander's triumphs, in allusion to those of the great Louis, were turned out to order, and Versailles to this day is tapestried with battle-pieces in which Louis is always victor. Considering the amount of work done, Lebrun showed great fecundity and industry, but none of it has much more than a mechanical ingenuity about it. It was rather original in composition, but poor in drawing, lighting, and coloring; and its example upon the painters of the time was pernicious.

His contemporary, **Le Sueur** (1616-1655), was a more sympathetic and sincere painter, if not a much better technician. Both were pupils of Vouet, but Le Sueur's art was religious in subject, while Lebrun's was military and monarchical. Le Sueur had a feeling for his theme, but was a weak painter, inclined to the sentimental, thin in coloring, and not at all certain in his drawing. French allusions to him as "the French Raphael" show more national complacency than correctness.**Sebastian Bourdon** (1616-1671) was another painter of history, but a little out of the Lebrun circle. He was not, however, free from the influence of Italy, where he spent three years studying color more than drawing. This shows in his works, most of which are lacking in form.[139]

Contemporary with these men was a group of portrait-painters who gained celebrity perhaps as much by their subjects as by their own powers. They were facile flatterers given over to the pomps of the reign and mirroring all its absurdities of fashion. Their work has a graceful, smooth appearance, and, for its time, it was undoubtedly excellent portraiture. Even to this day it has qualities of drawing and coloring to commend it, and at times one meets with exceptionally good work. The leaders among these portrait-painters were **Philip de Champaigne** (1602-1674), the best of his time; **Pierre Mignard** (1610?-1695), a pupil of Vouet, who studied in Rome and afterward returned to France to become the successful rival of Lebrun; **Largillière** (1656-1746) and **Rigaud** (1659-1743).

EIGHTEENTH-CENTURY PAINTING: The painting of Louis XIV.'s time was continued into the eighteenth century for some fifteen years or more with little change. With the advent of Louis XV. art took upon itself another character, and one that reflected perfectly the moral, social, and political France of the eighteenth century. The first Louis clamored for glory, the second Louis revelled in gayety, frivolity, and sensuality. This was the difference between both monarchs and both arts. The gay and the coquettish in painting had already been introduced by the Regent, himself a dilettante in art, and when Louis XV. came to the throne it passed from the gay to the insipid, the flippant, even the erotic. Shepherds and shepherdesses dressed in court silks and satins with cottony sheep beside them posed in stage-set Arcadias, pretty gods and goddesses reclined indolently upon gossamer clouds, and court gallants lounged under artificial trees by artificial ponds making love to pretty soubrettes from the theatre.

Yet, in spite of the lack of moral and intellectual elevation, in spite of frivolity and make-believe, this art was infinitely better than the pompous imitation of foreign ex[140]ample set up by Louis XIV. It was more spontaneous, more original, more French. The influence of Italy began to fail, and the painters began to mirror French life. It was largely court life, lively, vivacious, licentious, but in that very respect characteristic of the time. Moreover, there was another quality about it that showed French taste at its best—the decorative quality. It can hardly be supposed that the fairy creations of the age were intended to represent actual nature. They were designed to ornament hall and boudoir, and in pure decorative delicacy of design, lightness of touch, color charm, they have never been excelled. The serious spirit was lacking, but the gayety of line and color was well given.

FIG. 59.—BOUCHER. PASTORAL. LOUVRE.

Watteau (1684-1721) was the one chiefly responsible for the coquette and soubrette of French art, and Watteau was, practically speaking, the first French painter. His subjects[141] were trifling bits of fashionable love-making, scenes from the opera, fêtes, balls, and the like. All his characters played at life in parks and groves that never grew, and most of his color was beautifully unreal; but for all that the work was original, decorative, and charming. Moreover, Watteau was a brushman, and introduced not only a new spirit and new subject into art, but a new method. The epic treatment of the Italians was laid aside in favor of a genre treatment, and instead of line and flat surface Watteau introduced color and cleverly laid pigment. He was a brilliant painter; not a great man in thought or imagination, but one of fancy, delicacy, and skill. Unfortunately he set a bad example by his gay subjects, and those who came after him carried his gayety and lightness of spirit into exaggeration. Watteau's best pupils were **Lancret** (1690-1743) and **Pater** (1695-1736), who painted in his style with fair results.

After these men came **Van Loo** (1705-1765) and **Boucher** (1703-1770), who turned Watteau's charming fêtes, showing the costumes and manners of the Regency, into flippant extravagance. Not only was the moral tone and intellectual stamina of their art far below that of Watteau, but their workmanship grew defective. Both men possessed a remarkable facility of the hand and a keen decorative color-sense; but after a time both became stereotyped and mannered. Drawing and modelling were neglected, light was wholly conventional, and landscape turned into a piece of embroidered background with a Dresden china-tapestry effect about it. As decoration the general effect was often excellent, as a serious expression of life it was very weak, as an intellectual or moral force it was worse than worthless. **Fragonard** (1732-1806) followed in a similar style, but was a more knowing man, clever in color, and a much freer and better brushman.

A few painters in the time of Louis XV. remained appar[142]ently unaffected by the court influence, and stand in conspicuous isolation. **Claude Joseph Vernet** (1712-1789) was a landscape and marine painter of some repute in his time. He had a sense of the pictorial, but not a remarkable sense of the truthful in nature. **Chardin**(1699-1779) and **Greuze** (1725-1805), clung to portrayals of humble life and sought to popularize the *genre* subject. Chardin was not appreciated by the masses. His frank realism, his absolute sincerity of purpose, his play of light and its effect upon color, and his charming handling of textures were comparatively unnoticed. Yet as a colorist he may be ranked second to none in French art, and in freshness of handling his work is a model for present-day painters. Diderot early recognized Chardin's excellence, and many artists since his day have admired his pictures; but he is not now a well-known or popular painter. The populace fancies Greuze and his sentimental heads of young girls. They have a prettiness about them that is attractive, but as art they lack in force, and in workmanship they are too smooth, finical, and thin in handling.

PRINCIPAL WORKS: All of these French painters are best represented in the collections of the Louvre. Some of the other galleries, like the Dresden, Berlin, and National at London, have examples of their work; but the masterpieces are with the French people in the Louvre and in the other municipal galleries of France.

[143]

CHAPTER XIII.
FRENCH PAINTING.

THE NINETEENTH CENTURY.

BOOKS RECOMMENDED: As before, Stranahan, *et al.*; also Ballière, *Henri Regnault*; Blanc, *Les Artistes de mon Temps*; Blanc, *Histoire des Peintres français au XIXme Siècle*; Blanc, *Ingres et son Œuvre*; Bigot, *Peintres français contemporains*; Breton, *La Vie d'un Artiste(English Translation)*; Brownell, *French Art*; Burty, *Maîtres et Petit-Maîtres*; Chesneau, *Peinture française au XIXme Siècle*; Clément, *Études sur les Beaux Arts en France*; Clément, *Prudhon*; Delaborde, *Œuvre de Paul Delaroche*; Delécluze, *Jacques Louis David, son École, et son Temps*; Duret, *Les Peintres français en 1867*; Gautier, *L'Art Moderne*; Gautier, *Romanticisme*; Gonse, *Eugène Fromentin*; Hamerton, *Contemporary French Painting*; Hamerton, *Painting in France after the Decline of Classicism*; Henley, *Memorial Catalogue of French and Dutch Loan Collection* (1886); Henriet, *Charles Daubigny et son Œuvre*; Lenormant, *Les Artistes Contemporains*; Lenormant, *Ary Scheffer*; Merson, *Ingres, sa Vie et son Œuvre*; Moreau, *Decamps et son Œuvre*; Planche, *Études sur l'École française*; Robaut et Chesneau, *L'Œuvre complet d'Eugène Delacroix*; Sensier, *Théodore Rousseau*; Sensier, *Life and Works of J. F. Millet*; Silvestre, *Histoire des Artistes vivants et étrangers*; Strahan, *Modern French Art*; Thoré, *L'Art Contemporain*; Theuriet, *Jules Bastien-Lepage*; Van Dyke, *Modern French Masters*.

THE REVOLUTIONARY TIME: In considering this century's art in Europe, it must be remembered that a great social and intellectual change has taken place since the days of the Medici. The power so long pent up in Italy during the Renaissance finally broke and scattered itself upon the[144] western nations; societies and states were torn down and rebuilded, political, social, and religious ideas shifted into new garbs; the old order passed away.

FIG. 60.—DAVID. THE SABINES. LOUVRE.
Please click here for a modern color image

Religion as an art-motive, or even as an art-subject, ceased to obtain anywhere. The Church failed as an art-patron, and the walls of cloister and cathedral furnished no new Bible readings to the unlettered. Painting, from being a necessity of life, passed into a luxury, and the king, the state, or the private collector became the patron. Nature and actual life were about the only sources left from which original art could draw its materials. These have been freely used, but not so much in a national as in an individual manner. The tendency to-day is not to put forth a universal conception but an individual belief. Individualism—the same quality that appeared so strongly in Michael Angelo's art—has become a keynote in modern work. It[145] is not the only kind of art that has been shown in this century, nor is nature the only theme from which art has been derived. We must remember and consider the influence of the past upon modern men, and the attempts to restore the classic beauty of the Greek, Roman, and Italian, which practically ruled French painting in the first part of this century.

FRENCH CLASSICISM OF DAVID: This was a revival of Greek form in art, founded on the belief expressed by Winckelmann, that beauty lay in form, and was best shown by the ancient Greeks. It was the objective view of art which saw beauty in the external and tolerated no individuality in the artist except that which was shown in technical skill. It was little more than an imitation of the Greek and Roman marbles as types, with insistence upon perfect form, correct drawing, and balanced composition. In theme and spirit it was pseudo-heroic, the incidents of Greek and Roman history forming the chief subjects, and in method it rather despised color, light-and-shade, and natural surroundings. It was elevated, lofty, ideal in aspiration, but coldly unsympathetic because lacking in contemporary interest; and, though correct enough in classic form, was lacking in the classic spirit. Like all reanimated art, it was derivative as regards its forms and lacking in spontaneity. The reason for the existence of Greek art died with its civilization, and those, like the French classicists, who sought to revive it, brought a copy of the past into the present, expecting the world to accept it.

There was some social, and perhaps artistic, reason, however, for the revival of the classic in the French art of the late eighteenth century. It was a revolt, and at that time revolts were popular. The art of Boucher and Van Loo had become quite unbearable. It was flippant, careless, licentious. It had no seriousness or dignity about it. Moreover, it smacked of the Bourbon monarchy, which people had come to hate. Classicism was severe, elevated,[146] respectable at least, and had the air of the heroic republic about it. It was a return to a sterner view of life, with the martial spirit behind it as an impetus, and it had a great vogue. For many years during the Revolution, the Consulate, and the Empire, classicism was accepted by the sovereigns and the Institute of France, and to this day it lives in a modified form in that semi-classic work known as academic art.

THE CLASSIC SCHOOL: Vien (1716-1809) was the first painter to protest against the art of Boucher and Van Loo by advocating more nobility of form and a closer study of nature. He was, however, more devoted to the antique forms he had studied in Rome than to nature. In subject and line his tendency was classic, with a leaning toward the Italians of the Decadence. He lacked the force to carry out a complete reform in painting, but his pupil **David** (1748-1825) accomplished what he had begun. It was David who established the reign of classicism, and by native power became the leader. The time was appropriate, the Revolution called for pictures of Romulus, Brutus and Achilles, and Napoleon encouraged the military theme. David had studied the marbles at Rome, and he used them largely for models, reproducing scenes from Greek and Roman life in an elevated and sculpturesque style, with much archæological knowledge and a great deal of skill. In color, relief, sentiment, individuality, his painting was lacking. He despised all that. The rhythm of line, the sweep of composed groups, the heroic subject and the heroic treatment, made up his art. It was thoroughly objective, and what contemporary interest it possessed lay largely in the martial spirit then prevalent. Of course it was upheld by the Institute, and it really set the pace for French painting for nearly half a century. When David was called upon to paint Napoleonic pictures he painted them under protest, and yet these, with his portraits, constitute his[147] best work. In portraiture he was uncommonly strong at times.

FIG. 61.—INGRES. ŒDIPUS AND SPHINX. LOUVRE.
Please click here for a modern color image

After the Restoration David, who had been a revolutionist, and then an adherent of Napoleon, was sent into exile; but the influence he had left and the school he had established were carried on by his contemporaries and pupils. Of the former **Regnault** (1754-1829), **Vincent** (1746-1816), and **Prudhon** (1758-1823) were the most conspicuous. The last one was considered as out of the classic circle, but so far as making his art depend upon drawing and composition, he was a genuine classicist. His subjects, instead of being heroic, inclined to the mythological and the allegorical. In Italy he had been a student of the Renaissance painters, and from them borrowed a method of shadow gradation that[148] rendered his figures misty and phantom-like. They possessed an ease of movement sometimes called "Prudhonesque grace," and in composition were well placed and effective.

Of David's pupils there were many. Only a few of them, however, had pronounced ability, and even these carried David's methods into the theatrical. **Girodet**(1766-1824) was a draughtsman of considerable power, but with poor taste in color and little repose in composition. Most of his work was exaggeration and strained effect. **Lethière** (1760-1832) and **Guérin** (1774-1833), pupils of Regnault, were painters akin to Girodet, but inferior to him. **Gérard** (1770-1837) was a weak David follower, who gained some celebrity by painting portraits of celebrated men and women. The two pupils of David who brought him the most credit were **Ingres** (1780-1867) and **Gros** (1771-1835). Ingres was a cold, persevering man, whose principles had been well settled by David early in life, and were adhered to with conviction by the pupil to the last. He modified the classic subject somewhat, studied Raphael and the Italians, and reintroduced the single figure into art (the Source, and the Odalisque, for example). For color he had no fancy. "In nature all is form," he used to say. Painting he thought not an independent art, but "a development of sculpture." To consider emotion, color, or light as the equal of form was monstrous, and to compare Rembrandt with Raphael was blasphemy. To this belief he clung to the end, faithfully reproducing the human figure, and it is not to be wondered at that eventually he became a learned draughtsman. His single figures and his portraits show him to the best advantage. He had a strong grasp of modelling and an artistic sense of the beauty and dignity of line not excelled by any artist of this century. And to him more than any other painter is due the cultured draughtsmanship which is to-day the just pride of the French school.[149]

Gros was a more vacillating man, and by reason of forsaking the classic subject for Napoleonic battle-pieces, he unconsciously led the way toward romanticism. He excelled as a draughtsman, but when he came to paint the Field of Eylau and the Pest of Jaffa he mingled color, light, air, movement, action, sacrificing classic composition and repose to reality. This was heresy from the Davidian point of view, and David eventually convinced him of it. Gros returned to the classic theme and treatment, but soon after was so reviled by the changing criticism of the time that he committed suicide in the Seine. His art, however, was the beginning of romanticism.

The landscape painting of this time was rather academic and unsympathetic. It was a continuation of the Claude-Poussin tradition, and in its insistence upon line, grandeur of space, and imposing trees and mountains, was a fit companion to the classic figure-piece. It had little basis in nature, and little in color or feeling to commend it. **Watelet** (1780-1866), **Bertin** (1775-1842), **Michallon** (1796-1822), and **Aligny** (1798-1871), were its exponents.

A few painters seemed to stand apart from the contemporary influences. **Madame Vigée-Lebrun** (1755-1842), a successful portrait-painter of nobility, and **Horace Vernet** (1789-1863), a popular battle-painter, many of whose works are to be seen at Versailles, were of this class.

ROMANTICISM: The movement in French painting which began about 1822 and took the name of Romanticism was but a part of the "storm-and-stress" feeling that swept Germany, England, and France at the beginning of this century, appearing first in literature and afterward in art. It had its origin in a discontent with the present, a passionate yearning for the unattainable, an intensity of sentiment, gloomy melancholy imaginings, and a desire to express the inexpressible. It was emphatically subjective, self-conscious, a mood of mind or feeling. In this respect it was[150] diametrically opposed to the academic and the classic. In French painting it came forward in opposition to the classicism of David. People had begun to weary of Greek and Roman heroes and their deeds, of impersonal line-bounded statuesque art. There was a demand for something more representative, spontaneous, expressive of the intense feeling of the time. The very gist of romanticism was passion. Freedom to express itself in what form it would was a condition of its existence.

FIG. 62.—DELACROIX. MASSACRE OF SCIO. LOUVRE.
Please click here for a modern color image

The classic subject was abandoned by the romanticists for dramatic scenes of mediæval and modern times. The romantic hero and heroine in scenes of horror, perils by land and sea, flame and fury, love and anguish, came upon the[151] boards. Much of this was illustration of history, the novel, and poetry, especially the poetry of Goethe, Byron, and Scott. Line was slurred in favor of color, symmetrical composition gave way to wild disordered groups in headlong action, and atmospheres, skies, and lights were twisted and distorted to convey the sentiment of the story. It was thus, more by suggestion than realization, that romanticism sought to give the poetic sentiment of life. Its position toward classicism was antagonistic, a rebound, a flying to the other extreme. One virtually said that beauty was in the Greek form, the other that it was in the painter's emotional nature. The disagreement was violent, and out of it grew the so-called quarrel of the 1820's.

LEADERS OF ROMANTICISM: Symptoms of the coming movement were apparent long before any open revolt. Gros had made innovations on the classic in his battle-pieces, but the first positive dissent from classic teachings was made in the Salon of 1819 by **Géricault** (1791-1824) with his Raft of the Medusa. It represented the starving, the dead, and the dying of the Medusa's crew on a raft in mid-ocean. The subject was not classic. It was literary, romantic, dramatic, almost theatric in its seizing of the critical moment. Its theme was restless, harrowing, horrible. It met with instant opposition from the old men and applause from the young men. It was the trumpet-note of the revolt, but Géricault did not live long enough to become the leader of romanticism. That position fell to his contemporary and fellow-pupil, **Delacroix** (1799-1863). It was in 1822 that Delacroix's first Salon picture (the Dante and Virgil) appeared. A strange, ghost-like scene from Dante's *Inferno*, the black atmosphere of the nether world, weird faces, weird colors, weird flames, and a modelling of the figures by patches of color almost savage as compared to the tinted drawing of classicism. Delacroix's youth saved the picture from condemnation, but it was different with his Massacre of[152]Scio two years later. This was decried by the classicists, and even Gros called it "the massacre of art." The painter was accused of establishing the worship of the ugly, he was no draughtsman, had no selection, no severity, nothing but brutality. But Delacroix was as obstinate as Ingres, and declared that the whole world could not prevent him from seeing and painting things in his own way. It was thus the quarrel started, the young men siding with Delacroix, the older men following David and Ingres.

In himself Delacroix embodied all that was best and strongest in the romantic movement. His painting was intended to convey a romantic mood of mind by combinations of color, light, air, and the like. In subject it was tragic and passionate, like the poetry of Hugo, Byron, and Scott. The figures were usually given with anguish-wrung brows, wild eyes, dishevelled hair, and impetuous, contorted action. The painter never cared for technical details, seeking always to gain the effect of the whole rather than the exactness of the part. He purposely slurred drawing at times, and was opposed to formal composition. In color he was superior, though somewhat violent at times, and in brush-work he was often labored and patchy. His strength lay in imagination displayed in color and in action.

The quarrel between classicism and romanticism lasted some years, with neither side victorious. Delacroix won recognition for his view of art, but did not crush the belief in form which was to come to the surface again. He fought almost alone. Many painters rallied around him, but they added little strength to the new movement. **Devéria** (1805-1865) and **Champmartin** (1797-1883) were highly thought of at first, but they rapidly degenerated. **Sigalon** (1788-1837), **Cogniet**(1794-1880), **Robert-Fleury** (1797-), and **Boulanger** (1806-1867), were romanticists, but achieved more as teachers than as painters. **Delaroche** (1797-1856) was an eclectic—in fact, founded a school of that name[153]—thinking to take what was best from both parties. Inventing nothing, he profited by all invented. He employed the romantic subject and color, but adhered to classic drawing. His composition was good, his costume careful in detail, his brush-work smooth, and his story-telling capacity excellent. All these qualities made him a popular painter, but not an original or powerful one. **Ary**

Scheffer (1797-1858) was an illustrator of Goethe and Byron, frail in both sentiment and color, a painter who started as a romanticist, but afterward developed line under Ingres.

FIG. 63.—GÉRÔME. POLLICE VERSO.

Please click here for a modern color image

THE ORIENTALISTS: In both literature and painting one phase of romanticism showed itself in a love for the life, the light, the color of the Orient. From Paris **Decamps** (1803-1860) was the first painter to visit the East and paint Eastern life. He was a *genre* painter more than a figure painter, giving naturalistic street scenes in Turkey and Asia Minor, courts, and interiors, with great feeling for air,[154] warmth of color, and light. At about the same time **Marilhat** (1811-1847) was in Egypt picturing the life of that country in a similar manner; and later, **Fromentin** (1820-1876), painter and writer, following Delacroix, went to Algiers and portrayed there Arab life with fast-flying horses, the desert air, sky, light, and color. **Théodore Frere** and **Ziem** belong further on in the century, but were no less exponents of romanticism in the East.

Fifteen years after the starting of romanticism the movement had materially subsided. It had never been a school in the sense of having rules and laws of art. Liberty of thought and perfect freedom for individual expression were all it advocated. As a result there was no unity, for there was nothing to unite upon; and with every painter painting as he pleased, regardless of law, extravagance was inevitable. This was the case, and when the next generation came in romanticism began to be ridiculed for its excesses. A reaction started in favor of more line and academic training. This was first shown by the students of Delaroche, though there were a number of movements at the time, all of them leading away from romanticism. A recoil from too much color in favor of more form was inevitable, but romanticism was not to perish entirely. Its influence was to go on, and to appear in the work of later men.

ECLECTICS AND TRANSITIONAL PAINTERS: After Ingres his follower **Flandrin** (1809-1864) was the most considerable draughtsman of the time. He was not classic but religious in subject, and is sometimes called "the religious painter of France." He had a delicate beauty of line and a fine feeling for form, but never was strong in color, brush-work, or sentiment. His best work appears in his very fine portraits. **Gleyre** (1806-1874) was a man of classic methods, but romantic tastes, who modified the heroic into the idyllic and mythologic. He was a sentimental day-dreamer,[155] with a touch of melancholy about the vanished past, appearing in Arcadian fancies, pretty nymphs, and idealized memories of youth. In execution he was not at all romantic. His color was pale, his drawing delicate, and his lighting misty and uncertain. It was the etherealized classic method, and this method he transmitted to a little band of painters called the

NEW-GREEKS, who, in point of time, belong much further along in the century, but in their art are with Gleyre. Their work never rose above the idyllic and the graceful, and calls for no special mention. **Hamon** (1821-1874) and **Aubert** (1824-) belonged to the band, and **Gérôme** (1824-[6]) was at one time its leader, but he afterward emerged from it to a higher place in French art, where he will find mention hereafter.

[6]Died, 1904.

Couture (1815-1879) stood quite by himself, a mingling of several influences. His chief picture, The Romans of the Decadence, is classic in subject, romantic in sentiment (and this very largely expressed by warmth of color), and rather realistic in natural appearance. He was an eclectic in a way, and yet seems to stand as the forerunner of a large body of artists who find classification hereafter under the title of the Semi-Classicists.

PRINCIPAL WORKS: All the painters mentioned in this chapter are best represented in the Louvre at Paris, at Versailles, and in the museums of the chief French cities. Some works of the late or living men may be found in the Luxembourg, where pictures bought by the state are kept for ten years after the painter's death, and then are either sent to the Louvre or to the other municipal galleries of France. Some pictures by these men are also to be seen in the Metropolitan Museum, New York, the Boston Museum, and the Chicago Art Institute.

[156]

CHAPTER XIV.
FRENCH PAINTING.
THE NINETEENTH CENTURY (*Continued*).

BOOKS RECOMMENDED: The books before mentioned, consult also General Bibliography, (page xv.)

THE LANDSCAPE PAINTERS: The influence of either the classic or romantic example may be traced in almost all of the French painting of this century. The opposed teachings find representatives in new men, and under different names the modified dispute goes on—the dispute of the academic *versus* the individual, the art of form and line *versus* the art of sentiment and color.

With the classicism of David not only the figure but the landscape setting of it, took on an ideal heroic character. Trees and hills and rivers became supernaturally grand and impressive. Everything was elevated by method to produce an imaginary Arcadia fit for the deities of the classic world. The result was that nature and the humanity of the painter passed out in favor of school formula and academic traditions. When romanticism came in this was changed, but nature falsified in another direction. Landscape was given an interest in human affairs, and made to look gay or sad, peaceful or turbulent, as the day went well or ill with the hero of the story portrayed. It was, however, truer to the actual than the classic, more studied in the parts, more united in the whole. About the year 1830 the influence of romanticism began to show in a new landscape art. That is to[157] say, the emotional impulse springing from romanticism combined with the study of the old Dutch landscapists, and the English contemporary painters, Constable and Bonington, set a large number of painters to the close study of nature and ultimately developed what has been vaguely called the

FONTAINEBLEAU-BARBIZON SCHOOL: This whole school was primarily devoted to showing the sentiment of color and light. It took nature just as it found it in the forest of Fontainebleau, on the plain of Barbizon, and elsewhere, and treated it with a poetic feeling for light, shadow, atmosphere, color, that resulted in the best landscape painting yet known to us.

FIG. 64.—COROT. LANDSCAPE.

Corot (1796-1875) though classically trained under Bertin, and though somewhat apart from the other men in his life, belongs with this group. He was a man whose artistic life was filled with the beauty of light and air. These he painted with great singleness of aim and great poetic charm. Most of his work is in a light silvery key of color, usually slight[158] in composition, simple in masses of light and dark, and very broadly but knowingly handled with the brush. He began painting by using the minute brush, but changed it later on for a freer style which recorded only the great omnipresent truths and suppressed the small ones. He has never had a superior in producing the permeating light of morning and evening. For this alone, if for no other excellence, he deservedly holds high rank.

Rousseau (1812-1867) was one of the foremost of the recognized leaders, and probably the most learned landscapist of this century. A man of many moods and methods he produced in variety with rare versatility. Much of his work was experimental, but at his best he had a majestic conception of nature, a sense of its power and permanence, its volume and mass, that often resulted in the highest quality of pictorial poetry. In color he was rich and usually warm, in technic firm and individual, in sentiment at times quite sublime. At first he painted broadly and won friends among the artists and sneers from the public; then in his middle style he painted in detail, and had a period of popular success; in his late style he went back to the broad manner, and died amid quarrels and vexations of spirits. His long-time friend and companion, **Jules Dupré** (1812-1889), hardly reached up to him, though a strong painter in landscape and marine. He was a good but not great colorist, and, technically, his brush was broad enough but sometimes heavy. His late work is inferior in sentiment and labored in handling. **Diaz** (1808-1876) was allied to Rousseau in aim and method, though not so sure nor so powerful a painter. He had fancy and variety in creation that sometimes ran to license, and in color he was clear and brilliant. Never very well trained, his drawing is often indifferent and his light distorted, but these are more than atoned for by delicacy and poetic charm. At times he painted with much power. **Daubigny** (1817-1878) seemed[159] more like Corot in his charm of style and love of atmosphere and light than any of the others. He was fond of the banks of the Seine and the Marne at twilight, with evening atmospheres and dark trees standing in silent ranks against the warm sky. He was also fond of the gray day along the coast, and even the sea attracted him not a little. He was a painter of high abilities, and in treatment strongly individual, even distinguished, by his simplicity and directness. Unity of the whole, grasp of the mass entire, was his technical aim, and this he sought to get not so much by line as by color-tones of varying value. In this respect he seemed a connecting link between Corot and the present-day impressionists.**Michel** (1763-1842), **Huet** (1804-1869), **Chintreuil** (1814-1873),

and **Français** (1814-) were all allied in point of view with this group of landscape painters, and among the late men who have carried out their beliefs are **Cazin**,[7] **Yon**,[8] **Damoye, Pointelin, Harpignies** and **Pelouse**[9] seem a little more inclined to the realistic than the poetic view, though producing work of much virility and intelligence.

[7]Died, 1901.
[8]Died, 1897.
[9]Died, 1890.

47

Contemporary and associated with the Fontainebleau painters were a number of men who won high distinction as

PAINTERS OF ANIMALS: Troyon (1810-1865) was the most prominent among them. His work shows the same sentiment of light and color as the Fontainebleau landscapists, and with it there is much keen insight into animal life. As a technician he was rather hard at first, and he never was a correct draughtsman, but he had a way of giving the character of the objects he portrayed which is the very essence of truth. He did many landscapes with and without cattle. His best pupil was **Van Marcke** (1827-1890), who followed his methods but never possessed the feeling of his master. **Jacque** (1813-[10]) is also of the Fontainebleau-Barbizon group, and is justly celebrated for his paintings and etchings of sheep. The poetry of the school is his, and technically he [160]is fine in color at times, if often rather dark in illumination. Like Troyon he knows his subject well, and can show the nature of sheep with true feeling. **Rosa Bonheur** (1822-[11]) and her brother, **Auguste Bonheur** (1824-1884), have both dealt with animal life, but never with that fine artistic feeling which would warrant their popularity. Their work is correct enough, but prosaic and commonplace in spirit. They do not belong in the same group with Troyon and Rousseau.

[10]Died, 1894.
[11]Died, 1899.

FIG. 65.—ROUSSEAU, CHARCOAL BURNERS' HUT. FULLER COLLECTION.

THE PEASANT PAINTERS: Allied again in feeling and sentiment with the Fontainebleau landscapists were some celebrated painters of peasant life, chief among whom stood **Millet** (1814-1875), of Barbizon. The pictorial inclination of Millet was early grounded by a study of Delacroix, the master romanticist, and his work is an expression of[161] romanticism modified by an individual study of nature and applied to peasant life. He was peasant born, living and dying at Barbizon, sympathizing with his class, and painting them with great poetic force and simplicity. His sentiment sometimes has a literary bias, as in his far-famed but indifferent Angelus, but usually it is strictly pictorial and has to do with the beauty of light, air, color, motion, life, as shown in The Sower or The Gleaners. Technically he was not strong as a draughtsman or a brushman, but he had a large feeling for form, great simplicity in line, keen perception of the relations of light and dark, and at times an excellent color-sense. He was virtually the discoverer of the peasant as an art subject, and for this, as for his original point of view and artistic feeling, he is ranked as one of the foremost artists of the century.

Jules Breton (1827-), though painting little besides the peasantry, is no Millet follower, for he started painting peasant scenes at about the same time as Millet. His affinities were with the New-Greeks early in life, and ever since he has inclined toward the academic in style, though handling the rustic subject. He is a good technician, except in his late work; but as an original thinker, as a pictorial poet, he does not show the intensity or profundity of Millet. The followers of the Millet-Breton tradition are many. The blue-frocked and sabot-shod peasantry have appeared in salon and gallery for twenty years and more, but with not very good results. The imitators, as usual, have caught at the subject and missed the spirit. **Billet** and **Legros**, contemporaries of Millet, still living, and **Lerolle**, a man of present-day note, are perhaps the most considerable of the painters of rural subjects to-day.

THE SEMI-CLASSICISTS: It must not be inferred that the classic influence of David and Ingres disappeared from view with the coming of the romanticists, the Fontainebleau landscapists, and the Barbizon painters. On the contrary,[162] side by side with these men, and opposed to them, were the believers in line and academic formulas of the beautiful. The whole tendency of academic art in France was against Delacroix, Rousseau, and Millet. During their lives they were regarded as heretics in art and without the pale of the Academy. Their art, however, combined with nature study and the realism of Courbet, succeeded in modifying the severe classicism of Ingres into what has been called semi-classicism. It consists in the elevated, heroic, or historical theme, academic form well drawn, some show of bright colors, smoothness of brush-work, and precision and nicety of detail. In treatment it attempts the realistic, but in spirit it is usually stilted, cold, unsympathetic.

Cabanel (1823-1889) and **Bouguereau** (1825-1905) have both represented semi-classic art well. They are justly ranked as famous draughtsmen and good portrait-painters, but their work always has about it the stamp of the academy machine, a something done to order, knowing and exact, but lacking in the personal element. It is a weakness of the academic method that it virtually banishes the individuality of eye and hand in favor of school formulas. Cabanel and Bouguereau have painted many incidents of classic and historic story, but with never a dash of enthusiasm or a suggestion of the great qualities of painting. Their drawing has been as thorough as could be asked for, but their colorings have been harsh and their brushes cold and thin.

Gérôme (1824-[12]) is a man of classic training and inclination, but his versatility hardly allows him to be classified anywhere. He was first a leader of the New-Greeks, painting delicate mythological subjects; then a historical painter, showing deaths of Cæsar and the like; then an Orientalist, giving scenes from Cairo and Constantinople; then a *genre* painter, depicting contemporary subjects in the many lands through which he has travelled. Whatever he has done shows semi-classic drawing, ethnological and archæological [163]knowledge, Parisian technic, and exact detail. His travels have not changed his precise scientific point of view. He is a true academician at bottom, but a more versatile and cultured painter than either Cabanel or Bouguereau. He draws well, sometimes uses color well, and is an excellent painter of textures. A man of great learning in many departments he is no painter to be sneered at, and yet not a painter to make the pulse beat faster or to arouse the æsthetic emotions. His work is impersonal, objective fact, showing a brilliant exterior but inwardly devoid of feeling.

[12]Died, 1904.

FIG. 66.—MILLET. THE GLEANERS. LOUVRE.
Please click here for a modern color image

Paul Baudry (1828-1886), though a disciple of line, was not precisely a semi-classicist, and perhaps for that reason was superior to any of the academic painters of his time. He was a follower of the old masters in Rome more than the *École des Beaux Arts*. His subjects, aside from many splendid portraits, were almost all classical, allegorical, or mythological. He was a fine draughtsman, and, what is more[164] remarkable in conjunction therewith, a fine colorist. He was hardly a great originator, and had not passion, dramatic force, or much sentiment, except such as may be found in his delicate coloring and rhythm of line. Nevertheless he was an artist to be admired for his purity of purpose and breadth of accomplishment. His chief work is to be seen in the Opera at Paris. **Puvis de Chavannes**(1824-[13]) is quite a different style of painter, and is remarkable for fine delicate tones of color which hold their place well on wall or ceiling, and for a certain grandeur of composition. In his desire to revive the monumental painting of the Renaissance he has met with much praise and much blame. He is an artist of sincerity and learning, and as a wall-painter has no superior in contemporary France.

[13]Died, 1898.

Hébert (1817-1908), an early painter of academic tendencies, and **Henner** (1829-), fond of form and yet a brushman with an idyllic feeling for light and color in dark surroundings, are painters who may come under the semi-classic grouping. **Lefebvre** (1834-) is probably the most pronounced in academic methods among the present men, a draughtsman of ability.

PORTRAIT AND FIGURE PAINTERS: Under this heading may be included those painters who stand by themselves, showing no positive preference for either the classic or romantic followings. **Bonnat** (1833-) has painted all kinds of subjects—*genre*, figure, and historical pieces—but is perhaps best known as a portrait-painter. He has done forcible work. Some of it indeed is astonishing in its realistic modelling—the accentuation of light and shadow often causing the figures to advance unnaturally. From this feature on his detail he has been known for years as a "realist." His anatomical Christ on the Cross and mural paintings in the Pantheon are examples. As a portrait-painter he is acceptable, if at times a little raw in color. Another portrait-painter of celebrity is **Carolus-Duran** (1837-). He is rather [165]startling at times in his portrayal of robes and draperies, has a facility of the brush that is frequently deceptive, and in color is sometimes vivid. He has had great success as a teacher, and is, all told, a painter of high rank. **Delaunay** (1828-1892) in late years painted little besides portraits, and was one of the conservatives of French art. **Laurens** (1838-) has been more of a historical painter than the others, and has dealt largely with death scenes. He is often spoken of as "the painter of the dead," a man of sound training and excellent technical power. **Regnault** (1843-1871) was a figure and *genre* painter with much feeling for oriental light and color, who unfortunately was killed in battle at twenty-seven years of age. He was an artist of promise, and has left several notable canvases. Among the younger men who portray the historical subject in an elevated style mention should be made of **Cormon** (1845-), **Benjamin-Constant** (1845-[14]), and **Rochegrosse**. As painters of portraits **Aman-Jean** and **Carrière**[15] have long held rank, and each succeeding Salon brings new portraitists to the front.

[14]Died, 1902.

[15]Died, 1906.

THE REALISTS: About the time of the appearance of Millet, say 1848, there also came to the front a man who scorned both classicism and romanticism, and maintained that the only model and subject of art should be nature. This man, **Courbet** (1819-1878), really gave a third tendency to the art of this century in France, and his influence undoubtedly had much to do with modifying both the classic and romantic tendencies. Courbet was a man of arrogant, dogmatic disposition, and was quite heartily detested during his life, but that he was a painter of great ability few will deny. His theory was the abolition of both sentiment and academic law, and the taking of nature just as it was, with all its beauties and all its deformities. This, too, was his practice to a certain extent. His art is material, and yet at times lofty in conception even to the sublime. And while he believed in realism he did not believe in petty detail, but rather in the [166]great truths of nature. These he saw with a discerning eye and portrayed with a masterful brush. He believed in what he saw only, and had more the observing than the reflective or emotional disposition. As a technician he was coarse but superbly strong, handling sky, earth, air, with the ease and power of one well trained in his craft. His subjects were many—the peasantry of France, landscape, and the sea holding prominent places—and his influence, though not direct because he had no pupils of consequence, has been most potent with the late men.

FIG. 67.—CABANEL. PHÆDRA.
Please click here for a modern color image

The young painter of to-day who does things in a "realistic" way is frequently met with in French art. **L'hermitte** (1844-), **Julien Dupré** (1851-), and others have handled the peasant subject with skill, after the Millet-Courbet initiative; and **Bastien-Lepage** (1848-1884) excited a good deal of admiration in his lifetime for the truth and evident sincerity of his art. Bastien's point of view was realistic[167] enough, but somewhat material. He never handled the large composition with success, but in small pieces and in portraits he was quite above criticism. His following among the young men was considerable, and the so-called impressionists have ranked him among their disciples or leaders.

PAINTERS OF MILITARY SCENES, GENRE, ETC.: The art of **Meissonier** (1815-1891), while extremely realistic in modern detail, probably originated from a study of the seventeenth-century Dutchmen like Terburg and Metsu. It does not portray low life, but rather the half-aristocratic—the scholar, the cavalier, the gentleman of leisure. This is done on a small scale with microscopic nicety, and really more in the historical than the *genre* spirit. Single figures and interiors were his preference, but he also painted a cycle of Napoleonic battle-pictures with much force. There is little or no sentiment about his work—little more than in that of Gérôme. His success lay in exact technical accomplishment. He drew well, painted well, and at times was a superior colorist. His art is more admired by the public than by the painters; but even the latter do not fail to praise his skill of hand. He was a great craftsman in the infinitely little. As a great artist his rank is still open to question.

The *genre* painting of fashionable life has been carried out by many followers of Meissonier, whose names need not be mentioned since they have not improved upon their forerunner. **Toulmouche** (1829-), **Leloir** (1843-1884), **Vibert** (1840-), **Bargue** (?-1883), and others, though somewhat different from Meissonier, belong among those painters of *genre* who love detail, costumes, stories, and pretty faces. Among the painters of military *genre* mention should be made of **De Neuville** (1836-1885), **Berne-Bellecour** (1838-), **Detaille** (1848-), and **Aimé-Morot** (1850-), all of them painters of merit.

Quite a different style of painting—half figure-piece half[168] *genre*—is to be found in the work of **Ribot** (1823-), a strong painter, remarkable for his apposition of high flesh lights with deep shadows, after the manner of Ribera, the Spanish painter. **Roybet** (1840-) is fond of rich stuffs and tapestries with velvet-clad characters in interiors, out of which he makes good color effects. **Bonvin** (1817-1887) and **Mettling** have painted the interior with small figures, copper-kettles, and other still-life that have given brilliancy to their pictures. As a still-life painter **Vollon** (1833-) has never had a superior. His fruits, flowers, armors, even his small marines and harbor pieces, are painted with one of the surest brushes of this century. He is called the "painter's painter," and is a man of great force in handling color, and in large realistic effect. **Dantan** and **Friant** have both produced canvases showing figures in interiors.

A number of excellent *genre* painters have been claimed by the impressionists as belonging to their brotherhood. There is little to warrant the claim, except the adoption to some extent of the modern ideas of illumination and flat painting. **Dagnan-Bouveret** (1852-) is one of these men, a good draughtsman, and a finished clean painter who by his recent use of high color finds himself occasionally looked upon as an impressionist. As a matter of fact he is one of the most conservative of the moderns—a man of feeling and imagination, and a fine technician. **Fantin-Latour** (1836-1904) is half romantic, half allegorical in subject, and in treatment oftentimes designedly vague and shadowy, more suggestive than realistic. **Duez** (1843-) and **Gervex** (1848-) are perhaps nearer to impressionism in their works than the others, but they are not at all advance advocates of this latest phase of art. In addition there are **Cottet** and **Henri Martin**.

FIG. 68.—MEISSONIER. NAPOLEON IN 1814.

THE IMPRESSIONISTS: The name is a misnomer. Every painter is an impressionist in so far as he records his impressions, and all art is impressionistic. What **Manet** (1833-1883), the leader of the original movement, meant to say was[169] that nature should not be painted as it actually is, but as it "impresses" the painter. He and his few followers tried to change the name to Independents, but the original name has clung to them and been mistakenly fastened to a present band of landscape painters who are seeking effects of light and air and should be called luminists if it is necessary for them to be named at all. Manet was extravagant in method and disposed toward low life for a subject, which has always militated against his popularity; but he was a very important man for his technical discoveries regarding the relations of light and shadow, the flat appearance of nature, the exact value of color tones. Some of his works, like The Boy with a Sword and The Toreador[170] Dead, are excellent pieces of painting. The higher imaginative qualities of art Manet made no great effort at attaining.

Degas stands quite by himself, strong in effects of motion, especially with race-horses, fine in color, and a delightful brushman in such subjects as ballet-girls and scenes from the theatre. **Besnard** is one of the best of the present men. He deals with the figure, and is usually concerned with the problem of harmonizing color under conflicting lights, such as twilight and lamplight. **Béraud** and **Raffaelli** are exceedingly clever in street scenes and character pieces; **Pissarro**[16] handles the peasantry in high color; **Brown** (1829-1890), the race-horse, and **Renoir**, the middle class of social life. **Caillebotte**, **Roll**, **Forain**, and **Miss Cassatt**, an American, are also classed with the impressionists.

[16]Died, 1903.

IMPRESSIONIST LANDSCAPE PAINTERS: Of recent years there has been a disposition to change the key of light in landscape painting, to get nearer the truth of nature in the height of light and in the height of shadows. In doing this **Claude Monet**, the present leader of the movement, has done away with the dark brown or black shadow and substituted the light-colored shadow, which is nearer the actual truth of nature. In trying to raise the pitch of light he has not been quite so successful, though accomplishing something. His method is to use pure prismatic colors on the principle that color is light in a decomposed form, and that its proper juxtaposition on canvas will recompose into pure light again. Hence the use of light shadows and bright colors. The aim of these modern men is chiefly to gain the effect of light and air. They do not apparently care for subject, detail, or composition.

At present their work is in the experimental stage, but from the way in which it is being accepted and followed by the painters of to-day we may be sure the movement is of considerable importance. There will probably be a reaction [171]in favor of more form and solidity than the present men give, but the high key of light will be retained. There are so many painters following these modern methods, not only in France but all over the world, that a list of their names would be impossible. In France **Sisley** with Monet are the two important landscapists. In marines **Boudin** and **Montenard** should be mentioned.

PRINCIPAL WORKS: The modern French painters are seen to advantage in the Louvre, Luxembourg, Pantheon, Sorbonne, and the municipal galleries of France. Also Metropolitan Museum New York, Chicago Art Institute, Boston Museum, and many private collections in France and America. Consult for works in public or private hands, Champlin and Perkins, *Cyclopedia of Painters and Paintings*, under names of artists.

[172]

CHAPTER XV.
SPANISH PAINTING.

BOOKS RECOMMENDED: Bermudez, *Diccionario de las Bellas Artes en España*; Davillier, *Mémoire de Velasquez*; Davillier, *Fortuny*; Eusebi, *Los Differentes Escuelas de Pintura*; Ford, *Handbook of Spain*; Head, *History of Spanish and French Schools of Painting*; Justi,*Velasquez and his Times*; Lefort, *Velasquez*; Lefort, *Francisco Goya*; Lefort, *Murillo et son École*; Lefort, *La Peinture Espagnole*; Palomino de Castro y Velasco, *Vidas de los Pintores y Estatuarios Eminentes Españoles*; Passavant, *Die Christliche Kunst in Spanien*; Plon, *Les Maîtres Italiens au Service de la Maison d'Autriche*; Stevenson, *Velasquez*; Stirling, *Annals of the Artists of Spain*; Stirling,*Velasquez and his Works*; Tubino, *El Arte y los Artistas contemporáneos en la Peninsula*; Tubino, *Murillo*; Viardot, *Notices sur les Principaux Peintres de l'Espagne*; Yriarte, *Goya, sa Biographie*, etc.

SPANISH ART MOTIVES: What may have been the early art of Spain we are at a loss to conjecture. The reigns of the Moor, the Iconoclast, and, finally, the Inquisitor, have left little that dates before the fourteenth century. The miniatures and sacred relics treasured in the churches and said to be of the apostolic period, show the traces of a much later date and a foreign origin. Even when we come down to the fifteenth century and meet with art produced in Spain, we have a following of Italy or the Netherlands. In methods and technic it was derivative more than original, though almost from the beginning peculiarly Spanish in spirit.

FIG. 69.—SANCHEZ COELLO. CLARA EUGENIA, DAUGHTER OF PHILIP II. MADRID.

That spirit was a dark and savage one, a something that[173] cringed under the lash of the Church, bowed before the Inquisition, and played the executioner with the paint-brush. The bulk of Spanish art was Church art, done under ecclesiastical domination, and done in form without question or protest. The religious subject ruled. True enough, there was portraiture of nobility, and under Philip and Velasquez a half-monarchical art of military scenes and *genre*; but this was not the bent of Spanish painting as a whole. Even in late days, when Velasquez was reflecting the haughty court, Murillo was more widely and nationally[174] reflecting the believing provinces and the Church faith of the people. It is safe to say, in a general way, that the Church was responsible for Spanish art, and that religion was its chief motive.

There was no revived antique, little of the nude or the pagan, little of consequence in landscape, little, until Velasquez's time, of the real and the actual. An ascetic view of life, faith, and the hereafter prevailed. The pietistic, the fervent, and the devout were not so conspicuous as the morose, the ghastly, and the horrible. The saints and martyrs, the crucifixions and violent deaths, were eloquent of the torture-chamber. It was more ecclesiasticism by blood and violence than Christianity by peace and love. And Spain welcomed this. For of all the children of the Church she was the most faithful to rule, crushing out heresy with an iron hand, gaining strength from the Catholic reaction, and upholding the Jesuits and the Inquisition.

METHODS OF PAINTING: Spanish art worthy of mention did not appear until the fifteenth century. At that time Spain was in close relations with the Netherlands, and Flemish painting was somewhat followed. How much the methods of the Van Eycks influenced Spain would be hard to determine, especially as these Northern methods were mixed with influences coming from Italy. Finally, the Italian example prevailed by reason of Spanish students in Italy and Italian painters in Spain. Florentine line, Venetian color, and Neapolitan light-and-shade ruled almost everywhere, and it was not until the time of Velasquez—the period just before the eighteenth-century decline—that distinctly Spanish methods, founded on nature, really came forcibly to the front.

SPANISH SCHOOLS OF PAINTING: There is difficulty in classifying these schools of painting because our present knowledge of them is limited. Isolated somewhat from the rest[175] of Europe, the Spanish painters have never been critically studied as the Italians have been, and what is at present known about the schools must be accepted subject to critical revision hereafter.

FIG. 70.—MURILLO. ST. ANTHONY OF PADUA. BERLIN.

The earliest school seems to have been made up from a gathering of artists at Toledo, who limned, carved, and gilded in the cathedral; but this school was not of long duration. It was merged into the Castilian school, which, after the building of Madrid, made its home in that capital and drew its forces from the towns of Toledo, Valladolid, and Badajoz. The Andalusian school, which rose about the middle of the sixteenth century, was made up from the local schools of Seville, Cordova, and Granada. The[176] Valencian school, to the southeast, rose about the same time, and was finally merged into the Andalusian. The Aragonese school, to the east, was small and of no great consequence, though existing in a feeble way to the end of the seventeenth century. The painters of these schools are not very strongly marked apart by methods or school traditions, and perhaps the divisions would better be looked upon as more geographical than otherwise. None of the schools really began before the sixteenth century, though there are names of artists and some extant pictures before that date, and with the seventeenth century all art in Spain seems to have centred about Madrid.

Spanish painting started into life concurrently with the rise to prominence of Spain as a political kingdom. What, if any, direct effect the maritime discoveries, the conquests of Granada and Naples, the growth of literature, and the decline of Italy, may have had upon Spanish painting can only be conjectured; but certainly the sudden advance of the nation politically and socially was paralleled by the advance of its art.

THE CASTILIAN SCHOOL: This school probably had no so-called founder. It was a growth from early art traditions at Toledo, and afterward became the chief school of the kingdom owing to the patronage of Philip II. and Philip IV. at Madrid. The first painter of importance in the school seems to have been**Antonio Rincon** (1446?-1500?). He is sometimes spoken of as the father of Spanish painting, and as having studied in Italy with Castagno and Ghirlandajo, but there is little foundation for either statement. He painted chiefly at Toledo, painted portraits of Ferdinand and Isabella, and had some skill in hard drawing.**Berruguete** (1480?-1561) studied with Michael Angelo, and is supposed to have helped him in the Vatican. He afterward returned to Spain, painted many altar-pieces, and was patronized as painter, sculptor, and architect by[177] Charles V. and Philip II. He was probably the first to introduce pure Italian methods into Spain, with some coldness and dryness of coloring and handling. **Becerra** (1520?-1570) was born in Andalusia, but worked in Castile, and was a man of Italian training similar to Berruguete. He was an exceptional man, perhaps, in his use of mythological themes and nude figures.

There is not a great deal known about **Morales** (1509?-1586), called "the Divine," except that he was allied to the Castilian school, and painted devotional heads of Christ with the crown of thorns, and many afflicted and weeping madonnas. There was Florentine drawing in his work, great regard for finish, and something of Correggio's softness in shadows pitched in a browner key. His sentiment was rather exaggerated. **Sanchez-Coello** (1513?-1590) was painter and courtier to Philip II., and achieved reputation as a portrait-painter, though also doing some altar-pieces. It is doubtful whether he ever studied in Italy, but in Spain he was for a time with Antonio Moro, and probably learned from him something of rich costumes, ermines, embroideries, and jewels, for which his portraits were remarkable.**Navarette** (1526?-1579), called "El Mudo" (the dumb one), certainly was in Italy for something like twenty years, and was there a disciple of Titian, from whom he doubtless learned much of color and the free flow of draperies. He was one of the best of the middle-period painters. **Theotocopuli** (1548?-1625), called "El Greco" (the Greek), was another Venetian-influenced painter, with enough Spanish originality about him to make most of his pictures striking in color and drawing. **Tristan** (1586-1640) was his best follower.

FIG. 71.—RIBERA. ST. AGNES. DRESDEN.
Please click here for a modern color image

Velasquez (1599-1660) is the greatest name in the history of Spanish painting. With him Spanish art took upon itself a decidedly naturalistic and national stamp. Before his time Italy had been freely imitated; but though Velasquez[178] himself was in Italy for quite a long time, and intimately acquainted with great Italian art, he never seemed to have been led away from his own individual way of seeing and doing. He was a pupil of Herrera, afterward with Pacheco, and learned much from Ribera and Tristan, but more from a direct study of nature than from all the others. He was in a broad sense a realist—a man who recorded the material and the actual without emendation or transposition. He has never been surpassed in giving the solidity and substance of form and the placing of objects in atmosphere. And this, not in a small, finical way, but with a breadth of view and of treatment which are to-day the despair of painters. There was nothing of the ethereal, the spiritual,[179] the pietistic, or the pathetic about him. He never for a moment left the firm basis of reality. Standing upon earth he recorded the truths of the earth, but in their largest, fullest, most universal forms.

Technically his was a master-hand, doing all things with ease, giving exact relations of colors and lights, and placing everything so perfectly that no addition or alteration is thought of. With the brush he was light, easy, sure. The surface looks as though touched once, no more. It is the perfection of handling through its simplicity and certainty, and has not the slightest trace of affectation or mannerism. He was one of the few Spanish painters who were enabled to shake off the yoke of the Church. Few of his canvases are religious in subject. Under royal patronage he passed almost all of his life in painting portraits of the royal family, ministers of state, and great dignitaries. As a portrait-painter he is more widely known than as a figure-painter. Nevertheless he did many canvases like The Tapestry Weavers and The Surrender at Breda, which attest his remarkable genius in that field; and even in landscape, in *genre*, in animal painting, he was a very superior man. In fact Velasquez is one of the few great painters in European history for whom there is nothing but praise. He was the full-rounded complete painter, intensely individual and self-assertive, and yet in his art recording in a broad way the Spanish type and life. He was the climax of Spanish painting, and after him there was a rather swift decline, as had been the case in the Italian schools.

Mazo (1610?-1667), pupil and son-in-law of Velasquez, was one of his most facile imitators, and **Carreño de Miranda** (1614-1685) was influenced by Velasquez, and for a time his assistant. The Castilian school may be said to have closed with these late men and with **Claudio Coello** (1635?-1693), a painter with a style founded on Titian and Rubens, whose best work was of extraordinary power. Spanish[180] painting went out with Spanish power, and only isolated men of small rank remained.

ANDALUSIAN SCHOOL: This school came into existence about the middle of the sixteenth century. Its chief centre was at Seville, and its chief patron the Church rather than the king. **Vargas** (1502-1568) was probably the real founder of the school, though **De Castro** (fl. 1454) and others preceded him. Vargas was a man of much reputation and ability in his time, and introduced Italian methods and elegance into the Andalusian school after twenty odd years of residence in Italy. He is said to have studied under Perino del Vaga, and there is some sweetness of face and grace of form about his work that point that way, though his composition suggests Correggio. Most of his frescos have perished; some of his canvases are still in existence.

Cespedes (1538?-1608) is little known through extant works, but he achieved fame in many departments during his life, and is said to have been in Italy under Florentine influence. His coloring was rather cold, and his drawing large and flat. The best early painter of the school was **Roelas** (1558?-1625), the inspirer of Murillo and the master of Zurbaran. He is supposed to have studied at Venice, because of his rich, glowing color. Most of his works are religious and are found chiefly at Seville. He was greatly patronized by the Jesuits. **Pacheco** (1571-1654) was more of a pedant than a painter, a man of rule, who to-day might be written down an academician. His drawing was hard, and perhaps the best reason for his being remembered is that he was one of the masters and the father-in-law of Velasquez. His rival, **Herrera the Elder** (1576?-1656) was a stronger man—in fact, the most original artist of his school. He struck off by himself and created a bold realism with a broad brush that anticipated Velasquez—in fact, Velasquez was under him for a time.

The pure Spanish school in Andalusia, as distinct from[181] Italian imitation, may be said to have started with Herrera. It was further advanced by another independent painter, **Zurbaran** (1598-1662), a pupil of Roelas. He was a painter of the emaciated monk in ecstasy, and many other rather dismal religious subjects expressive of tortured rapture. From using a rather dark shadow he acquired the name of the Spanish Caravaggio. He had a good deal of Caravaggio's strength, together with a depth and breadth of color suggestive of the Venetians. **Cano** (1601-1667), though he never was in Italy, had the name of the Spanish Michael Angelo, probably because he was sculptor, painter, and architect. His painting was rather sharp in line and statuesque in pose, with a coloring somewhat like that of Van Dyck. It was eclectic rather than original work.

FIG. 72.—FORTUNY. SPANISH MARRIAGE.

Murillo (1618-1682) is generally placed at the head of the Andalusian school, as Velasquez at the head of the Castilian. There is good reason for it, for though Murillo was not the great painter he was sometime supposed, yet he was[182] not the weak man his modern critics would make him out. A religious painter largely, though doing some *genre* subjects like his beggar-boy groups, he sought for religious fervor and found, only too often, sentimentality. His madonnas are usually after the Carlo Dolci pattern, though never so excessive in sentiment. This was not the case with his earlier works, mostly of humble life, which were painted in rather a hard, positive manner. Later on he became misty, veiled in light and effeminate in outline, though still holding grace. His color varied with his early and later styles. It was usually gay and a little thin. While basing his work on nature like Velasquez, he never had the supreme poise of that master, either mentally or technically; howbeit he was an excellent painter, who perhaps justly holds second place in Spanish art.

SCHOOL OF VALENCIA: This school rose contemporary with the Andalusian school, into which it was finally merged after the importance of Madrid had been established. It was largely modelled upon Italian painting, as indeed were all the schools of Spain at the start. **Juan de Joanes** (1507?-1579) apparently was its founder, a man who painted a good portrait, but in other respects was only a fair imitator of Raphael, whom he had studied at Rome. A stronger man was **Francisco de Ribalta** (1550?-1628), who was for a time in Italy under the Caracci, and learned from them free draughtsmanship and elaborate composition. He was also fond of Sebastiano del Piombo, and in his best works (at Valencia) reflected him. Ribalta gave an early training to **Ribera** (1588-1656), who was the most important man of this school. In reality Ribera was more Italian than Valencian, for he spent the greater part of his life in Italy, where he was called Lo Spagnoletto, and was greatly influenced by Caravaggio. He was a Spaniard in the horrible subjects that he chose, but in coarse strength of line, heaviness of shadows, harsh handling of the brush, he was a true[183] Neapolitan Darkling. A pronounced mannerist he was no less a man of strength, and even in his shadow-saturated colors a painter with the color instinct. In Italy his influence in the time of the Decadence was wide-spread, and in Spain his Italian pupil, Giordano, introduced his methods for late imitation. There were no other men of much rank in the Valencian school, and, as has been said, the school was eventually merged in Andalusian painting.

EIGHTEENTH AND NINETEENTH-CENTURY PAINTING IN SPAIN: Almost directly after the passing of Velasquez and Murillo Spanish art failed. The eighteenth-century, as in Italy, was quite barren of any considerable art until near its close. Then **Goya** (1746-1828) seems to have made a partial restoration of painting. He was a man of peculiarly Spanish turn of mind, fond of the brutal and the bloody, picturing inquisition scenes, bull-fights, battle pieces, and revelling in caricature, sarcasm, and ridicule. His imagination was grotesque and horrible, but as a painter his art was based on the natural, and was exceedingly strong. In brush-work he followed Velasquez; in a peculiar forcing of contrasts in light and dark he was apparently quite himself, though possibly influenced by Ribera's work. His best work shows in his portraits and etchings.

After Goya's death Spanish art, such as it was, rather followed France, with the extravagant classicism of David as a model. What was produced may be seen to this day in the Madrid Museum. It does not call for mention here. About the beginning of the 1860's Spanish painting made a new advance with **Mariano Fortuny** (1838-1874). In his early years he worked at historical painting, but later on he went to Algiers and Rome, finding his true vent in a bright sparkling painting of *genre* subjects, oriental scenes, streets, interiors, single figures, and the like. He excelled in color, sunlight effects, and particularly in a vivacious facile handling of the brush. His work is brilliant, and in his late productions often spotty from excessive use of points of light in high color. He was a technician of much brilliancy and originality, his work exciting great admiration in his day, and leading the younger painters of Spain into that ornate handling visible in their works at the present time. Many of these latter, from association with art and artists in Paris, have adopted French methods, and hardly show such a thing as Spanish nationality. Fortuny's brother-in-law, **Madrazo** (1841-), is an example of a Spanish painter turned French in his methods—a facile and brilliant portrait-painter. **Zamacois** (1842-1871) died early, but with a reputation as a successful portrayer of seventeenth-century subjects a little after the style of Meissonier and not unlike Gérôme. He was a good colorist and an excellent painter of textures.

FIG. 73.—MADRAZO, UNMASKED.

The historical scene of Mediæval or Renaissance times, pageants and fêtes with rich costume, fine architecture and vivid effects of color, are characteristic of a number of the modern Spaniards—**Villegas, Pradilla, Alvarez**. As a general thing their canvases are a little flashy, likely to please at first sight but grow wearisome after a time. **Palmaroli** has a style that resembles a mixture of Fortuny and Meissonier; and some other painters, like **Luis Jiminez Aranda, Sorolla, Zuloaga, Anglada, Garcia y Remos, Vierge, Roman Ribera,** and **Domingo**, have done excellent work. In landscape and Venetian scenes **Rico** leads among the Spaniards with a vivacity and brightness not always seen to good advantage in his late canvases.

PRINCIPAL WORKS: Generally speaking, Spanish art cannot be seen to advantage outside of Spain. Both its ancient and modern masterpieces are at Madrid, Seville, Toledo, and elsewhere. The Royal Gallery at Madrid has the most and the best examples.

CASTILIAN SCHOOL—**Rincon**, altar-piece church of Robleda de Chavilla; **Berruguete**, altar-pieces Saragossa, Valladolid, Madrid, Toledo; **Morales**, Madrid and Louvre; **Sanchez-Coello**, Madrid and Brussels Mus.; **Navarette**, Escorial, Madrid, St. Petersburg; **Theotocupuli**, Cathedral and S. Tomé Toledo, Madrid Mus.; **Velasquez**, best works in Madrid Mus., Escorial, Salamanca, Montpensier Gals., Nat. Gal. Lon., Infanta Marguerita Louvre, Borro portrait (?) Berlin, Innocent X. Doria Rome; **Mazo**, landscapes Madrid Mus.; **Carreño de Miranda**, Madrid Mus.; **Claudio Coello**, Escorial, Madrid, Brussels, Berlin, and Munich Mus.

ANDALUSIAN SCHOOL—**Vargas**, Seville Cathedral; **Cespedes**, Cordova Cathedral; **Roelas**, S. Isidore Cathedral, Museum Seville; **Pacheco**, Madrid Mus.; **Herrera**, Seville Cathedral and Mus. and Archbishop's Palace, Dresden Mus.; **Zurbaran**, Seville Cathedral and Mus. Madrid, Dresden, Louvre, Nat. Gal. Lon.; **Cano**, Madrid, Seville Mus. and Cathedral, Berlin, Dresden, Munich; **Murillo**, best pictures in Madrid Mus. and Acad. of S. Fernando Madrid, Seville Mus. Hospital and Capuchin Church, Louvre, Nat. Gal. Lon., Dresden, Munich, Hermitage.

VALENCIAN SCHOOL—**Juan de Joanes**, Madrid Mus., Cathedral Valencia, Hermitage; **Ribalta**, Madrid and Valencian Mus., Hermitage; **Ribera**, Louvre, Nat. Gal. Lon., Dresden, Naples, Hermitage, and other European museums, chief works at Madrid.

MODERN MEN AND THEIR WORKS—**Goya**, Madrid Mus., Acad. of S. Fernando, Valencian Cathedral and Mus., two portraits in Louvre. The works of the contemporary painters are largely in private hands where reference to them is of little use to the average student. Thirty Fortunys are in the collection of William H. Stewart in Paris. His best work, The Spanish Marriage, belongs to Madame de Cassin, in Paris. Examples of Villegas, Madrazo, Rico, Domingo, and others, in the Vanderbilt Gallery, Metropolitan Mus., New York; Boston, Chicago, and Philadelphia Mus.

CHAPTER XVI.
FLEMISH PAINTING.

BOOKS RECOMMENDED: Busscher, *Recherches sur les Peintres Gantois*; Crowe and Cavalcaselle, *Early Flemish Painters*; Cust, *Van Dyck*; Dehaisnes, *L'Art dans la Flandre*; Du Jardin, *L'art Flamand*; Eisenmann, *The Brothers Van Eyck*; Fétis, *Les Artistes Belges à l'Étranger*;

Fromentin, *Old Masters of Belgium and Holland*; Gerrits, *Rubens zyn Tyd*, etc.; Guiffrey, *Van Dyck*; Hasselt, *Histoire de Rubens*; (Waagen's) Kügler, *Handbook of Painting—German, Flemish, and Dutch Schools*; Lemonnier, *Histoire des Arts en Belgique*; Mantz, *Adrien Brouwer*; Michel, *Rubens*; Michiels, *Rubens en l'École d'Anvers*; Michiels, *Histoire de la Peinture Flamande*; Stevenson, *Rubens*; Van den Branden, *Geschiedenis der Antwerpsche Schilderschool*; Van Mander, *Le Livre des Peintres*; Waagen, *Uber Hubert und Jan Van Eyck*; Waagen, *Peter Paul Rubens*; Wauters, *Rogier van der Weyden*; Wauters, *La Peinture Flamande*; Weale, *Hans Memling(Arundel Soc.)*; Weale, *Notes sur Jean Van Eyck*.

THE FLEMISH PEOPLE: Individually and nationally the Flemings were strugglers against adverse circumstances from the beginning. A realistic race with practical ideas, a people rather warm of impulse and free in habits, they combined some German sentiment with French liveliness and gayety. The solidarity of the nation was not accomplished until after 1385, when the Dukes of Burgundy began to extend their power over the Low Countries. Then the Flemish people became strong enough to defy both Germany and France, and wealthy enough, through their com[187]merce with Spain, Italy, and France to encourage art not only at the Ducal court but in the churches, and among the citizens of the various towns.

FIG. 74.—VAN EYCKS. ST. BAVON ALTAR-PIECE (WING). BERLIN.
Please click here for a modern color image

FLEMISH SUBJECTS AND METHODS: As in all the countries of Europe, the early Flemish painting pictured Christian subjects primarily. The great bulk of it was church altar-pieces, though side by side with this was an admirable portraiture, some knowledge of landscape, and some exposition of allegorical subjects. In means and methods it was quite original. The early history is lost, but if Flemish painting was beholden to the painting of any other nation, it was to the miniature painting of France. There is, however, no positive record of this. The Flemings seem to have begun by themselves, and pictured the life about them in their own way. They were apparently not influenced at first by Italy. There were no antique influences, no excavated marbles to copy, no Byzantine traditions left[188] to follow. At first their art was exact and minute in detail, but not well grasped in the mass. The compositions were huddled, the landscapes pure but finical, the figures inclined to slimness, awkwardness, and angularity in the lines of form or drapery, and uncertain in action. To offset this there was a positive realism in textures, perspective, color, tone, light, and atmosphere. The effect of the whole was odd and strained, but the effect of the part was to convince one that the Flemish painters were excellent craftsmen in detail, skilled with the brush, and shrewd observers of nature in a purely picturesque way.

To the Flemish painters of the fifteenth century belongs, not the invention of oil-painting, for it was known before their time, but its acceptable application in picture-making. They applied oil with color to produce brilliancy and warmth of effect, to insure firmness and body in the work, and to carry out textural effects in stuffs, marbles, metals, and the like. So far as we know there never was much use of distemper, or fresco-work upon the walls of buildings. The oil medium came into vogue when the miniatures and illuminations of the early days had expanded into panel pictures. The size of the miniature was increased, but the minute method of finishing was not laid aside. Some time afterward painting with oil upon canvas was adopted.

SCHOOL OF BRUGES: Painting in Flanders starts abruptly with the fifteenth century. What there was before that time more than miniatures and illuminations is not known. Time and the Iconoclasts have left no remains of consequence. Flemish art for us begins with **Hubert van Eyck** (?-1426) and his younger brother **Jan van Eyck**(?-1440). The elder brother is supposed to have been the better painter, because the most celebrated work of the brothers—the St. Bavon altar-piece, parts of which are in Ghent, Brussels, and Berlin—bears the inscription that Hubert began it [189]and Jan finished it. Hubert was no doubt an excellent painter, but his pictures are few and there is much discussion whether he or Jan painted them. For historical purposes Flemish art was begun, and almost completed, by Jan van Eyck. He had all the attributes of the early men, and was one of the most perfect of Flemish painters. He painted real forms and real life, gave them a setting in true perspective and light, and put in background landscapes with a truthful if minute regard for the facts. His figures in action had some awkwardness, they were small of head, slim of body, and sometimes stumbled; but his modelling of faces, his rendering of textures in cloth, metal, stone, and the like, his delicate yet firm *facture* were all rather remarkable for his time. None of this early Flemish art has the grandeur of Italian composition, but in realistic detail, in landscape, architecture, figure, and dress, in pathos, sincerity, and sentiment it is unsurpassed by any fifteenth-century art.

FIG. 75.—MEMLING (?). ST. LAWRENCE (DETAIL).
NAT. GAL., LONDON.

Little is known of the personal history of either of the Van Eycks. They left an influence and had many followers, but whether these were direct pupils or not is an open question. **Peter**

Cristus (1400?-1472) was perhaps a pupil of Jan, though more likely a follower of his methods in color and general technic. **Roger van der Weyden** (1400?-1464), whether a pupil of the Van Eycks or a rival, produced a similar style of art. His first master was an obscure Robert Campin. He was afterward at Bruges, and from there went to Brussels and founded a school of his own called the

SCHOOL OF BRABANT: He was more emotional and dramatic than Jan van Eyck, giving much excited action and[190] pathetic expression to his figures in scenes from the passion of Christ. He had not Van Eyck's skill, nor his detail, nor his color. More of a draughtsman than a colorist, he was angular in figure and drapery, but had honesty, pathos, and sincerity, and was very charming in bright background landscapes. Though spending some time in Italy, he was never influenced by Italian art. He was always Flemish in type, subject, and method, a trifle repulsive at first through angularity and emotional exaggeration, but a man to be studied.

By **Van der Goes** (1430?-1482) there are but few good examples, the chief one being an altar-piece in the Uffizi at Florence. It is angular in drawing but full of character, and in beauty of detail and ornamentation is a remarkable picture. He probably followed Van der Weyden, as did also **Justus van Ghent** (last half of fifteenth century). Contemporary with these men **Dierick Bouts** (1410-1475) established a school at Haarlem. He was Dutch by birth, but after 1450 settled in Louvain, and in his art belongs to the Flemish school. He was influenced by Van der Weyden, and shows it in his detail of hands and melancholy face, though he differed from him in dramatic action and in type. His figure was awkward, his color warm and rich, and in landscape backgrounds he greatly advanced the painting of the time.

Memling (1425?-1495?), one of the greatest of the school, is another man about whose life little is known. He was probably associated with Van der Weyden in some way. His art is founded on the Van Eyck school, and is remarkable for sincerity, purity, and frankness of attitude. As a religious painter, he was perhaps beyond all his contemporaries in tenderness and pathos. In portraiture he was exceedingly strong in characterization, and in his figures very graceful. His flesh painting was excellent, but in textures or landscape work he was not remarkable. His best followers were **Van der Meire** (1427?-1474?) and **Gheeraert**[191] **David** (1450?-1523). The latter was famous for the fine, broad landscapes in the backgrounds of his pictures, said, however, by critics to have been painted by Joachim Patinir. He was realistically horrible in many subjects, and though a close recorder of detail he was much broader than any of his predecessors.

FLEMISH SCHOOLS OF THE SIXTEENTH CENTURY: In this century Flemish painting became rather widely diffused. The schools of Bruges and Ghent gave place to the schools in the large commercial cities like Antwerp and Brussels, and the commercial relations between the Low Countries and Italy finally led to the dissipation of national characteristics in art and the imitation of the Italian Renaissance painters. There is no sharp line of demarcation between those painters who clung to Flemish methods and those who adopted Italian methods. The change was gradual.

FIG. 76.—MASSYS. HEAD OF VIRGIN. ANTWERP.

Quentin Massys (1460?-1530) and **Mostert** (1474-1556?), a Dutchman by birth, but, like Bouts, Flemish by influence, were among the last of the Gothic painters in Flanders, and yet they began the introduction of Italian features in their painting. Massys led in architectural backgrounds, and from that the Italian example spread to subjects, figures, methods, until the indigenous Flemish art became a thing of the past. Massys was, at Antwerp, the most important painter of his day, following the old Flemish methods with many improvements. His work was detailed, and yet executed with a broader, freer brush than formerly, and with more variety in color, modelling, expression of character. He increased figures to almost life-size, giving them greater importance than landscape or architecture. The type was[192] still lean and angular, and often contorted with emotion. His Money-Changers and Misers (many of them painted by his son) were a *genre* of his own. With him closed the Gothic school, and with him began the

ANTWERP SCHOOL, the pupils of which went to Italy, and eventually became Italianized. **Mabuse** (1470?-1541) was the first to go. His early work shows the influence of Massys and David. He was good in composition, color, and brush-work, but lacked in originality, as did all the imitators of Italy. **Franz Floris** (1518?-1570) was a man of talent, much admired in his time, because he brought back reminiscences of Michael Angelo to Antwerp. His influence was fatal upon his followers, of whom there were many, like the **Franckens** and **De Vos**. Italy and Roman methods, models, architecture, subjects, began to rule everywhere.

From Brussels **Barent van Orley** (1491?-1542) left early for Italy, and became essentially Italian, though retaining some Flemish color. He painted in oil, tempera, and for glass, and is supposed to have gained his brilliant colors by using a gilt ground. His early works remind one of David. **Cocxie** (1499-1592), the Flemish Raphael, was but an indifferent imitator of the Italian

Raphael. At Liége the Romanists, so called, began with **Lambert Lombard** (1505-1566), of whose work nothing authentic remains except drawings. At Bruges **Peeter Pourbus** (1510?-1584) was about the last one of the good portrait-painters of the time. Another excellent portrait-painter, a pupil of Scorel, was **Antonio Moro** (1512?-1578?). He had much dignity, force, and elaborateness of costume, and stood quite by himself. There were other painters of the time who were born or trained in Flanders, and yet became so naturalized in other countries that in their work they do not belong to Flanders. **Neuchatel** (1527?-1590?), **Geldorp** (1553-1616?), **Calvaert** (1540?-1619), **Spranger** (1546-1627?), and others, were of this group.[193]

Among all the strugglers in Italian imitation only a few landscapists held out for the Flemish view. **Paul Bril** (1554-1626) was the first of them. He went to Italy, but instead of following the methods taught there, he taught Italians his own view of landscape. His work was a little dry and formal, but graceful in composition, and good in light and color. The **Brueghels**—there were three of them—also stood out for Flemish landscape, introducing it nominally as a background for small figures, but in reality for the beauty of the landscape itself.

FIG. 77.—RUBENS. PORTRAIT OF YOUNG WOMAN.
HERMITAGE, ST. PETERSBURGH.

Please click here for a modern color image

SEVENTEENTH-CENTURY PAINTING: This was the great century of Flemish painting, though the painting was not entirely Flemish in method or thought. The influence of Italy had done away with the early simplicity, purity, and religious pathos of the Van Eycks. During the sixteenth century everything had run to bald imitation of Renaissance methods. Then came a new master-genius, **Rubens** (1577-1640), who formed a new art founded in method upon Italy, yet distinctly northern in character. Rubens chose all subjects for his brush, but the religious altar-piece probably[194] occupied him as much as any. To this he gave little of Gothic sentiment, but everything of Renaissance splendor. His art was more material than spiritual, more brilliant and startling in sensuous qualities, such as line and color, than charming by facial expression or tender feeling. Something of the Paolo Veronese cast of mind, he conceived things largely, and painted them proportionately—large Titanic types, broad schemes and masses of color, great sweeping lines of beauty. One value of this largeness was its ability to hold at a distance upon wall or altar. Hence, when seen to-day, close at hand, in museums, people are apt to think Rubens's art coarse and gross.

There is no prettiness about his type. It is not effeminate or sentimental, but rather robust, full of life and animal spirits, full of blood, bone, and muscle—of majestic dignity, grace, and power, and glowing with splendor of color. In imagination, in conception of art purely as art, and not as a mere vehicle to convey religious or mythological ideas, in mental grasp of the pictorial world, Rubens stands with Titian and Velasquez in the very front rank of painters. As a technician, he was unexcelled. A master of composition, modelling, and drawing, a master of light, and a color-harmonist of the rarest ability, he, in addition, possessed the most certain, adroit, and facile hand that ever handled a paint-brush. Nothing could be more sure than the touch of Rubens, nothing more easy and masterful. He was trained in both mind and eye, a genius by birth and by education, a painter who saw keenly, and was able to realize what he saw with certainty.

Well-born, ennobled by royalty, successful in both court and studio, Rubens lived brilliantly and his life was a series of triumphs. He painted enormous canvases, and the number of pictures, altar-pieces, mythological decorations, landscapes, portraits scattered throughout the galleries of Europe, and attributed to him, is simply amazing. He was[195] undoubtedly helped in many of his canvases by his pupils, but the works painted by his own hand make a world of art in themselves. He was the greatest painter of the North, a full-rounded, complete genius, comparable to Titian in his universality. His precursors and masters, **Van Noort** (1562-1641) and **Vaenius** (1558-1629), gave no strong indication of the greatness of Ruben's art, and his many pupils, though echoing his methods, never rose to his height in mental or artistic grasp.

FIG. 78.—VAN DYCK. PORTRAIT OF CORNELIUS VAN DER GEEST.
NAT. GAL. LONDON.

Please click here for a modern color image

Van Dyck (1599-1641) was his principal pupil. He followed Rubens closely at first, though in a slighter manner technically, and with a cooler coloring. After visiting Italy he took up with the warmth of Titian. Later, in England,[196] he became careless and less certain. His rank is given him not for his figure-pieces. They were not always successful, lacking as they did in imagination and originality, though done with force. His best work was his portraiture, for which he became famous, painting nobility in every country of Europe in which he visited. At his best he was a portrait-painter of great power, but not to be placed in the same rank with Titian, Rubens, Rembrandt, and Velasquez. His characters are gracefully posed, and appear to be aristocratic. There is a noble distinction about them, and yet even this has the feeling of being somewhat affected. The serene complacency of his lords and ladies finally became almost a mannerism with him, though never a disagreeable one. He died early, a painter of mark, but not the greatest portrait-painter of the world, as is sometimes said of him.

There were a number of Rubens's pupils, like **Diepenbeeck** (1596-1675), who learned from their master a certain brush facility, but were not sufficiently original to make deep impressions. When Rubens died the best painter left in Belgium was **Jordaens** (1593-1678). He was a pupil of Van Noort, but submitted to the Rubens influence and followed in Rubens's style, though more florid in coloring and grosser in types. He painted all sorts of subjects, but was seen at his best in mythological scenes with groups of drunken satyrs and bacchants, surrounded by a close-placed landscape. He was the most independent and original of the followers, of whom there was a host. **Crayer** (1582-1669), **Janssens** (1575-1632), **Zegers** (1591-1651), **Rombouts** (1597-1637), were the prominent ones. They all took an influence more or less pronounced from Rubens. **Cornelius de Vos** (1585-1651) was a more independent man—a realistic portrait-painter of much ability. **Snyders** (1579-1657), and **Fyt** (1609?-1661), devoted their brushes to the painting of still-life, game, fruits, flowers, landscape—Snyders often in collaboration with Rubens himself.[197]

FIG. 79.—TENIERS THE YOUNGER. PRODIGAL SON. LOUVRE.
Please click here for a modern color image

Living at the same time with these half-Italianized painters, and continuing later in the century, there was another group of painters in the Low Countries who were emphatically of the soil, believing in themselves and their own country and picturing scenes from commonplace life in a manner quite their own. These were the "Little Masters," the *genre* painters, of whom there was even a stronger representation appearing contemporaneously in Holland. In Belgium there were not so many nor such talented men, but some of them were very interesting in their work as in their subjects. **Teniers the Younger** (1610-1690) was among the first of them to picture peasant, burgher, alewife, and nobleman in all scenes and places. Nothing escaped him as a subject, and yet his best work was shown in the handling of low life in taverns. There is coarse wit in his work, but[198] it is atoned for by good color and easy handling. He was influenced by Rubens, though decidedly different from him in many respects. **Brouwer** (1606?-1638) has often been catalogued with the Holland school, but he really belongs with Teniers, in Belgium. He died early, but left a number of pictures remarkable for their fine "fat" quality and their beautiful color. He was not a man of Italian imagination, but a painter of low life, with coarse humor and not too much good taste, yet a superb technician and vastly beyond many of his little Dutch contemporaries at the North. Teniers and Brouwer led a school and had many followers.

In a slightly different vein was **Gonzales Coques** (1618-1684), who is generally seen to advantage in pictures of interiors with family groups. In subject he was more refined than the other *genre* painters, and was influenced to some extent by Van Dyck. As a colorist he held rank, and his portraiture (rarely seen) was excellent. At this time there were also many painters of landscape, marine, battles, still-life—in fact Belgium was alive with painters—but none of them was sufficiently great to call for individual mention. Most of them were followers of either Holland or Italy, and the gist of their work will be spoken of hereafter under Dutch painting.

EIGHTEENTH-CENTURY PAINTING IN BELGIUM: Decline had set in before the seventeenth century ended. Belgium was torn by wars, her commerce flagged, her art-spirit seemed burned out. A long line of petty painters followed whose works call for silence. One man alone seemed to stand out like a star by comparison with his contemporaries, **Verhagen** (1728-1811), a portrait-painter of talent.

NINETEENTH-CENTURY PAINTING IN BELGIUM: During this century Belgium has been so closely related to France that the influence of the larger country has been quite apparent upon the art of the smaller. In 1816 David, the leader of the French classic school, sent into exile by the Restoration,[199] settled at Brussels, and immediately drew around him many pupils. His influence was felt at once, and **Francois Navez** (1787-1869) was the chief one among his pupils to establish the revived classic art in Belgium. In 1830, with Belgian independence and almost concurrently with the romantic movement in France, there began a romantic movement in Belgium with **Wappers** (1803-1874). His art was founded substantially on Rubens; but, like the Paris romanticists, he chose the dramatic subject of the times and treated it more for color than for line. He drew a number of followers to himself, but the movement was not more lasting than in France.

Wiertz (1806-1865), whose collection of works is to be seen in Brussels, was a partial exposition of romanticism mixed with a what-not of eccentricity entirely his own. Later on came a comparatively new man, **Louis Gallait** (1810-?), who held in Brussels substantially the same position that Delaroche did in Paris. His art was eclectic and never strong, though he had many pupils at Brussels, and started there a rivalry to Wappers at Antwerp. **Leys** (1815-1869) holds a rather unique position in Belgian art by reason of his affectation. He at first followed Pieter de Hooghe and other early painters. Then, after a study of the old German painters like Cranach, he developed an archaic style, producing a Gothic quaintness of line and composition, mingled with old Flemish coloring. The result was something popular, but not original or far-reaching, though technically well done. His chief pupil was **Alma Tadema** (1836-), alive to-day in London, and belonging to no school in particular. He is a technician of ability, mannered in composition and subject, and somewhat perfunctory in execution. His work is very popular with those who enjoy minute detail and smooth texture-painting.

In 1851 the influence of the French realism of Courbet began to be felt at Brussels, and since then Belgian art has[200] followed closely the art movements at Paris. Men like **Alfred Stevens** (1828-), a pupil of Navez, are really more French than Belgian. Stevens is one of the best of the moderns, a painter of power in fashionable or high-life *genre*, and a colorist of the first rank in modern art. Among the recent painters but a few can be mentioned. **Willems** (1823-), a weak painter of fashionable *genre*; **Verboeckhoven** (1799-1881), a vastly over-estimated animal painter; **Clays** (1819-), an excellent marine painter; **Boulanger**, a landscapist; **Wauters** (1846-), a history, and portrait-painter; **Jan van Beers** and **Robie**. The new men are **Claus, Buysse, Frederic, Khnopff, Lempoels**.

FIG. 80.—ALFRED STEVENS. ON THE BEACH.

[201]
PRINCIPAL WORKS:—**Hubert van Eyck**, Adoration of the Lamb (with Jan van Eyck) St. Bavon Ghent (wings at Brussels and Berlin supposed to be by Jan, the rest by Hubert); **Jan van Eyck**, as above, also Arnolfini portraits Nat. Gal. Lon., Virgin and Donor Louvre, Madonna Staedel Mus., Man with Pinks Berlin, Triumph of Church Madrid; **Van der Weyden**, a number of pictures in Brussels and Antwerp Mus., also at Staedel Mus., Berlin, Munich, Vienna; **Cristus**, Berlin, Staedel Mus., Hermitage, Madrid; **Justus van Ghent**, Last Supper Urbino Gal.; **Bouts**, St. Peter Louvain, Munich, Berlin, Brussels, Vienna; **Memling**, Brussels Mus. and Bruges Acad., and Hospital Antwerp, Turin, Uffizi, Munich, Vienna; **Van der Meire**, triptych St. Bavon Ghent; **Ghaeraert David**, Bruges, Berlin, Rouen, Munich.

Massys, Brussels, Antwerp, Berlin, St. Petersburg; best works Deposition in Antwerp Gal. and Merchant and Wife Louvre; **Mostert**, altar-piece Notre Dame Bruges; **Mabuse**, Madonnas Palermo, Milan Cathedral, Prague, other works Vienna, Berlin, Munich, Antwerp;**Floris**, Antwerp, Amsterdam, Brussels, Berlin, Munich, Vienna; **Barent van Orley**, altar-pieces Church of the Saviour Antwerp, and Brussels Mus.; **Cocxie**, Antwerp, Brussels, and Madrid Mus.; **Pourbus**, Bruges, Brussels, Vienna Mus.; **Moro**, portraits Madrid, Vienna, Hague, Brussels, Cassel, Louvre, St. Petersburg Mus.; **Bril**, landscapes Madrid, Louvre, Dresden, Berlin Mus.; the landscapes of the three**Breughels** are to be seen in most of the museums of Europe, especially at Munich, Dresden, and Madrid.

Rubens, many works, 93 in Munich, 35 in Dresden, 15 at Cassel, 16 at Berlin, 14 in London, 90 in Vienna, 66 in Madrid, 54 in Paris, 63 at St. Petersburg (as given by Wauters), best works at Antwerp, Vienna, Munich, and Madrid; **Van Noort**, Antwerp, Brussels Mus., Ghent and Antwerp Cathedrals; **Van Dyck**, Windsor Castle, Nat. Gal. Lon., 41 in Munich, 19 in Dresden, 15 in Cassel, 13 in Berlin, 67 in Vienna, 21 in Madrid, 24 in Paris, and 38 in St. Petersburg (Wauters), best examples in Vienna, Louvre, Nat. Gal. Lon.; and Madrid, good example in Met. Mus. N. Y.; **Diepenbeeck**, Antwerp Churches and Mus., Berlin, Vienna, Munich, Frankfort; **Jordaens**, Brussels, Antwerp, Munich, Vienna, Cassel, Madrid, Paris; **Crayer**, Brussels, Munich, Vienna; **Janssens**, Antwerp Mus., St. Bavon Ghent, Brussels and Cologne Mus.; **Zegers**, Cathedral Ghent, Notre Dame Bruges, Antwerp Mus.; **Rombouts**, Mus. and Cathedral Ghent, Antwerp Mus., Beguin Convent Mechlin, Hospital of St. John Bruges; **De Vos**, Cathedral and Mus. Antwerp, Munich, Oldenburg, Berlin Mus.; **Snyders**, Munich, Dresden, Vienna, Madrid, Paris, St. Petersburg; **Fyt**, Munich, Dresden, Cassel, [202]Berlin, Vienna, Madrid, Paris; **Teniers the Younger**, 29 pictures in Munich, 24 in Dresden, 8 in Berlin, 19 in Nat. Gal. Lon., 33 in Vienna, 52 in Madrid, 34 in Louvre, 40 in St. Petersburg (Wauters); **Brauwer**, 19 in Munich, 6 in Dresden, 4 in Berlin, 5 in Paris, 5 in St. Petersburgh (Wauters);**Coques**, Nat. Gal. Lon., Amsterdam, Berlin, Munich Mus.

Verhagen, Antwerp, Brussels, Ghent, and Vienna Mus.; **Navez**, Ghent, Antwerp, and Amsterdam Mus., Nat. Gal. Berlin; **Wappers**, Amsterdam, Brussels, Versailles Mus.; **Wiertz**, in Wiertz Gal. Brussels; **Gallait**, Liége, Versailles, Tournay, Brussels, Nat. Gal. Berlin;**Leys**, Amsterdam Mus., New Pinacothek, Munich, Brussels, Nat. Gal. Berlin, Antwerp Mus. and City Hall; **Alfred Stevens**, Marseilles, Brussels, frescos Royal Pal. Brussels; **Willems**, Brussels Mus. and Foder Mus. Amsterdam, Met. Mus. N. Y.; **Verboeckhoven**, Amsterdam, Foder, Nat. Gal.

Berlin, New Pinacothek, Brussels, Ghent, Met. Mus. N. Y.; **Clays**, Ghent Mus.; **Wauters**, Brussels, Liége Mus.; **Van Beers**, Burial of Charles the Good Amsterdam Mus.

[203]
CHAPTER XVII.
DUTCH PAINTING.

BOOKS RECOMMENDED: As before Fromentin, (Waagen's) Kügler; Amand-Durand, *Œuvre de Rembrandt*; *Archief voor Nederlandsche Kunst-geschiedenis*; Blanc, *Œuvre de Rembrandt*; Bode, *Franz Hals und seine Schule*; Bode, *Studien zur Geschichte der Hollandischen Malerei*; Bode, *Adriaan van Ostade*; Brown, *Rembrandt*; Burger (Th. Thoré), *Les Musées de la Hollande*; Havard, *La Peinture Hollandaise*; Michel, *Rembrandt*; Michel, *Gerard Terburg et sa Famille*; Mantz, *Adrien Brouwer*; Rooses, *Dutch Painters of the Nineteenth Century*; Rooses, *Rubens*; Schmidt, *Das Leben des Malers Adriaen Brouwer*; Van der Willigen, *Les Artistes de Harlem*; Van Mander, *Leven der Nederlandsche en Hoogduitsche Schilders*; Vosmaer, *Rembrandt, sa Vie et ses Œuvres*; Westrheene, *Jan Steen, Étude sur l'Art en Hollande*; Van Dyke, *Old Dutch and Flemish Masters*.

THE DUTCH PEOPLE AND THEIR ART: Though Holland produced a somewhat different quality of art from Flanders and Belgium, yet in many respects the people at the north were not very different from those at the south of the Netherlands. They were perhaps less versatile, less volatile, less like the French and more like the Germans. Fond of homely joys and the quiet peace of town and domestic life, the Dutch were matter-of-fact in all things, sturdy, honest, coarse at times, sufficient unto themselves, and caring little for what other people did. Just so with their painters. They were realistic at times to grotesqueness. Little troubled with fine poetic frenzies they painted their own lives in street, town-hall, tavern, and kitchen, conscious that it was good because true to themselves.[204]

At first Dutch art was influenced, even confounded, with that of Flanders. The Van Eycks led the way, and painters like Bouts and others, though Dutch by birth, became Flemish by adoption in their art at least. When the Flemish painters fell to copying Italy some of the Dutch followed them, but with no great enthusiasm. Suddenly, at the beginning of the seventeenth century, when Holland had gained political independence, Dutch art struck off by itself, became original, became famous. It pictured native life with verve, skill, keenness of insight, and fine pictorial view. Limited it was; it never soared like Italian art, never became universal or world-embracing. It was distinct, individual, national, something that spoke for Holland, but little beyond it.

In subject there were few historical canvases such as the Italians and French produced. The nearest approach to them were the paintings of shooting companies, or groups of burghers and syndics, and these were merely elaborations and enlargements of the portrait which the Dutch loved best of all. As a whole their subjects were single figures or small groups in interiors, quiet scenes, family conferences, smokers, card-players, drinkers, landscapes, still-life, architectural pieces. When they undertook the large canvas with many figures, they were often unsatisfactory. Even Rembrandt was so. The chief medium was oil, used upon panel or canvas. Fresco was probably used in the early days, but the climate was too damp for it and it was abandoned. It was perhaps the dampness of the northern climate that led to the adaptation of the oil medium, something the Van Eycks are credited with inaugurating.

FIG. 81.—HALS. PORTRAIT OF A LADY.

THE EARLY PAINTING: The early work has, for the great part, perished through time and the fierceness with which the Iconoclastic warfare was waged. That which remains to-day is closely allied in method and style to Flemish painting under the Van Eycks. **Ouwater** is one of the[205] earliest names that appears, and perhaps for that reason he has been called the founder of the school. He was remarked in his time for the excellent painting of background landscapes; but there is little authentic by him left to us from which we may form an opinion.[17] **Geertjen van St. Jan** (about 1475) was evidently a pupil of his, and from him there are two wings of an altar in the Vienna Gallery, supposed to be genuine. Bouts and Mostert have been spoken of under the Flemish school. **Bosch** (1460?-1516) was a man of some individuality who produced fantastic purgatories that were popular in their time and are known to-day through engravings.**Engelbrechsten** (1468-1533) was Dutch by birth and in his art, and yet probably got his inspiration from the Van Eyck school. The works attributed to him are doubtful, though two in the Leyden Gallery seem to be authentic. He was the master of **Lucas van Leyden** (1494-1533), the leading artist of the early period. Lucas van Leyden was a personal friend of Albrecht Dürer, the German painter, and in his art he was not unlike [206]him. A man with a singularly lean type, a little awkward in composition, brilliant in color, and warm in tone, he was, despite his archaic-looking work, an artist of much ability and originality. At first he was inclined toward Flemish methods, with an exaggerated realism in facial expression. In his middle period he was distinctly Dutch, but in his later days he came under Italian influence, and with a weakening effect upon his art. Taking his work as a whole, it was the strongest of all the early Dutch painters.

[17]A Raising of Lazarus is in the Berlin Gallery.

SIXTEENTH CENTURY: This century was a period of Italian imitation, probably superinduced by the action of the Flemings at Antwerp. The movement was somewhat like the Flemish one, but not so extensive or so productive. There was hardly a painter of rank in Holland during the whole century. **Scorel** (1495-1562) was the leader, and he probably got his first liking for Italian art through Mabuse at Antwerp. He afterward went to Italy, studied Raphael and Michael Angelo, and returned to Utrecht to open a school and introduce Italian art into Holland. A large number of pupils followed him, but their work was lacking in true originality. **Heemskerck** (1498-1574) and **Cornelis van Haarlem** (1562-1638), with **Steenwyck** (1550?-1604), were some of the more important men of the century, but none of them was above a common average.

SEVENTEENTH CENTURY: Beginning with the first quarter of this century came the great art of the Dutch people, founded on themselves and rooted in their native character. Italian methods were abandoned, and the Dutch told the story of their own lives in their own manner, with truth, vigor, and skill. There were so many painters in Holland during this period that it will be necessary to divide them into groups and mention only the prominent names.

PORTRAIT AND FIGURE PAINTERS: The real inaugurators of Dutch portraiture were Mierevelt, Hals, Ravesteyn, and De Keyser. **Mierevelt** (1567-1641) was one of the earliest,[207] a prolific painter, fond of the aristocratic sitter, and indulging in a great deal of elegance in his accessories of dress and the like. He had a slight, smooth brush, much detail, and a profusion of color. Quite the reverse of him was **Franz Hals** (1584?-1666), one of the most remarkable painters of portraits with which history acquaints us. In giving the sense of life and personal physical presence, he was unexcelled by any one. What he saw he could portray with the most telling reality. In drawing and modelling he was usually good; in coloring he was excellent, though in his late work sombre; in brush-handling he was one of the great masters. Strong, virile, yet easy and facile, he seemed to produce without effort. His brush was very broad in its sweep, very sure, very true. Occasionally in his late painting facility ran to the ineffectual, but usually he was certainty itself. His best work was in portraiture, and the most important of this is to be seen at Haarlem, where he died after a rather careless life. As a painter, pure and simple, he is almost to be ranked beside Velasquez; as a poet, a thinker, a man of lofty imagination, his work gives us little enlightenment except in so far as it shows a fine feeling for masses of color and problems of light. Though excellent portrait-painters, **Ravesteyn** (1572?-1657) and **De Keyser** (1596?-1679) do not provoke enthusiasm. They were quiet, conservative, dignified, painting civic guards and societies with a knowing brush and lively color, giving the truth of physiognomy, but not with that verve of the artist so conspicuous in Hals, nor with that unity of the group so essential in the making of a picture.

FIG. 82.—REMBRANDT. HEAD OF WOMAN. NAT. GAL. LONDON.

The next man in chronological order is **Rembrandt** (1607?-1669), the greatest painter in Dutch art. He was a pupil of Swanenburch and Lastman, but his great knowledge of nature and his craft came largely from the direct study of the model. Settled at Amsterdam, he quickly rose to fame, had a large following of pupils, and his influence was felt[208] through all Dutch painting. The portrait was emphatically his strongest work. The many-figured group he was not always successful in composing or lighting. His method of work rather fitted him for the portrait and unfitted him for the large historical piece. He built up the importance of certain features by dragging down all other features. This was largely shown in his handling of illumination. Strong in a few high lights on cheek, chin, or white linen, the rest of the picture was submerged in shadow, under which color was unmercifully sacrificed. This was not the best method for a large, many-figured piece, but was singularly well suited to the portrait. It produced strength by contrast. "Forced" it was undoubtedly, and not always true to nat[209]ure, yet nevertheless most potent in Rembrandt's hands. He was an arbitrary though perfect master of light-and-shade, and unusually effective in luminous and transparent shadows. In color he was again arbitrary but forcible and harmonious. In brush-work he was at times labored, but almost always effective.

Mentally he was a man keen to observe, assimilate, and express his impressions in a few simple truths. His conception was localized with his own people and time (he never built up the imaginary or followed Italy), and yet into types taken from the streets and shops of Amsterdam he infused the very largest humanity through his inherent sympathy with man. Dramatic, even tragic, he was; yet this was not so apparent in vehement action as in passionate expression. He had a powerful way of striking universal truths through the human face, the turned head, bent body, or outstretched hand. His people have character, dignity, and a pervading feeling that they are the great types of the Dutch race—people of substantial physique, slow in thought and impulse, yet capable of feeling, comprehending, enjoying, suffering.

His landscapes, again, were a synthesis of all landscapes, a grouping of the great truths of light, air, shadow, space. Whatever he turned his hand to was treated with that breadth of view that overlooked the little and grasped the great. He painted many subjects. His earliest work dates from 1627, and is a little hard and sharp in detail and cold in coloring. After 1654 he grew broader in handling and warmer in tone, running to golden browns, and, toward the end of his career, to rather hot tones. His life was embittered by many misfortunes, but these never seem to have affected his art except to deepen it. He painted on to the last, convinced that his own view was the true one, and producing works that rank second to none in the history of painting.[210]

Rembrandt's influence upon Dutch art was far-reaching, and appeared immediately in the works of his many pupils. They all followed his methods of handling light-and-shade, but no one of them ever equalled him, though they produced work of much merit. **Bol** (1611-1680) was chiefly a portrait-painter, with a pervading yellow tone and some pallor of flesh-coloring—a man of ability who mistakenly followed Rubens in the latter part of his life. **Flinck** (1615-1660) at one time followed Rembrandt so closely that his work has passed for that of the master; but latterly he, too, came under Flemish influence. Next to Eeckhout he was probably the nearest to Rembrandt in methods of all the pupils. **Eeckhout** (1621-1674) was really a Rembrandt imitator, but his hand was weak and his color hot.**Maes** (1632-1693) was the most successful manager of light after the school formula, and succeeded very well with warmth and richness of color, especially with his reds. The other Rembrandt pupils and followers were **Poorter** (fl. 1635-1643), **Victoors** (1620?-1672?), **Koninck** (1619-1688), **Fabritius** (1624-1654), and**Backer** (1608?-1651).

Van der Helst (1612?-1670) stands apart from this school, and seems to have followed more the portrait style of De Keyser. He was a realistic, precise painter, with much excellence of modelling in head and hands, and with fine carriage and dignity in the figure. In composition he hardly held his characters in group owing to a sacrifice of values, and in color he was often "spotty," and lacking in the unity of mass.

THE GENRE PAINTERS: This heading embraces those who may be called the "Little Dutchmen," because of the small scale of their pictures and their *genre*subjects. **Gerard Dou** (1613-1675) is indicative of the class without fully representing it. He was a pupil of Rembrandt, but his work gave little report of this. It was smaller, more delicate in detail, more petty in conception. He was a man great in[211] little things, one who wasted strength on the minutiæ of dress, or table-cloth, or the texture of furniture without grasping the mass or color significance of the whole scene. There was infinite detail about his work, and that gave it popularity; but as art it held, and holds to-day, little higher place than the work of **Metsu** (1630-1667), **Van Mieris** (1635-1681), **Netscher** (1639-1684), or **Schalcken** (1643-1706), all of whom produced the interior piece with figures elaborate in accidental effects. **Van Ostade** (1610-1685), though dealing with the small canvas, and portraying peasant life with perhaps unnecessary coarseness, was a much stronger painter than the men just mentioned. He was the favorite pupil of Hals and the master of Jan Steen. With little delicacy in choice of subject he had much delicacy in color, taste in arrangement, and skill in handling. His brush was precise but not finical.

FIG. 83.—J. VAN RUISDAEL. LANDSCAPE.

[212]

By far the best painter among all the "Little Dutchmen" was **Terburg** (1617?-1681), a painter of interiors, small portraits, conversation pictures, and the like. Though of diminutive scale his work has the largeness of view characteristic of genius, and the skilled technic of a thorough craftsman. Terburg was a travelled man, visiting Italy, where he studied Titian, returning to Holland to study Rembrandt, finally at Madrid studying Velasquez. He was a painter of much culture, and the keynote of his art is refinement. Quiet and dignified he carried taste through all branches of his art. In subject he was rather elevated, in color subdued with broken tones, in composition simple, in brush-work sure, vivacious, and yet unobtrusive. Selection in his characters was followed by reserve in using them. Detail was not very apparent. A few people with some accessory objects were all that he required to make a picture. Perhaps his best qualities appear in a number of small portraits remarkable for their distinction and aristocratic grace.

Steen (1626?-1679) was almost the opposite of Terburg, a man of sarcastic flings and coarse humor who satirized his own time with little reserve. He developed under Hals and Van Ostade, favoring the latter in his interiors, family scenes, and drunken debauches. He was a master of physiognomy, and depicted it with rare if rather unpleasant truth. If he had little refinement in his themes he certainly handled them as a painter with delicacy. At his best his many figured groups were exceedingly well composed, his color was of good quality (with a fondness for yellows), and his brush was as limpid and graceful as though painting angels instead of Dutch boors. He was really one of the fine brushmen of Holland, a man greatly admired by Sir Joshua Reynolds, and many an artist since; but not a man of high intellectual pitch as compared with Terburg, for instance.[213]

Pieter de Hooghe (1632?-1681) was a painter of purely pictorial effects, beginning and ending a picture in a scheme of color, atmosphere, clever composition, and above all the play of light-and-shade. He was one of the early masters of full sunlight, painting it falling across a courtyard or streaming through a window with marvellous truth and poetry. His subjects were commonplace enough. An interior with a figure or two in the middle distance, and a passage-way leading into a lighted background were sufficient for him. These formed a skeleton which he clothed in a half-tone shadow, pierced with warm yellow light, enriched with rare colors, usually garnet reds and deep yellows repeated in the different planes, and surrounded with a subtle pervading atmosphere. As a brushman he was easy but not distinguished, and often his drawing was not correct; but in the placing of color masses and in composing by color and light he was a master of the first rank. Little is known about his life. He probably formed himself on Fabritius or Rembrandt at second-hand, but little trace of the latter is apparent in his work. He seems not to have achieved much fame until late years, and then rather in England than in his own country.

Jan van der Meer of Delft (1632-1675), one of the most charming of all the *genre* painters, was allied to De Hooghe in his pictorial point of view and interior subjects. Unfortunately there is little left to us of this master, but the few extant examples serve to show him a painter of rare qualities in light, in color, and in atmosphere. He was a remarkable man for his handling of blues, reds, and yellows; and in the tonic relations of a picture he was a master second to no one. Fabritius is supposed to have influenced him.

THE LANDSCAPE PAINTERS: The painters of the Netherlands were probably the first, beginning with Bril, to paint landscape for its own sake, and as a picture motive in itself. Before them it had been used as a background for[214] the figure, and was so used by many of the Dutchmen themselves. It has been said that these landscape-painters were also the first ones to paint landscape realistically, but that is true only in part. They studied natural forms, as did, indeed, Bellini in the Venetian school; they learned something of perspective, air, tree anatomy, and the appearance of water; but no Dutch painter of landscape in the seventeenth century grasped the full color of Holland or painted its many varied lights. They indulged in a meagre conventional palette of grays, greens, and browns, whereas Holland is full of brilliant hues.

FIG. 84.—HOBBEMA. THE WATER-WHEEL. AMSTERDAM MUS.

Van Goyen (1596-1656) was one of the earliest of the seventeenth-century landscapists. In subject he was fond of the Dutch bays, harbors, rivers, and canals with shipping, windmills, and houses. His sky line was generally given low, his water silvery, and his sky misty and lumi[215]nous with bursts of white light. In color he was subdued, and in perspective quite cunning at times. **Salomon van Ruisdael** (1600?-1670) was his follower, if not his pupil. He had the same sobriety of color as his master, and was a mannered and prosaic painter in details, such as leaves and tree-branches. In composition he was good, but his art had only a slight basis upon reality, though it looks to be realistic at first sight. He had a formula for doing landscape which he varied only in a slight way, and this conventionality ran through all his work. **Molyn** (1600?-1661) was a painter who showed limited truth to nature in flat and hilly landscapes, transparent skies, and warm coloring. His extant works are few in number. **Wynants** (1615?-1679?) was more of a realist in natural appearance than any of the others, a man who evidently studied directly from nature in details of vegetation, plants, trees, roads, grasses, and the like. Most of the figures and animals in his landscapes were painted by other hands. He himself was a pure landscape-painter, excelling in light and aërial perspective, but not remarkable in color. **Van der Neer** (1603-1677) and **Everdingen** (1621?-1675) were two other contemporary painters of merit.

The best landscapist following the first men of the century was **Jacob van Ruisdael** (1625?-1682), the nephew of Salomon van Ruisdael. He is put down, with perhaps unnecessary emphasis, as the greatest landscape-painter of the Dutch school. He was undoubtedly the equal of any of his time, though not so near to nature, perhaps, as Hobbema. He was a man of imagination, who at first pictured the Dutch country about Haarlem, and afterward took up with the romantic landscape of Van Everdingen. This landscape bears a resemblance to the Norwegian country, abounding, as it does, in mountains, heavy dark woods, and rushing torrents. There is considerable poetry in its composition, its gloomy skies, and darkened lights. It is[216] mournful, suggestive, wild, usually unpeopled. There was much of the methodical in his putting together, and in color it was cold, and limited to a few tones. Many of Ruisdael's works have darkened through time. Little is known about the painter's life except that he was not appreciated in his own time and died in the almshouse.

Hobbema (1638?-1709) was probably the pupil of Jacob van Ruisdael, and ranks with him, if not above him, in seventeenth-century landscape painting. Ruisdael hardly ever painted sunlight, whereas Hobbema rather affected it in quiet wood-scenes or roadways with little pools of water and a mill. He was a freer man with the brush than Ruisdael, and knew more about the natural appearance of trees, skies, and lights; but, like his master, his view of nature found no favor in his own land. Most of his work is in England, where it had not a little to do with influencing such painters as Constable and others at the beginning of the nineteenth century.

FIG. 85.—ISRAELS. ALONE IN THE WORLD.

LANDSCAPE WITH CATTLE: Here we meet with **Wouverman** (1619-1668), a painter of horses, cavalry, battles, and riding parties placed in landscape. His landscape is bright and his horses are spirited in action. There is some mannerism apparent in his reiterated concentration of light on a white horse, and some repetition in his canvases, of which there are many; but on the whole he was an interesting, if smooth and neat painter. **Paul Potter** (1625-1654) hardly merited his great repute. He was a harsh, exact recorder of facts, often tin-like or wooden, in his cattle, and not in any way remarkable in his landscapes, least of all in their composition. The Young Bull at the Hague is an ambitious piece of drawing, but is not successful in color, light, or *ensemble*. It is a brittle work all through, and not nearly so good as some smaller things in the National Gallery London, and in the Louvre. **Adrien van de Velde** (1635?-1672) was short-lived, like Potter, but managed to do[217] a prodigious amount of work, showing cattle and figures in landscape with much technical ability and good feeling. He was particularly good in composition and the subtle gradation of neutral tints. A little of the Italian influence appeared in his work, and with the men who came with him and after him the Italian imitation became very pronounced. **Aelbert Cuyp** (1620-1691) was a many-sided painter, adopting at various times different styles, but was enough of a genius to be himself always. He is best known to us, perhaps, by his yellow sunlight effects along rivers, with cattle in the foreground, though he painted still-life, and even portraits and marines. In composing a group he was knowing, recording natural effects with power; in light and atmosphere he was one of the best of his time, and in texture and color refined, and frequently brilliant. **Both** (1610-1650?), **Berchem** (1620-1683), **Du Jardin** (1622?-1678), followed the Italian tradition of Claude Lorrain, producing semi-classic landscapes, never very convincing in their[218] originality. **Van der Heyden** (1637-1712), should be mentioned as an excellent, if minute, painter of architecture with remarkable atmospheric effects.

MARINE AND STILL-LIFE PAINTERS: There were two pre-eminent marine painters in this seventeenth century, **Willem van de Velde** (1633-1707) and **Backhuisen** (1631-1708). The sea was not an unusual subject with the Dutch landscapists. Van Goyen, **Simon de Vlieger** (1601?-1660?), Cuyp, **Willem van de Velde the Elder** (1611?-1693), all employed it; but it was Van de Velde the Younger who really stood at the head of the marine painters. He knew his subject thoroughly, having been well grounded in it by his father and De Vlieger, so that the painting of the Dutch fleets and harbors was a part of his nature. He preferred the quiet haven to the open sea. Smooth water, calm skies, silvery light, and boats lying listlessly at anchor with drooping sails, made up his usual subject. The color was almost always in a key of silver and gray, very charming in its harmony and serenity, but a little thin. Both he and his father went to England and entered the service of the English king, and thereafter did English fleets rather than Dutch ones. Backhuisen was quite the reverse of Van de Velde in preferring the tempest to the calm of the sea. He also used more brilliant and varied colors, but he was not so happy in harmony as Van de Velde. There was often dryness in his handling, and something too much of the theatrical in his wrecks on rocky shores.

The still-life painters of Holland were all of them rather petty in their emphasis of details such as figures on table-covers, water-drops on flowers, and fur on rabbits. It was labored work with little of the art spirit about it, except as the composition showed good masses. A number of these painters gained celebrity in their day by their microscopic labor over fruits, flowers, and the like, but they have no great rank at the present time. **Jan van Heem** (1600?[219]1684?) was perhaps the best painter of flowers among them. **Van Huysum** (1682-1749) succeeded with the same subject beyond his deserts. **Hondecoeter** (1636-1695) was a unique painter of poultry; **Weenix** (1640-1719) and **Van Aelst** (1620-1679), of dead game; **Kalf** (1630?-1693), of pots, pans, dishes, and vegetables.

EIGHTEENTH CENTURY: This was a period of decadence during which there was no originality worth speaking about among the Dutch painters. Realism in minute features was carried to the extreme, and imitation of the early men took the place of invention. Everything was prettified and elaborated until there was a porcelain smoothness and a photographic exactness inconsistent with true art. **Adriaan van der Werff** (1659-1722), and **Philip van Dyck** (1683-1753) with their "ideal" inanities are typical of the century's art. There was nothing to commend it. The lowest point of affectation had been reached.

NINETEENTH CENTURY: The Dutch painters, unlike the Belgians, have almost always been true to their own traditions and their own country. Even in decadence the most of them feebly followed their own painters rather than those of Italy and France, and in the early nineteenth century they were not affected by the French classicism of David. Later on there came into vogue an art that had some affinity with that of Millet and Courbet in France. It was the Dutch version of modern sentiment about the laboring classes, founded on the modern life of Holland, yet in reality a continuation of the style or *genre* practised by the early Dutchmen. **Israels** (1824-) is a revival or a survival of Rembrandtesque methods with a sentiment and feeling akin to the French Millet. He deals almost exclusively with peasant life, showing fisher-folk and the like in their cottage interiors, at the table, or before the fire, with good effects of light, atmosphere, and much pathos. Technically he is rather labored and heavy in handling, but usually[220] effective with sombre color in giving the unity of a scene. **Artz** (1837-1890) considered himself in measure a follower of Israels, though he never studied under him. His pictures in subject are like those of Israels, but without the depth of the latter. **Blommers** (1845-) is another peasant painter who follows Israels at a distance, and **Neuhuys** (1844-) shows a similar style of work. **Bosboom** (1817-1891) excelled in representing interiors, showing, with much pictorial effect, the light, color, shadow, and feeling of space and air in large cathedrals.

FIG. 86.—MAUVE. SHEEP.

The brothers Maris have made a distinct impression on modern Dutch art, and, strange enough, each in a different way from the others. **James Maris** (1837-) studied at Paris, and is remarkable for fine, vigorous views of canals, towns, and landscapes. He is broad in handling, rather bleak in coloring, and excels in fine luminous skies and voyaging clouds. **Matthew Maris** (1835-), Parisian trained like his brother, lives in London, where little is seen of his work. He paints for himself and his friends, and is rather melancholy and mystical in his art. He is a recorder of visions[221] and dreams rather than the substantial things of the earth, but always with richness of color and a fine decorative feeling. **Willem Maris** (1839-), sometimes called the "Silvery Maris," is a portrayer of cattle and landscape in warm sunlight and haze with a charm of color and tone often suggestive of Corot. **Jongkind** (1819-1891) stands by himself, **Mesdag** (1831-) is a fine painter of marines and sea-shores, and **Mauve** (1838-1888), a cattle and sheep painter, with nice sentiment and tonality, whose renown is just now somewhat disproportionate to his artistic ability. In addition there are **Kever, Poggenbeek, Bastert, Baur, Breitner, Witsen, Haverman, Weissenbruch.**

EXTANT WORKS: Generally speaking the best examples of the Dutch schools are still to be seen in the local museums of Holland, especially the Amsterdam and Hague Mus.; **Bosch**, Madrid, Antwerp, Brussels Mus.; **Lucas van Leyden**, Antwerp, Leyden, Munich Mus.; **Scorel**, Amsterdam, Rotterdam, Haarlem Mus.; **Heemskerck**, Amsterdam, Hague, Berlin, Cassel, Dresden; Steenwyck, Amsterdam, Hague, Brussels; **Cornelis van Haarlem**, Amsterdam, Haarlem, Brunswick.

PORTRAIT AND FIGURE PAINTERS—**Mierevelt**, Hague, Amsterdam, Rotterdam, Brunswick, Dresden, Copenhagen; **Hals**, best works to be seen at Haarlem, others at Amsterdam, Brussels, Hague, Berlin, Cassel, Louvre, Nat. Gal. Lon., Met. Mus. New York, Art Institute Chicago; **Rembrandt**, Amsterdam, Hermitage, Louvre, Munich, Berlin, Dresden, Madrid, London; **Bol**, Amsterdam, Hague, Dresden, Louvre; **Flinck**, Amsterdam, Hague, Berlin; **Eeckhout**, Amsterdam, Brunswick, Berlin, Munich; **Maes**, Nat. Gal. Lon., Rotterdam, Amsterdam, Hague, Brussels; **Poorter**, Amsterdam, Brussels, Dresden; **Victoors**, Amsterdam, Copenhagen, Brunswick, Dresden; **Fabritius**, Rotterdam, Amsterdam, Berlin; **Van der Helst**, best works at Amsterdam Mus.

GENRE PAINTERS—Examples of **Dou, Metsu, Van Mieris, Netscher, Schalcken, Van Ostade**, are to be seen in almost all the galleries of Europe, especially the Dutch, Belgian, German, and French galleries; **Terburg**, Amsterdam, Louvre, Dresden, Berlin (fine portraits); **Steen**, Amsterdam, Louvre, Rotterdam, Hague, Berlin, Cassel, Dresden, Vienna; **De Hooghe**, Nat. Gal. Lon., Louvre, Amsterdam, Hermitage; **Van der Meer of Delft**, Louvre, Hague, Amsterdam, Berlin, Dresden, Met. Mus. New York.[222]

LANDSCAPE PAINTERS—**Van Goyen**, Amsterdam, Fitz-William Mus. Cambridge, Louvre, Brussels, Cassel, Dresden, Berlin; **Salomon van Ruisdael**, Amsterdam, Brussels, Berlin, Dresden, Munich; **Van der Neer**, Nat. Gal. Lon., Louvre, Brussels, Amsterdam, Berlin, Dresden; **Everdingen**, Amsterdam, Berlin, Louvre, Brunswick, Dresden, Munich, Frankfort; **Jacob van Ruisdael**, Nat. Gal. Lon., Louvre, Amsterdam, Berlin, Dresden; **Hobbema**, best works in England, Nat. Gal. Lon., Amsterdam, Rotterdam, Dresden; **Wouvermans**, many works, best at Amsterdam, Cassel, Louvre; Potter, Amsterdam, Hague, Louvre, Nat. Gal. Lon.; **Van de Velde**, Amsterdam, Hague, Cassel, Dresden, Frankfort,

Munich, Louvre; **Cuyp**, Amsterdam, Nat. Gal. Lon., Louvre, Munich, Dresden; examples of **Both, Berchem, Du Jardin,** and **Van der Heyden**, in almost all of the Dutch and German galleries, besides the Louvre and Nat. Gal. Lon.

MARINE PAINTERS—**Willem van de Velde Elder and Younger, Backhuisen, Vlieger,** together with the flower and fruit painters like**Huysum, Hondecoeter, Weenix**, have all been prolific workers, and almost every European gallery, especially those at London, Amsterdam, and in Germany, have examples of their works; **Van der Werff** and **Philip van Dyck** are seen at their best at Dresden.

The best works of the modern men are in private collections, many in the United States, some examples of them in the Amsterdam and Hague Museums. Also some examples of the old Dutch masters in New York Hist. Society Library, Yale School of Fine Arts, Met. Mus. New York, Boston Mus., and Chicago Institute.

[223]

CHAPTER XVIII.
GERMAN PAINTING.

BOOKS RECOMMENDED: Colvin, *A. Durer, his Teachers, his Rivals, and his Scholars*; Eye, *Leben und Werke Albrecht Durers*; Förster,*Peter von Cornelius*; Förster, *Geschichte der Deutschen Kunst*; Keane, *Early Teutonic, Italian, and French Painters*; Kügler, *Handbook to German and Netherland Schools*, trans. by *Crowe*; Merlo, *Die Meister der altkolnischer Malerschule*; Moore, *Albert Durer*, Pecht,*Deutsche Kunstler des Neunzehnten Jahrhunderts*; Reber, *Geschichte der neueren Deutschen Kunst*; Riegel, *Deutsche Kunststudien*; Rosenberg, *Die Berliner Malerschule*; Rosenberg, *Sebald und Barthel Beham*; Rumohr, *Hans Holbein der Jungere*; Sandrart, *Teutsche Akademie der Edlen Bau, Bild-und Malerey-Kunste*; Schuchardt, *Lucas Cranach's Leben*; Thausig, *Albert Durer, His Life and Works*; Waagen, *Kunstwerke und Kunstler in Deutschland*; E. aus'm Weerth, *Wandmalereien des Mittelalters in den Rheinlanden*; Wessely,*Adolph Menzel*; Woltmann, *Holbein and his Time*; Woltmann, *Geschichte der Deutschen Kunst im Elsass*; Wurtzbach, *Martin Schongauer*.

EARLY GERMAN PAINTING: The Teutonic lands, like almost all of the countries of Europe, received their first art impulse from Christianity through Italy. The centre of the faith was at Rome, and from there the influence in art spread west and north, and in each land it was modified by local peculiarities of type and temperament. In Germany, even in the early days, though Christianity was the theme of early illuminations, miniatures, and the like, and though there was a traditional form reaching back to Italy and Byzantium, yet under it was the Teutonic type—the material, awkward, rather coarse Germanic point of view. The wish[224]to realize native surroundings was apparent from the beginning.

It is probable that the earliest painting in Germany took the form of illuminations. At what date it first appeared is unknown. In wall-painting a poor quality of work was executed in the churches as early as the ninth century, and probably earlier. The oldest now extant are those at Oberzell, dating back to the last part of the tenth century. Better examples are seen in the Lower Church of Schwarzrheindorf, of the twelfth century, and still better in the choir and transept of the Brunswick cathedral, ascribed to the early thirteenth century.

FIG. 87.—LOCHNER. STS. JOHN, CATHERINE, AND MATTHEW. NAT. GAL. LONDON.

Please click here for a modern color image

All of these works have an archaic appearance about[225] them, but they are better in composition and drawing than the productions of Italy and Byzantium at that time. It is likely that all the German churches at this time were decorated, but most of the paintings have been destroyed. The usual method was to cover the walls and wooden ceilings with blue grounds, and upon these to place figures surrounded by architectural ornaments. Stained glass was also used extensively. Panel painting seems to have come into existence before the thirteenth century (whether developed from miniature or wall-painting is unknown), and was used for altar decorations. The panels were done in tempera with figures in light colors upon gold grounds. The spirituality of the age with a mingling of northern sentiment appeared in the figure. This figure was at times graceful, and again awkward and archaic, according to the place of production and the influence of either France or Italy. The oldest panels extant are from the Wiesenkirche at Soest, now in the Berlin Museum. They do not date before the thirteenth century.

FOURTEENTH AND FIFTEENTH CENTURIES: In the fourteenth century the influence of France began to show strongly in willowy figures, long flowing draperies, and sentimental poses. The artists along the Rhine showed this more than those in the provinces to the east, where a ruder if freer art appeared. The best panel-painting of the time was done at Cologne, where we meet with the name of the first painter, **Meister Wilhelm**, and where a school was established usually known as the

SCHOOL OF COLOGNE: This school probably got its sentimental inclination, shown in slight forms and tender expression, from France, but derived much of its technic from the Netherlands. Stephen Lochner, or **Meister Stephen**, (fl. 1450) leaned toward the Flemish methods, and in his celebrated picture, the Madonna of the Rose Garden, in the Cologne Museum, there is an indication of this; but there[226] is also an individuality showing the growth of German independence in painting. The figures of his Dombild have little manliness or power, but considerable grace, pathos, and religious feeling. They are not abstract types but the[227]spiritualized people of the country in native costumes, with much gold, jewelry, and armor. Gold was used instead of a landscape background, and the foreground was spattered with flowers and leaves. The outlines are rather hard, and none of the aërial perspective of the Flemings is given. After a time French sentiment was still further encroached upon by Flemish realism, as shown in the works of the **Master of the Lyversberg Passion** (fl. about 1463-1480), to be seen in the Cologne Museum.

FIG. 88.—WOLGEMUT. CRUCIFIXION. MUNICH.

BOHEMIAN SCHOOL: It was not on the Lower Rhine alone that German painting was practised. The Bohemian school, located near Prague, flourished for a short time in the fourteenth century, under Charles IV., with **Theodorich of Prague** (fl. 1348-1378), **Wurmser**, and **Kunz**, as the chief masters. Their art was quite the reverse of the Cologne painters. It was heavy, clumsy, bony, awkward. If more original it was less graceful, not so pathetic, not so religious. Sentiment was slurred through a harsh attempt at realism, and the religious subject met with something of a check in the romantic mediæval chivalric theme, painted quite as often on the castle wall as the scriptural theme on the church wall. After the close of the fourteenth century wall-painting began to die out in favor of panel pictures.

NUREMBERG SCHOOL: Half-way between the sentiment of Cologne and the realism of Prague stood the early school of Nuremberg, with no known painter at its head. Its chief work, the Imhof altar-piece, shows, however, that the Nuremberg masters of the early and middle fifteenth century were between eastern and western influences. They inclined to the graceful swaying figure, following more the sculpture of the time than the Cologne type.

FIFTEENTH AND SIXTEENTH CENTURIES: German art, if begun in the fourteenth century, hardly showed any depth[228] or breadth until the fifteenth century, and no real individual strength until the sixteenth century. It lagged behind the other countries of Europe and produced the cramped archaic altar-piece. Then when printing was invented the painter-engraver came into existence. He was a man who painted panels, but found his largest audience through the circulation of engravings. The two kinds of arts being produced by the one man led to much detailed line work with the brush. Engraving is an influence to be borne in mind in examining the painting of this period.

FIG. 89.—DÜRER. PRAYING VIRGIN. AUGSBURG.

FRANCONIAN SCHOOL: Nuremberg was the centre of this school, and its most famous early master was **Wolgemut** (1434-1519), though **Plydenwurff** is the first-named painter. After the latter's death Wolgemut married his widow and became the head of the school. His paintings were chiefly altar-pieces, in which the figures were rather lank and narrow-shouldered, with sharp outlines, indicative perhaps of the influence of wood-engraving, in which he was much interested. There was, however, in his work an advance in characterization, nobility of expression, and quiet dignity, and it was his good fortune to be the master of one of the[229] most thoroughly original painters of all the German schools—**Albrecht Dürer** (1471-1528).

With Dürer and Holbein German art reached its apogee in the first half of the sixteenth century, yet their work was not different in spirit from that of their predecessors. Painting simply developed and became forceful and expressive technically without abandoning its early character. There is in Dürer a naive awkwardness of figure, some angularity of line, strain of pose, and in composition oftentimes huddling and overloading of the scene with details. There is not that largeness which seemed native to his Italian contemporaries. He was hampered by that German exactness, which found its best expression in engraving, and which, though unsuited to painting, nevertheless crept into it. Within these limitations Dürer produced the typical art of Germany in the Renaissance time—an art more attractive for the charm and beauty of its parts than for its unity, or its general impression. Dürer was a travelled man, visited Italy and the Netherlands, and, though he always remained a German in art, yet he picked up some Italian methods from Bellini and Mantegna that are faintly apparent in some of his works. In subject he was almost exclusively religious, painting the altar-piece with infinite care upon wooden panel, canvas, or parchment. He never worked in fresco, preferring oil and tempera. In drawing he was often harsh and faulty, in draperies cramped at times, and then, again, as in the Apostle panels at Munich, very broad, and effective. Many of his pictures show a hard, dry brush, and a few, again, are so free and mellow that they look as though done by another hand. He was usually minute in detail, especially in such features as hair, cloth, flesh. His portraits were uneven and not his best productions. He was too close a scrutinizer of the part and not enough of an observer of the whole for good portraiture. Indeed, that is the criticism to be made upon all his work. He was an ex[230]quisite realist of certain features, but not always of the *ensemble*. Nevertheless he holds first rank in the German art of the Renaissance, not only on account of his technical ability, but also because of his imagination, sincerity, and striking originality.

FIG. 90.—HOLBEIN THE YOUNGER. PORTRAIT. HAGUE MUS.
Please click here for a modern color image

Dürer's influence was wide-spread throughout Germany, especially in engraving, of which he was a master. In painting **Schäufelin** (1490?-1540?) was probably his apprentice, and in his work followed the master so closely that many of his works have been attributed to Dürer. This is true in measure of **Hans Baldung**(1476?-1552?). **Hans von Kulmbach** (?-1522) was a painter of more than ordinary importance, brilliant in coloring, a follower of Dürer, who was in[231]clined toward Italian methods, an inclination that afterward developed all through German art. Following Dürer's formulas came a large number of so-called "Little Masters" (from the size of their engraved plates), who were more engravers than painters. Among the more important of those who were painters as well as engravers were **Altdorfer** (1480?-1538), a rival rather than an imitator of Dürer; **Barthel Beham** (1502-1540), **Sebald Beham** (1500-1550), **Pencz** (1500?-1550), **Aldegrever** (1502-1558), and **Bink** (1490?-1569?).

SWABIAN SCHOOL: This school includes a number of painters who were located at different places, like Colmar and Ulm, and later on it included the Holbeins at Augsburg, who were really the consummation of the school. In the fifteenth century one of the early leaders was **Martin Schöngauer** (1446?-1488), at Colmar. He is supposed to have been a pupil of Roger Van der Weyden, of the Flemish school, and is better known by his engravings than his paintings, none of the latter being positively authenticated. He was thoroughly German in his type and treatment, though, perhaps, indebted to the Flemings for his coloring. There was some angularity in his figures and draperies, and a tendency to get nearer nature and further away from the ecclesiastical and ascetic conception in all that he did.

At Ulm a local school came into existence with **Zeitblom** (fl. 1484-1517), who was probably a pupil of Schüchlin. He had neither Schöngauer's force nor his fancy, but was a simple, straightforward painter of one rather strong type. His drawing was not good, except in the draperies, but he was quite remarkable for the solidity and substance of his painting, considering the age he lived in was given to hard, thin brush-work. **Schaffner** (fl. 1500-1535) was another Ulm painter, a junior to Zeitblom, of whom little is known, save from a few pictures graceful and free in composition.[232] A recently discovered man, **Bernard Strigel** (1461?-1528?) seems to have been excellent in portraiture.

FIG. 91.—PILOTY. WISE AND FOOLISH VIRGINS.

At Augsburg there was still another school, which came into prominence in the sixteenth century with Burkmair and the Holbeins. It was only a part of the Swabian school, a concentration of artistic force about Augsburg, which, toward the close of the fifteenth century, had come into competition with Nuremberg, and rather outranked it in splendor. It was at Augsburg that the Renaissance art in Germany showed in more restful composition, less angularity, better modelling and painting, and more sense of the *ensemble* of a picture. **Hans Burkmair** (1473-1531) was the founder of the school, a pupil of Schöngauer, later influenced by Dürer, and finally showing the influence of Italian art. He was not, like Dürer, a religious painter, though doing religious subjects. He was more concerned with worldly appearance, of which he had a large knowledge, as may be seen from his illustrations for engraving. As a painter he was a rather fine colorist, indulging in the[233] fantastic of architecture but with good taste, crude in drawing but forceful, and at times giving excellent effects of motion. He was rounder, fuller, calmer in composition than Dürer, but never so strong an artist.

Next to Burkmair comes the celebrated Holbein family. There were four of them all told, but only two of them, Hans the Elder and Hans the Younger, need be mentioned. **Holbein the Elder** (1460?-1524), after Burkmair, was the best painter of his time and school without being in himself a great artist. Schöngauer was at first his guide, though he soon submitted to some Flemish and Cologne influence, and later on followed Italian form and method in composition to some extent. He was a good draughtsman, and very clever at catching realistic points of physiognomy—a gift he left his son Hans. In addition he had some feeling for architecture and ornament, and in handling was a bit hard, and oftentimes careless. The best half of his life fell in the latter part of the fifteenth century, and he never achieved the free painter's quality of his son.

Hans Holbein the Younger (1497-1543) holds, with Dürer, the high place in German art. He was a more mature painter than Dürer, coming as he did a quarter of a century later. He was the Renaissance artist of Germany, whereas Dürer always had a little of the Gothic clinging to him. The two men were widely different in their points of view and in their work. Dürer was an idealist seeking after a type, a religious painter, a painter of panels with the spirit of an engraver. Holbein was emphatically a realist finding material in the actual life about him, a designer of cartoons and large wall paintings in something of the Italian spirit, a man who painted religious themes but with little spiritual significance.

It is probable that he got his first instruction from his father and from Burkmair. He was an infant prodigy, developed early, saw much foreign art, and showed a number[234] of tendencies in his work. In composition and drawing he appeared at times to be following Mantegna and the northern Italians; in brush-work he resembled the Flemings, especially Massys; yet he was never an imitator of either Italian or Flemish painting. Decidedly a self-sufficient and an observing man, he travelled in Italy and the Netherlands, and spent much of his life in England, where he met with great success at court as a portrait-painter. From seeing much he assimilated much, yet always remained German, changing his style but little as he grew older. His wall paintings have perished, but the drawings from them are preserved and show him as an artist of much invention. He is now known chiefly by his portraits, of which there are many of great excellence. His facility in grasping physiognomy and realizing character, the quiet dignity of his composition, his firm modelling, clear outline, harmonious coloring, excellent detail, and easy solid painting, all place him in the front rank of great painters. That he was not always bound down to literal facts may be seen in his many designs for wood-engravings. His portrait of Hubert Morett, in the Dresden Gallery, shows his art to advantage, and there are many portraits by him of great spirit in England, in the Louvre, and elsewhere.

SAXON SCHOOL: Lucas Cranach (1472-1553) was a Franconian master, who settled in Saxony and was successively court-painter to three Electors and the leader of a small local school there. He, perhaps, studied under **Grünewald**, but was so positive a character that he showed no strong school influence. His work was fantastic, odd in conception and execution, sometimes ludicrous, and always archaic-looking. His type was rather strained in proportions, not always well drawn, but graceful even when not truthful. This type was carried into all his works, and finally became a mannerism with him. In subject he was religious, mythological, romantic, pastoral, with a preference for the[235] nude figure. In coloring he was at first golden, then brown, and finally cold and sombre. The lack of aërial perspective and shadow masses gave his work a queer look, and he was never much of a brushman. His pictures were typical of the time and country, and for that and for their strong individuality they are ranked among the most interesting paintings of the German school. Perhaps his most satisfactory works are his portraits. **Lucas Cranach the Younger** (1515-1586) was the best of the elder Cranach's pupils. Many of his pictures are attributed to his father. He followed the elder closely, but was a weaker man, with a smoother brush and a more rosy color. Though there were many pupils the school did not go beyond the Cranach family. It began with the father and died with the son.

FIG. 92.—LEIBL. IN CHURCH.

Please click here for a modern color image

SEVENTEENTH AND EIGHTEENTH CENTURIES: These were unrelieved centuries of decline in German painting. After Dürer, Holbein, and Cranach had passed there came about a senseless imitation of Italy, combined with an equally senseless imitation of detail in nature that produced nothing worthy of the name of original or genuine art. It is not probable that the Reformation had any more to do with this than with the decline in Italy. It was a period of barrenness in both countries. The Italian imitators in Germany were chiefly **Rottenhammer** (1564-1623), and**Elzheimer**[236] (1574?-1620). After them came the representative of the other extreme in **Denner** (1685-1749), who thought to be great in portraiture by the minute imitation of hair, freckles, and three-days'-old beard—a petty and unworthy realism which excited some curiosity but never held rank as art. **Mengs** (1728-1779) sought for the sublime through eclecticism, but never reached it. His work, though academic and correct, is lacking in spirit and originality. **Angelica Kauffman** (1741-1807) succeeded in pleasing her inartistic age with the simply pretty, while **Carstens** (1754-1798) was a conscientious if mistaken student of the great Italians—a man of some severity in form and of academic inclinations.

NINETEENTH CENTURY: In the first part of this century there started in Germany a so-called "revival of art" led by **Overbeck** (1789-1869), **Cornelius** (1783-1867), **Veit** (1793-1877), and **Schadow** (1789-1862), but like many another revival of art it did not amount to much. The attempt to "revive" the past is usually a failure. The forms are caught, but the spirit is lost. The nineteenth-century attempt in Germany was brought about by the study of monumental painting in Italy, and the taking up of the religious spirit in a pre-Raphaelite manner. Something also of German romanticism was its inspiration. Overbeck remained in Rome, but the others, after some time in Italy, returned to Germany, diffused their teaching, and really formed a new epoch in German painting. A modern art began with ambitions and subjects entirely disproportionate to its skill. The monumental, the ideal, the classic, the exalted, were spread over enormous spaces, but there was no reason for such work in the contemporary German life, and nothing to warrant its appearance save that its better had appeared in Italy during the Renaissance. Cornelius after his return became the head of the

MUNICH SCHOOL and painted pictures of the heroes of the[237] classic and the Christian world upon a large scale. Nothing but their size and good intention ever brought them into notice, for their form and coloring were both commonplace. **Schnorr** (1794-1872) followed in the same style with the Niebelungen Lied, Charlemagne, and Barbarossa for subjects. **Kaulbach** (1805-1874) was a pupil of Cornelius, and had some ability but little taste, and not enough originality to produce great art. **Piloty** (1826-1886) was more realistic, more of a painter and ranks as one of the best of the early Munich masters. After him Munich art became *genre*-like in subject, with greater attention given to truthful representation in light, color, texture. To-day there are a large number of painters in the school who are remarkable for realistic detail.

DUSSELDORF SCHOOL: After 1826 this school came into prominence under the guidance of Schadow. It did not fancy monumental painting so much as the common easel picture, with the sentimental, the dramatic, or the romantic subject. It was no better in either form or color than the Munich school, in fact not so good, though there were painters who emanated from it who had ability. At Berlin the inclination was to follow the methods and ideas held at Dusseldorf.

The whole academic tendency of modern painting in Germany and Austria for the past fifty years has not been favorable to the best kind of pictorial art. There is a disposition on the part of artists to tell stories, to encroach upon the sentiment of literature, to paint with a dry brush in harsh unsympathetic colors, to ignore relations of light-and-shade, and to slur beauties of form. The subject seems to count for more than the truth of representation, or the individuality of view. From time to time artists of much ability have appeared, but these form an exception rather than a rule. The men to-day who are the great artists of Germany are less followers of the German tradition than individuals each working in a style peculiar to himself. A few only of[238] them call for mention. **Menzel** (1815-1905) is easily first, a painter of group pictures, a good colorist, and a powerful pen-and-ink draughtsman; **Lenbach** (1836-1904), a forceful portraitist; **Uhde** (1848-), a portrayer of scriptural scenes in modern costumes with much sincerity, good color, and light; **Leibl** (1844-1900), an artist with something of the Holbein touch and realism; **Thoma**, a Frankfort painter of decorative friezes and panels; **Liebermann, Gotthardt Kuehl, Franz Stuck, Max Klinger, Greiner, Trübner, Bartels, Keller.**

FIG. 93.—MENZEL. A READER.

Aside from these men there are several notable painters with German affinities, like **Makart** (1840-1884), an Austrian, who possessed good technical qualities and indulged in a profusion of color; **Munkacsy** (1846-1900), a Hungarian, who is perhaps more Parisian than German in technic, and **Böcklin** (1827-1901), a Swiss, who is quite by himself in fantastic and grotesque subjects, a weird and uncanny imagination, and a brilliant prismatic coloring.[239]

PRINCIPAL WORKS: BOHEMIAN SCHOOL—**Theoderich of Prague**, Karlstein chap. and University Library Prague, Vienna Mus.;**Wurmser**, same places.

FRANCONIAN SCHOOL—**Wolgemut**, Aschaffenburg, Munich, Nuremberg, Cassel Mus.; **Dürer**, Crucifixion Dresden, Trinity Vienna Mus., other works Munich, Nuremberg, Madrid Mus.; **Schäufelin**, Basle, Bamberg, Cassel, Munich, Nuremberg, Nordlingen Mus., and Ulm Cathedral; **Baldung**, Aschaffenburg, Basle, Berlin, Kunsthalle Carlsruhe, Freiburg Cathedral; **Kulmbach**, Munich, Nuremberg, Oldenburg; **Altdorfer** and the "Little Masters" are seen in the Augsburg, Nuremberg, Berlin, Munich and Fürstenberg Mus.

SWABIAN SCHOOL—**Schöngauer**, attributed pictures Colmar Mus.; **Zeitblom**, Augsburg, Berlin, Carlsruhe, Munich, Nuremberg, Simaringen Mus.; **Schaffner**, Munich, Schliessheim, Nuremberg, Ulm Cathedral; **Strigel**, Berlin, Carlsruhe, Munich, Nuremberg;**Burkmair**, Augsburg, Berlin, Munich, Maurice chap. Nuremberg; **Holbein the Elder**, Augsburg, Nuremberg, Basle, Städel Mus., Frankfort; **Holbein the Younger**, Basle, Carlsruhe, Darmstadt, Dresden, Berlin, Louvre, Windsor Castle, Vienna Mus.

SAXON SCHOOL—**Cranach**, Bamberg Cathedral and Gallery, Munich, Vienna, Dresden, Berlin, Stuttgart, Cassel; **Cranach the Younger**, Stadtkirche Wittenberg, Leipsic, Vienna, Nuremberg Mus.

SEVENTEENTH AND EIGHTEENTH-CENTURY PAINTERS: Rottenhammer, Louvre, Berlin, Munich, Schliessheim, Vienna, Kunsthalle

Hamburg; **Elzheimer**, Stadel, Brunswick, Louvre, Munich, Berlin, Dresden; **Denner**, Kunsthalle Hamburg, Berlin, Brunswick, Dresden, Vienna, Munich; **Mengs**, Madrid, Vienna, Dresden, Munich, St. Petersburg; **Angelica Kauffman**, Vienna, Hermitage, Turin, Dresden, Nat. Gal. Lon., Phila. Acad.

NINETEENTH-CENTURY PAINTERS: Overbeck, frescos in S. Maria degli Angeli Assisi, Villa Massimo Rome, Carlsruhe, New Pinacothek, Munich, Städel Mus., Dusseldorf; **Cornelius**, frescos Glyptothek and Ludwigkirche Munich, Casa Zuccaro Rome, Royal Cemetery Berlin; **Veit**, frescos Villa Bartholdi Rome, Städel, Nat. Gal. Berlin; **Schadow**, Nat. Gal. Berlin, Antwerp, Städel, Munich Mus., frescos Villa Bartholdi Rome; **Schnorr**, Dresden, Cologne, Carlsruhe, New Pinacothek Munich, Städel Mus.; **Kaulbach**, wall paintings Berlin Mus., Raczynski Gal. Berlin, New Pinacothek Munich, Stuttgart, Phila. Acad.; **Piloty**, best pictures in the New Pinacothek and Maximilianeum Munich, Nat. Gal. Berlin; **Menzel**, Nat. Gal., Raczynski Mus. Berlin, Breslau Mus.; **Lenbach**, Nat. Gal. Berlin, New [240]Pinacothek Munich, Kunsthalle Hamburg, Zürich Gal.; **Uhde**, Leipsic Mus.; **Leibl**, Dresden Mus. The contemporary paintings have not as yet found their way, to any extent, into public museums, but may be seen in the expositions at Berlin and Munich from year to year. **Makart** has one work in the Metropolitan Mus., N. Y., as has also **Munkacsy**; other works by them and by **Böcklin**may be seen in the Nat. Gal. Berlin.

[241]
CHAPTER XIX.
BRITISH PAINTING.

BOOKS RECOMMENDED: Armstrong, *Sir Henry Raeburn*; Armstrong, *Gainsborough*; Armstrong, *Sir Joshua Reynolds*; Burton, *Catalogue of Pictures in National Gallery*; Chesneau, *La Peinture Anglaise*; Cook, *Art in England*; Cunningham, *Lives of the most Eminent British Artists*; Dobson, *Life of Hogarth*; Gilchrist, *Life of Etty*; Gilchrist, *Life of Blake*; Hamerton, *Life of Turner*; Henderson, *Constable*; Hunt,*The Pre-Raphaelite Brotherhood (Contemporary Review, Vol. 49)*; Leslie, *Sir Joshua Reynolds*; Leslie, *Life of Constable*; Martin and Newbery, *Glasgow School of Painting*; McKay, *Scottish School of Painting*; Monkhouse, *British Contemporary Artists*; Redgrave,*Dictionary of Artists of the English School*; Romney, *Life of George Romney*; Rossetti, *Fine Art, chiefly Contemporary*; Ruskin, *Pre-Raphaelitism*; Ruskin, *Art of England*; Sandby, *History of Royal Academy of Arts*; William Bell Scott, *Autobiography*; Scott, *British Landscape Painters*; Stephens, *Catalogue of Prints and Drawings in the British Museum*; Swinburne, *William Blake*; Temple, *Painting in the Queen's Reign*; Van Dyke, *Old English Masters*; Wedmore, *Studies in English Art*; Wilmot-Buxton, *English Painters*; Wright, *Life of Richard Wilson*.

FIG. 94.—HOGARTH. SHORTLY AFTER MARRIAGE. NAT. GAL. LONDON.

Please click here for a modern color image

BRITISH PAINTING: It may be premised in a general way, that the British painters have never possessed the pictorial cast of mind in the sense that the Italians, the French, or the Dutch have possessed it. Painting, as a purely pictorial arrangement of line and color, has been somewhat foreign to their conception. Whether this failure to appreciate painting as painting is the result of geographical position, isolation, race temperament, or mental disposition, would be hard to determine. It is quite[242] certain that from time immemorial the English people have not been lacking in the appreciation of beauty; but beauty has appealed to them, not so much through the eye in painting and sculpture, as through the ear in poetry and literature. They have been thinkers, reasoners, moralists, rather than observers and artists in color. Images have been brought to their minds by words rather than by forms. English poetry has existed since the days of Arthur and the Round Table, but English painting is of comparatively modern origin, and it is not wonderful that the original leaning of the people toward literature and its sentiment should find its way into pictorial representation. As a result one may say in a very general way that English painting is more illustrative than creative. It endeavors to record things that might be more pertinently and com[243]pletely told in poetry, romance, or history. The conception of large art—creative work of the Rubens-Titian type—has not been given to the English painters, save in exceptional cases. Their success has been in portraiture and landscape, and this largely by reason of following the model.

EARLY PAINTING: The earliest decorative art appeared in Ireland. It was probably first planted there by missionaries from Italy, and it reached its height in the seventh century. In the ninth and tenth centuries missal illumination of a Byzantine cast, with local modifications, began to show. This lasted, in a feeble way, until the fifteenth century, when work of a Flemish and French nature took its place. In the Middle Ages there were wall paintings and church decorations in England, as elsewhere in Europe, but these have now perished, except some fragments in Kempley Church, Gloucestershire, and Chaldon Church, Surrey. These are supposed to date back to the twelfth century, and there are some remains of painting in Westminster Abbey that are said to be of thirteenth and fourteenth-century origin. From the fifteenth to the eighteenth century the English people depended largely upon foreign painters who came and lived in England. Mabuse, Moro, Holbein, Rubens, Van Dyck, Lely, Kneller—all were there at different times, in the service of royalty, and influencing such local English painters as then lived. The outcome of missal illumination and Holbein's example produced in the sixteenth and seventeenth centuries a local school of miniature-painters of much interest, but painting proper did not begin to rise in England until the beginning of the eighteenth century—that century so dead in art over all the rest of Europe.

FIGURE AND PORTRAIT PAINTERS: Aside from a few inconsequential precursors the first English artist of note was **Hogarth** (1697-1764). He was an illustrator, a moralist, and a satirist as well as a painter. To point a moral upon[244] canvas by depicting the vices of his time was his avowed aim, but in doing so he did not lose sight of pictorial beauty. Charm of color, the painter's taste in arrangement, light, air, setting, were his in a remarkable degree. He was not successful in large compositions, but in small pictures like those of the Rake's Progress he was excellent. An early man, a rigid stickler for the representation, a keen observer of physiognomy, a satirist with a sense of the absurd, he was often warped in his art by the necessities of his subject and was sometimes hard and dry in method, but in his best work he was quite a perfect painter. He was the first of the English school, and perhaps the most original of that school. This is quite as true of his technic as of his point of view. Both were of his own creation. His subjects have been talked about a great deal in the past; but his painting is not to this day valued as it should be.

FIG. 95.—REYNOLDS. COUNTESS SPENCER AND LORD ALTHORP.
Please click here for a modern color image

The next man to be mentioned, one of the most considerable of all the English school, is **Sir Joshua Reynolds** (1723-1792). He was a pupil of Hudson, but owed his art to many sources. Besides the influence of Van Dyck he[245] was for some years in Italy, a diligent student of the great Italians, especially the Venetians, Correggio, and the Bolognese Eclectics. Sir Joshua was inclined to be eclectic himself, and from Italy he brought back a formula of art which, modified by his own individuality, answered him for the rest of his life. He was not a man of very lofty imagination or great invention. A few figure-pieces, after the Titian initiative, came from his studio, but his reputation rests upon his many portraits. In portraiture he was often beyond criticism, giving the realistic representation with dignity, an elevated spirit, and a suave brush. Even here he was more impressive by his broad truth of facts than by his artistic feeling. He was not a painter who could do things enthusiastically or excite enthusiasm in the spectator. There was too much of rule and precedent, too much regard for the traditions, for him to do anything strikingly original. His brush-work and composition were more learned than individual, and his color, though usually good, was oftentimes conventional in contrasts. Taking him for all in all he was a very cultivated painter, a man to be respected and admired, but he had not quite the original spirit that we meet with in Gainsborough.

Reynolds was well-grounded in Venetian color, Bolognese composition, Parmese light-and-shade, and paid them the homage of assimilation; but if **Gainsborough** (1727-1788) had such school knowledge he positively disregarded it. He disliked all conventionalities and formulas. With a natural taste for form and color, and with a large decorative sense, he went directly to nature, took from her the materials which he fashioned into art after his own peculiar manner. His celebrated Blue Boy was his protest against the conventional rule of Reynolds that a composition should be warm in color and light. All through his work we meet with departures from academic ways. By dint of native force and grace he made rules unto himself.[246]Some of them were not entirely successful, and in drawing he might have profited by school training; but he was of a peculiar poetic temperament, with a dash of melancholy about him, and preferred to work in his own way. In portraiture his color was rather cold; in landscape much warmer. His brush-work was as odd as himself, but usually effective, and his accessories in figure-painting were little more than decorative after-thoughts. Both in portraiture and landscape he was one of the most original and most English of all the English painters—a man not yet entirely appreciated, though from the first ranked among the foremost in English art.

FIG. 96.—GAINSBOROUGH. BLUE BOY.
Please click here for a modern color image

Romney (1734-1802), a pupil of Steele, was often quite as masterful a portrait-painter as either Reynolds or Gainsborough. He was never an artist elaborate in composition, and his best works are bust-portraits with a plain background. These he did with much dash and vivacity of manner. His women, particularly, are fine in life-like pose and winsomeness of mood. He was a very cunning observer, and knew how to arrange for grace of line and charm of color.

After Romney came **Beechey** (1753-1839), **Raeburn** (1756-1823), **Opie** (1761-1807), and **John Hoppner** (1759-1810).[247] Then followed **Lawrence** (1769-1830), a mixture of vivacious style and rather meretricious method. He was the most celebrated painter of his time, largely because he painted nobility to look more noble and grace to look more gracious. Fond of fine types, garments, draperies, colors, he was always seeking the sparkling rather than the true, and forcing artificial effects for the sake of startling one rather than stating facts simply and frankly. He was facile with the brush, clever in line and color, brilliant to the last degree, but lacking in that simplicity of view and method which marks the great mind. His composition was rather fine in its decorative effect, and, though his lights were often faulty when compared with nature, they were no less telling from the stand-point of picture-making. He is much admired by artists to-day, and, as a technician, he certainly had more than average ability. He was hardly an artist like Reynolds or Gainsborough, but among the mediocre painters of his day he shone like a star. It is not worth while to say much about his contemporaries. **Etty** (1787-1849) was one of the best of the figure men, but his Greek types and classic aspirations grow wearisome on acquaintance; and**Sir Charles Eastlake** (1793-1865), though a learned man in art and doing great service to painting as a writer, never was a painter of importance.

William Blake (1757-1827) was hardly a painter at all, though he drew and colored the strange figures of his fancy and cannot be passed over in any history of English art. He was perhaps the most imaginative artist of English birth, though that imagination was often disordered and almost incoherent. He was not a correct draughtsman, a man with no great color-sense, and a workman without technical training; and yet, in spite of all this, he drew some figures that are almost sublime in their sweep of power. His decorative sense in filling space with lines is well shown in his illustrations to the Book of Job. In grace[248] of form and feeling of motion he was excellent. Weird and uncanny in thought, delving into the unknown, he opened a world of mystery, peopled with a strange Apocalyptic race, whose writhing, flowing bodies are the epitome of graceful grandeur.

FIG. 97.—CONSTABLE. CORN FIELD. NAT. GAL. LONDON.
Please click here for a modern color image

GENRE-PAINTERS: From Blake to **Morland** (1763-1804) is a step across space from heaven to earth. Morland was a realist of English country life, horses at tavern-doors, cattle, pigs. His life was not the most correct, but his art in truthfulness of representation, simplicity of painting, richness of color and light, was often of a fine quality. As a skilful technician he stood quite alone in his time, and seemed to show more affinity with the Dutch *genre*-painters[249] than his own countrymen. His works are much prized to-day, and were so during the painter's life.

Sir David Wilkie (1785-1841) was also somewhat like the Dutch in subject, a *genre*-painter, fond of the village fête and depicting it with careful detail, a limpid brush, and good textural effects. In 1825 he travelled abroad, was gone some years, was impressed by Velasquez, Correggio, and Rembrandt, and completely changed his style. He then became a portrait and historical painter. He never outlived the nervous constraint that shows in all his pictures, and his brush, though facile within limits, was never free or bold as compared with a Dutchman like Steen. In technical methods **Landseer** (1802-1873), the painter of animals, was somewhat like him. That is to say, they both had a method of painting surfaces and rendering textures that was more "smart" than powerful. There is little solidity or depth to the brush-work of either, though both are impressive to the spectator at first sight. Landseer knew the habits and the anatomy of animals very well, but he never had an appreciation of the brute in the animal, such as we see in the pictures of Velasquez or the bronzes of Barye. The Landseer animal has too much sentiment about it. The dogs, for instance, are generally given those emotions pertinent to humanity, and which are only exceptionally true of the canine race. This very feature—the tendency to humanize the brute and make it tell a story—accounts in large measure for the popularity of Landseer's art. The work is perhaps correct enough, but the aim of it is somewhat afield from pure painting. It illustrates the literary rather than the pictorial. Following Wilkie the most distinguished painter was **Mulready** (1786-1863), whose pictures of village boys are well known through engravings.

FIG. 98.—TURNER. FIGHTING TÉMÉRAIRE. NAT. GAL. LONDON.
Please click here for a modern color image

THE LANDSCAPE PAINTERS: In landscape the English have had something to say peculiarly their own. It has not always been well said, the coloring is often hot, the[250] brush-work brittle, the attention to detail inconsistent with the large view of nature, yet such as it is it shows the English point of view and is valuable on that account. **Richard Wilson** (1713-1782) was the first landscapist of importance, though he was not so English in view as some others to follow. In fact, Wilson was nurtured on Claude Lorrain and Joseph Vernet and instead of painting the realistic English landscape he painted the pseudo-Italian landscape. He began working in portraiture under the tutorship of Wright, and achieved some success in this department; but in 1749 he went to Italy and devoted himself wholly to landscapes. These were of the classic type and somewhat conventional. The composition was usually a dark foreground with trees or buildings to right and left, an opening in the middle distance leading into the background, and a broad expanse of sunset sky. In the foreground he usually introduced a[251] few figures for romantic or classic association. Considerable elevation of theme and spirit marks most of his pictures. There was good workmanship about the skies and the light, and an attentive study of nature was shown throughout. His canvases did not meet with much success at the time they were painted. In more modern days Wilson has been ranked as the true founder of landscape in England, and one of the most sincere of English painters.

THE NORWICH SCHOOL: Old Crome (1769-1821), though influenced to some extent by Wilson and the Dutch painters, was an original talent, painting English scenery with much simplicity and considerable power. He was sometimes rasping with his brush, and had a small method of recording details combined with mannerisms of drawing and composition, and yet gave an out-of-doors feeling in light and air that was astonishing. His large trees have truth of mass and accuracy of drawing, and his foregrounds are painted with solidity. He was a keen student of nature, and drew about him a number of landscape painters at Norwich, who formed the Norwich School. Crome was its leader, and the school made its influence felt upon English landscape painting. **Cotman** (1782-1842) was the best painter of the group after Crome, a man who depicted landscape and harbor scenes in a style that recalls Girtin and Turner.

The most complete, full-rounded landscapist in England was **John Constable** (1776-1837). His foreign bias, such as it was, came from a study of the Dutch masters. There were two sources from which the English landscapists drew. Those who were inclined to the ideal, men like Wilson, **Calcott** (1779-1844), and Turner, drew from the Italian of Poussin and Claude; those who were content to do nature in her real dress, men like Gainsborough and Constable, drew from the Dutch of Hobbema and his contemporaries. A certain sombreness of color and manner of composition show in Constable that may be attributed to Holland; but[252]these were slight features as compared with the originality of the man. He was a close student of nature who painted what he saw in English country life, especially about Hampstead, and painted it with a knowledge and an artistic sensitiveness never surpassed in England. The rural feeling was strong with him, and his evident pleasure in simple scenes is readily communicated to the spectator. There is no attempt at the grand or the heroic. He never cared much for mountains or water, but was fond of cultivated uplands, trees, bowling clouds, and torn skies. Bursts of sunlight, storms, atmospheres, all pleased him. With detail he was little concerned. He saw landscape in large patches of form and color, and so painted it. His handling was broad and solid, and at times a little heavy. His light was often forced by sharp contrast with shadows, and often his pictures appear spotty from isolated glitters of light strewn here and there. In color he helped eliminate the brown landscape and substituted in its place the green and blue of nature. In atmosphere he was excellent. His influence upon English art was impressive, and in 1824 the exhibition at Paris of his Hay Wain, together with some work by Bonington and Fielding had a decided effect upon the then rising landscape school of France. The French realized that nature lay at the bottom of Constable's art, and they profited, not by imitating Constable, but by studying his nature model.

FIG. 99.—BURNE JONES. FLAMMA VESTALIS.
Please click here for a modern color image

Bonington (1801-1828) died young, and though of English[253] parents his training was essentially French, and he really belonged to the French school, an associate of Delacroix. His study of the Venetians turned his talent toward warm coloring, in which he excelled. In landscape his broad handling was somewhat related to that of Constable, and from the fact of their works appearing together in the Salon of 1824 they are often spoken of as influencers of the modern French landscape painters.

Turner (1775-1851) is the best known name in English art. His celebrity is somewhat disproportionate to his real merits, though it is impossible to deny his great ability. He was a man learned in all the forms of nature and schooled in all the formulas of art; yet he was not a profound lover of nature nor a faithful recorder of what things he saw in nature, except in his early days. In the bulk of his work he shows the traditions of Claude, with additions of his own. His taste was classic (he possessed all the knowledge and the belongings of the historical landscape), and he delighted in great stretches of country broken by sea-shores, rivers, high mountains, fine buildings, and illumined by blazing sunlight and gorgeous skies. His composition was at times grotesque in imagination; his light was usually bewildering in intensity and often unrelieved by shadows of sufficient depth; his tone was sometimes faulty; and in color he was not always harmonious, but inclined to be capricious, uneven, showing fondness for arbitrary schemes of color. The object of his work seems to have been to dazzle, to impress with a wilderness of lines and hues, to overawe by imposing scale and grandeur. His paintings are impressive, decoratively splendid, but they often smack of the stage, and are more frequently grandiloquent than grand. His early works, especially in water-colors, where he shows himself a follower of Girtin, are much better than his later canvases in oil, many of which have changed color. The water-colors are carefully done, subdued in color, and true in light. From[254] 1802, or thereabouts, to 1830 was his second period, in which Italian composition and much color were used. The last twenty years of his life he inclined to the *bizarre*, and turned his canvases into almost incoherent color masses. He had an artistic feeling for composition, linear perspective, and the sweep of horizon lines; skies and hills he knew and drew with power; color he comprehended only as decoration; and light he distorted for effect. Yet with all his shortcomings Turner was an artist to be respected and admired. He knew his craft, in fact, knew it so well that he relied too much on artificial effects, drew away from the model of nature, and finally passed into the extravagant.

THE WATER-COLORISTS: About the beginning of this century a school of water-colorists, founded originally by **Cozens** (1752-1799) and **Girtin** (1775-1802), came into prominence and developed English art in a new direction. It began to show with a new force the transparency of skies, the luminosity of shadows, the delicacy and grace of clouds, the brilliancy of light and color. Cozens and Blake were primitives in the use of the medium, but **Stothard** (1755-1834) employed it with much sentiment, charm, and *plein-air*effect. Turner was quite a master of it, and his most permanent work was done with it. Later on, when he rather abandoned form to follow color, he also abandoned water-color for oils. **Fielding** (1787-1849) used water-color effectively in giving large feeling for space and air, and also for fogs and mists; **Prout** (1783-1852) employed it in architectural drawings of the principal cathedrals of Europe; and **Cox** (1783-1859), **Dewint** (1784-1849), **Hunt** (1790-1864), **Cattermole** (1800-1868), **Lewis** (1805-1876), men whose names only can be mentioned, all won recognition with this medium. Water-color drawing is to-day said to be a department of art that expresses the English pictorial feeling better than any other, though this is not an undisputed statement.[255]

FIG. 100.—LEIGHTON. HELEN OF TROY.
Please click here for a modern color image

Perhaps the most important movement in English painting of recent times was that which took the name of

PRE-RAPHAELITISM: It was started about 1847, primarily by **Rossetti** (1828-1882), **Holman Hunt** (1827-), and **Sir John Millais** (1829-1896), associated with several sculptors and poets, seven in all. It was an emulation of the sincerity, the loving care, and the scrupulous exactness in truth that characterized the Italian painters before Raphael. Its advocates, including Mr. Ruskin the critic, maintained that after Raphael came that fatal facility in art which seeking grace of composition lost truth of fact, and that the proper course for modern painters was to return to the sincerity and veracity of the early masters. Hence the name pre-Ra[256]phaelitism, and the signatures on their early pictures, P. R. B., pre-Raphaelite Brother. To this attempt to gain the true regardless of the sensuous, was added a morbidity of thought mingled with mysticism, a moral and religious pose, and a studied simplicity. Some of the painters of the Brotherhood went even so far as following the habits of the early Italians, seeking retirement from the world and carrying with them a Gothic earnestness of air. There is no doubt about the sincerity that entered into this movement. It was an honest effort to gain the true, the good, and as a result, the beautiful; but it was no less a striven-after honesty and an imitated earnestness. The Brotherhood did not last for long, the members drifted from each other and began to paint each after his own style, and pre-Raphaelitism passed away as it had arisen, though not without leaving a powerful stamp on English art, especially in decoration.

Rossetti, an Italian by birth though English by adoption, was the type of the Brotherhood. He was more of a poet than a painter, took most of his subjects from Dante, and painted as he wrote, in a mystical romantic spirit. He was always of a retiring disposition and never exhibited publicly after he was twenty-eight years of age. As a draughtsman he was awkward in line and not always true in modelling. In color he was superior to his associates and had considerable decorative feeling. The shortcoming of his art, as with that of the others of the Brotherhood, was that in seeking truth of detail he lost truth of *ensemble*. This is perhaps better exemplified in the works of Holman Hunt. He has spent infinite pains in getting the truth of detail in his pictures, has travelled in the East and painted types, costumes, and scenery in Palestine to gain the historic truths of his Scriptural scenes; but all that he has produced has been little more than a survey, a report, a record of the facts. He has not made a picture. The insistence upon every detail has isolated all the facts and left them isolated in the[257] picture. In seeking the minute truths he has overlooked the great truths of light, air, and setting. His color has always been crude, his values or relations not well preserved, and his brush-work hard and tortured.

Millais showed some of this disjointed effect in his early work when he was a member of the Brotherhood. He did not hold to his early convictions however, and soon abandoned the pre-Raphaelite methods for a more conventional style. He has painted some remarkable portraits and some excellent figure pieces, and to-day holds high rank in English art; but he is an uneven painter, often doing weak, harshly-colored work. Moreover, the English tendency to tell stories with the paint-brush finds in Millais a faithful upholder. At his best he is a strong painter.

Madox Brown (1821-1893) never joined the Brotherhood, though his leaning was toward its principles. He had considerable dramatic power, with which he illustrated historic scenes, and among contemporary artists stood well. The most decided influence of pre-Raphaelitism shows in **Burne-Jones** (1833-), a pupil of Rossetti, and perhaps the most original painter now living[18] of the English school. From Rossetti he got mysticism, sentiment, poetry, and from association with Swinburne and William Morris, the poets, something of the literary in art, which he has put forth with artistic effect. He has not followed the Brotherhood in its pursuit of absolute truth of fact, but has used facts for decorative effect in line and color. His ability to fill a given space gracefully, shows with fine results in his pictures, as in his stained-glass designs. He is a good draughtsman and a rather rich colorist, but in brush-work somewhat labored, stippled, and unique in dryness. He is a man of much imagination, and his conceptions, though illustrative of literature, do not suffer thereby, because his treatment does not sacrifice the artistic. He has been the butt of considerable shallow laughter from time to time, like many another [258]man of power. **Albert Moore** (1840-1893), a graceful painter of a decorative ideal type, rather follows the Rossetti-Burne-Jones example, and is an illustration of the influence of pre-Raphaelitism.

[18]Died 1898.

OTHER FIGURE AND PORTRAIT PAINTERS: Among the contemporary painters **Sir Frederick Leighton** (1830-1896), President of the Royal Academy, is ranked as a fine academic draughtsman, but not a man with the color-sense or the brushman's quality in his work. **Watts** (1818-1904) is perhaps an inferior technician, and in color is often sombre and dirty; but he is a man of much imagination, occasionally rises to grandeur in conception, and has painted some superb portraits, notably the one of Walter Crane. **Orchardson** (1835-) is more of a painter, pure and simple, than any of his contemporaries, and is a knowing if somewhat mannered colorist. **Erskine Nicol** (1825-), **Faed**[19] (1826-), **Calderon** (1833-), **Boughton** (1834-1905), **Frederick Walker** (1840-1875), **Stanhope Forbes**, **Stott of Oldham** and in portraiture **Holl** (1845-1890) and **Herkomer** may be mentioned.

[19]Died 1900.

FIG. 101.—WATTS. LOVE AND DEATH.
Please click here for a modern color image

LANDSCAPE AND MARINE PAINTERS: In the department of landscape there are many painters in England of contemporary importance. **Vicat Cole** (1833-1893) had considerable exaggerated reputation as a depicter of sunsets and twilights; **Cecil Lawson** (1851-1882) gave promise of great accomplishment, and lived long enough to do some excellent work in the style [259]of the French Rousseau, mingled with an influence from Gainsborough; **Alfred Parsons** is a little hard and precise in his work, but one of the best of the living men; and **W. L. Wyllie** is a painter of more than average merit. In marines **Hook**(1819-) belongs to the older school, and is not entirely satisfactory. The most modern and the best sea-painter in England is **Henry Moore** (1831-1895), a man who paints well and gives the large feeling of the ocean with fine color qualities. Some other men of mark are **Clausen, Brangwyn, Ouless, Steer, Bell, Swan, McTaggart, Sir George Reid**.

MODERN SCOTCH SCHOOL: There is at the present time a school of art in Scotland that seems to have little or no affinity with the contemporary school of England. Its painters are more akin to the Dutch and the French, and in their coloring resemble, in depth and quality, the work of Delacroix. Much of their art is far enough removed from the actual appearance of nature, but it is strong in the sentiment of color and in decorative effect. The school is represented by such men as **James Guthrie, E. A. Walton, James Hamilton, George Henry, E. A. Hornel, Lavery, Melville, Crawhall, Roche, Lawson, McBride, Morton, Reid Murray, Spence, Paterson**.

PRINCIPAL WORKS: English art cannot be seen to advantage, outside of England. In the Metropolitan Museum, N. Y., and in private collections like that of Mr. William H. Fuller in New York,[20] there are some good examples of the older men—Reynolds, Constable, Gainsborough, and their contemporaries. In the Louvre there are some indifferent Constables and some good Boningtons. In England the best collection is in the National Gallery. Next to this the South Kensington Museum for Constable sketches. Elsewhere the Glasgow, Edinburgh, Liverpool, Windsor galleries, and the private collections of the late Sir Richard Wallace, the Duke of Westminster, and others. Turner is well represented in the National Gallery, though his oils

have suffered through time and the use of fugitive pigments. For the living men, their work may be seen in the yearly exhibitions at the Royal Academy and elsewhere. There are comparatively few English pictures in America.
[20]Dispersed, 1898.

[260]

CHAPTER XX.
AMERICAN PAINTING.

BOOKS RECOMMENDED: *American Art Review*; Amory, *Life of Copley*; *The Art Review*; Benjamin, *Contemporary Art in America*; *Century Magazine*; Caffin, *American Painters*; Clement and Hutton, *Artists of the Nineteenth Century*; Cummings, *Historic Annals of the National Academy of Design*; Downes, *Boston Painters (in Atlantic Monthly Vol. 62)*; Dunlap, *Arts of Design in United States*; Flagg, *Life and Letters of Washington Allston*; Galt, *Life of West*; Isham, *History of American Painting*; Knowlton, *W. M. Hunt*; Lester, *The Artists of America*; Mason, *Life and Works of Gilbert Stuart*; Perkins, *Copley*; *Scribner's Magazine*; Sheldon, *American Painters*; Tuckerman, *Book of the Artists*; Van Dyke, *Art for Art's Sake*; Van Rensselaer, *Six Portraits*; Ware, *Lectures on Allston*; White, *A Sketch of Chester A. Harding*.

AMERICAN ART: It is hardly possible to predicate much about the environment as it affects art in America. The result of the climate, the temperament, and the mixture of nations in the production or non-production of painting in America cannot be accurately computed at this early stage of history. One thing only is certain, and that is, that the building of a new commonwealth out of primeval nature does not call for the production of art in the early periods of development. The first centuries in the history of America were devoted to securing the necessities of life, the energies of the time were of a practical nature, and art as an indigenous product was hardly known.

After the Revolution, and indeed before it, a hybrid portraiture, largely borrowed from England, began to appear, and after 1825 there was an attempt at landscape painting;[261] but painting as an art worthy of very serious consideration, came in only with the sudden growth in wealth and taste following the War of the Rebellion and the Centennial Exhibition of 1876. The best of American art dates from about 1878, though during the earlier years there were painters of note who cannot be passed over unmentioned.

FIG. 102.—WEST. PETER DENYING CHRIST. HAMPTON CT.

THE EARLY PAINTERS: The "limner," or the man who could draw and color a portrait, seems to have existed very early in American history. **Smibert** (1684-1751), a Scotch painter, who settled in Boston, and **Watson** (1685?-1768), another Scotchman, who settled in New Jersey, were of this class—men capable of giving a likeness, but little more. They were followed by English painters of even less consequence. Then came **Copley** (1737-1815) and **West** (1738-1820), with whom painting in America really began. They were good men for their time, but it must be borne in mind that the times for art were not at all favorable. West was a man about whom all the infant prodigy tales have been told, but he never grew to be a great artist. He was ambitious beyond his power, indulged in theatrical composition, was hot in color, and never was at ease in handling the brush. Most of his life was passed in England, where he had a vogue, was elected President of the Royal Academy, and became practically a British painter. Copley was more of an American than West, and more of a painter. Some of his portraits are exceptionally fine, and his figure pieces, like Charles I. demanding the Five Members of House of Commons are excellent in color and composition. **C. W. Peale** (1741-1827), a pupil of both Copley and West, was perhaps [262]more fortunate in having celebrated characters like Washington for sitters than in his art. **Trumbull** (1756-1843) preserved on canvas the Revolutionary history of America and, all told, did it very well. Some of his compositions, portraits, and miniature heads in the Yale Art School at New Haven are drawn and painted in a masterful manner and are as valuable for their art as for the incidents which they portray.

FIG. 103.—GILBERT STUART. WASHINGTON (UNFINISHED). BOSTON MUS.

Please click here for a modern color image

Gilbert Stuart (1755-1828) was the best portrait-painter of all the early men, and his work holds very high rank even in the schools of to-day. He was one of the first in American art-history to show skilful accuracy of the brush, a good knowledge of color, and some artistic sense of dignity and carriage in the sitter. He was not always a good draughtsman, and he had a manner of laying on pure colors without blending them that sometimes produced sharpness in modelling; but as a general rule he painted a portrait with force and with truth. He was a pupil of Alexander, a Scotchman, and afterward an assistant to West. He settled in Boston, and during his life painted most of the great men of his time, including Washington.[263]

FIG. 104.—W. M. HUNT. LUTE PLAYER.

Vanderlyn (1776-1852) met with adversity all his life long, and perhaps never expressed himself fully. He was a pupil of Stuart, studied in Paris and Italy, and his associations with Aaron Burr made him quite as famous as his pictures. **Washington Allston** (1779-1843) was a painter whom the Bostonians have ranked high in their art-history, but he hardly deserved such position. Intellectually he was a man of lofty and poetic aspirations, but as an artist he never had the painter's sense or the painter's skill. He was an aspiration rather than a consummation. He cherished notions about ideals, dealt in imaginative allegories, and failed to observe the pictorial character of the world about him. As a result of this, and poor artistic training, his art had too little basis on nature, though it was very often satisfactory as decoration.**Rembrandt Peale** (1787-1860), like his father, was a painter of Washington portraits of mediocre quality.**Jarvis** (1780-1834) and **Sully** (1783-1872) were both British born, but their work belongs here in America, where most of their days were spent. Sully could paint a very good portrait occasionally, though he always inclined toward the weak and the sentimental, especially[264]in his portraits of women. **Leslie** (1794-1859) and **Newton** (1795-1835) were Americans, but, like West and Copley, they belong in their art more to England than to America. In all the early American painting the British influence may be traced, with sometimes an inclination to follow Italy in large compositions.

THE MIDDLE PERIOD in American art dates from 1825 to about 1878. During that time, something distinctly American began to appear in the landscape work of **Doughty** (1793-1856) and **Thomas Cole** (1801-1848). Both men were substantially self-taught, though Cole received some instruction from a portrait-painter named Stein. Cole during his life was famous for his Hudson River landscapes, and for two series of pictures called The Voyage of Life and The Course of Empire. The latter were really epic poems upon canvas, done with much blare of color and literary explanation in the title. His best work was in pure landscape, which he pictured with considerable accuracy in drawing, though it was faulty in lighting and gaudy in coloring. Brilliant autumn scenes were his favorite subjects. His work had the merit of originality and, moreover, it must be remembered that Cole was one of the beginners in American landscape art. **Durand** (1796-1886) was an engraver until 1835, when he began painting portraits, and afterward developed landscape with considerable power. He was usually simple in subject and realistic in treatment, with not so much insistence upon brilliant color as some of his contemporaries. **Kensett** (1818-1872) was a follower in landscape of the so-called Hudson River School of Cole and others, though he studied seven years in Europe. His color was rather warm, his air hazy, and the general effect of his landscape that of a dreamy autumn day with poetic suggestions. **F. E. Church** (1826-[A]) was a pupil of Cole, and has followed him in seeking the grand and the startling in mountain scenery. With Church should be mentioned a [265]number of artists—**Hubbard** (1817-1888), **Hill** (1829-,) **Bierstadt** (1830-),[21] **Thomas Moran** (1837-)—who have achieved reputation by canvases of the Rocky Mountains and other expansive scenes. Some other painters of smaller canvases belong in point of time, and also in spirit, with the Hudson River landscapists—painters, too, of considerable merit, as **David Johnson** (1827-), **Bristol** (1826-), **Sandford Gifford** (1823-1880), **McEntee** (1828-1891), and**Whittredge** (1820-), the last two very good portrayers of autumn scenes; **A. H. Wyant** (1836-1892), one of the best and strongest of the American landscapists;**Bradford** (1830-1892) and **W. T. Richards** (1833-), the marine-painters.

[21]Died, 1900.

FIG. 105.—EASTMAN JOHNSON. CHURNING.

PORTRAIT, HISTORY, AND GENRE-PAINTERS: Contemporary with the early landscapists were a number of figure-painters, most of them self-taught, or taught badly by foreign or native artists, and yet men who produced creditable work. **Chester Harding** (1792-1866) was one of the early portrait-painters of this century who achieved celebrity in Boston to be the subject of what was called "the Harding craze." **Elliott**(1812-1868) was a pupil of Trumbull, and a man of considerable reputation, as was also [266]**Inman** (1801-1846), a portrait and *genre*-painter with a smooth, detailed brush. **Page** (1811-1885), **Baker** (1821-1880), **Huntington**(1816-), the third President of the Academy of Design; **Healy** (1808-[22]), a portrait-painter of more than average excellence; **Mount** (1807-1868), one of the earliest of American *genre*-painters, were all men of note in this middle period.

[22]Died 1894.

Leutze (1816-1868) was a German by birth but an American by adoption, who painted many large historical scenes of the American Revolution, such as Washington Crossing the Delaware, besides many scenes taken from European history. He was a pupil of Lessing at Dusseldorf, and had something to do with introducing Dusseldorf methods into America. He was a painter of ability, if at times hot in color and dry in handling. Occasionally he did a fine portrait, like the Seward in the Union League Club, New York.

During this period, in addition to the influence of Dusseldorf and Rome upon American art, there came the influence of French art with **Hicks** (1823-1890) and **Hunt** (1824-1879), both of them pupils of Couture at Paris, and Hunt also of Millet at Barbizon. Hunt was the real introducer of Millet and the Barbizon-Fontainebleau artists to the American people. In 1855 he established himself at Boston, had a large number of pupils, and met with great success as a teacher. He was a painter of ability, but perhaps his greatest influence was as a teacher and an instructor in what was good art as distinguished from what was false and meretricious. He certainly was the first painter in America who taught catholicity of taste, truth and sincerity in art, and art in the artist rather than in the subject. Contemporary with Hunt lived **George Fuller** (1822-1884), a unique man in American art for the sentiment he conveyed in his pictures by means of color and atmosphere. Though never proficient in the grammar of art he managed by blendings of color to suggest certain[267] sentiments regarding light and air that have been rightly esteemed poetic.

FIG. 106.—INNESS. LANDSCAPE.

THE THIRD PERIOD in American art began immediately after the Centennial Exhibition at Philadelphia in 1876. Undoubtedly the display of art, both foreign and domestic, at that time, together with the national prosperity and great growth of the United States had much to do with stimulating activity in painting. Many young men at the beginning of this period went to Europe to study in the studios at Munich, and later on at Paris. Before 1880 some of them had returned to the United States, bringing with them knowledge of the technical side of art, which they immediately began to give out to many pupils. Gradually the influence of the young men from Munich and Paris spread. The Art Students' League, founded in 1875, was incorporated in 1878, and the Society of American Artists was established in the same year. Societies and painters began to spring up all over the country, and as a result there is in the United States to-day an artist body technically as well trained and[268] in spirit as progressive as in almost any country of Europe. The late influence shown in painting has been largely a French influence, and the American artists have been accused from time to time of echoing French methods. The accusation is true in part. Paris is the centre of all art-teaching to-day, and the Americans, in common with the European nations, accept French methods, not because they are French, but because they are the best extant. In subjects and motives, however, the American school is as original as any school can be in this cosmopolitan age.

PORTRAIT, FIGURE, AND GENRE PAINTERS (1878-1894): It must not be inferred that the painters now prominent in American art are all young men schooled since 1876. On the contrary, some of the best of them are men past middle life who began painting long before 1876, and have by dint of observation and prolonged study continued with the modern spirit. For example, **Winslow Homer** (1836-) is one of the strongest and most original of all the American artists, a man who never had the advantage of the highest technical training, yet possesses a feeling for color, a dash and verve in execution, an originality in subject, and an individuality of conception that are unsurpassed. **Eastman Johnson** (1824-) is one of the older portrait and figure-painters who stands among the younger generations without jostling, because he has in measure kept himself informed with modern thought and method. He is a good, conservative painter, possessed of taste, judgment, and technical ability. **Elihu Vedder** (1836-) is more of a draughtsman than a brushman. His color-sense is not acute nor his handling free, but he has an imagination which, if somewhat more literary than pictorial, is nevertheless very effective. **John La Farge** (1835-) and **Albert Ryder** (1847-) are both colorists, and La Farge in artistic feeling is a man of much power. Almost all of his pictures have fine decorative quality in line and color and are thoroughly pictorial.[269]

FIG. 107.—WINSLOW HOMER. UNDERTOW.
Please click here for a modern color image

The "young men," so-called, though some of them are now on toward middle life, are perhaps more facile in brush-work and better trained draughtsmen than those we have just mentioned. They have cultivated vivacity of style and cleverness in statement, frequently at the expense of the larger qualities of art. **Sargent**(1856-) is, perhaps, the most considerable portrait-painter now living, a man of unbounded resources technically and fine natural abilities. He is draughtsman, colorist, brushman—in fact, almost everything in art that can be cultivated. His taste is not yet mature, and he is just now given to dashing effects that are more clever than permanent; but that he is a master in portraiture has already been abundantly demonstrated. **Chase** (1849-) is also an exceptionally good portrait painter, and he handles the *genre* subject with brilliant color and a swift, sure brush. In brush-work he is exceed[270]ingly clever, and is an excellent technician in almost every respect. Not always profound in matter he generally manages to be entertaining in method. **Blum** (1857-) is well known to magazine readers through many black-and-white illustrations. He is also a painter of *genre* subjects taken from many lands, and handles his brush with brilliancy and force. **Dewing** (1851-) is a painter with a refined sense not only in form but in color. His pictures are usually small, but exquisite in delicacy and decorative charm. **Thayer** (1849-) is fond of large canvases, a man of earnestness, sincerity, and imagination, but not a good draughtsman, not a good colorist, and a rather clumsy brushman. He has, however, something to say, and in a large sense is an artist of uncommon ability. **Kenyon Cox** (1856-) is a draughtsman, with a strong command of line and taste in its arrangement. He is not a strong colorist, though in recent work he has shown a new departure in this feature that promises well. He renders the nude with power, and is fond of the allegorical subject.

FIG. 108.—WHISTLER. WHITE GIRL.
Please click here for a modern color image

The number of good portrait-painters at present working in America is quite large, and mention can be made of but a few in addition to those already spoken of—**Lockwood, McLure Hamilton, Tarbell, Beckwith, Benson, Vinton**. In figure and *genre*-painting the list of really good painters could be drawn out indefinitely, and again mention must be confined to a few only, like **Simmons, Shirlaw, Smedley, Brush, Millet, Hassam, Reid, Wiles, Mowbray, Reinhart, Blashfield, Metcalf, Low, C. Y. Turner, Henri**.

Most of the men whose names are given above are resident in America; but, in addition, there is a large contingent of young men, American born but resident abroad, who can hardly be claimed by the American school, and yet belong to it as much as to any school. They are cosmopolitan in their art, and reside in Paris, Munich, London, or elsewhere, as the spirit moves them. Sargent, the[271] portrait-painter, really belongs to this group, as does also **Whistler** (1834-[23]), one of the most artistic of all the moderns. Whistler was long resident in London, but has now removed to Paris. He belongs to no school, and such art as he produces is peculiarly his own, save a leaven of influences from Velasquez and the Japanese. His art is the perfection of delicacy, both in color and in line. Apparently very sketchy, it is in reality the maximum of effect with the minimum of display. It has the pictorial charm of mystery and suggestiveness, and the technical effect of light, air, and space. There is nothing better produced in modern painting than his present work, and in earlier years he painted portraits like that of his mother, which are justly ranked as great art. **E. A. Abbey** (1852-) is better known by his pen-and-ink work than by his paintings, [272]howbeit he has done good work in color. He is resident in England.

[23]Died, 1903.

In Paris there are many American-born painters, who really belong more with the French school than the American. **Bridgman** is an example, and **Dannat, Alexander Harrison, Hitchcock, McEwen, Melchers, Pearce, Julius Stewart, Weeks** (1849-1903), **J. W. Alexander, Walter Gay, Sergeant Kendall** have nothing distinctly American about their art. It is semi-cosmopolitan with a leaning toward French methods. There are also some American-born painters at Munich, like **C. F. Ulrich; Shannon** is in London and **Coleman** in Italy.[273]

FIG. 109.—SARGENT. "CARNATION LILY, LILY ROSE."
Please click here for a modern color image

LANDSCAPE AND MARINE PAINTERS, 1878-1894: In the department of landscape America has had since 1825 something distinctly national, and has at this day. In recent years the impressionist *plein-air* school of France has influenced many painters, and the prismatic landscape is quite as frequently seen in American exhibitions as in the Paris salons; but American landscape art rather dates ahead of French impressionism. The strongest landscapist of our times, **George Inness** (1825-[24]), is not a young man except in his artistic aspirations. His style has undergone many changes, yet still remains distinctly individual. He has always been an experimenter and an uneven painter, at times doing work of wonderful force, and then again falling into weakness. The solidity of nature, the mass and bulk of landscape, he has shown with a power second to none. He is fond of the sentiment of nature's light, air, and color, and has put it forth more in his later than in his earlier canvases. At his best, he is one of the first of the American landscapists. Among his contemporaries Wyant (already mentioned), **Swain Gifford**,[25] **Colman, Gay, Shurtleff**, have all done excellent work uninfluenced by foreign schools of to-day. **Homer Martin's**[26] landscapes, from their breadth of treatment, are popularly considered rather indifferent work, but in reality they are excellent in color and poetic feeling.

[24]Died 1894.
[25]Died 1905.
[26]Died 1897.

The "young men" again, in landscape as in the figure, are working in the modern spirit, though in substance they are based on the traditions of the older American landscape school. There has been much achievement, and there is still greater promise in such landscapists as **Tryon, Platt, Murphy, Dearth, Crane, Dewey,Coffin, Horatio Walker, Jonas Lie**. Among those who favor the so-called impressionistic view are **Weir, Twachtman,** and **Robinson**,[27] three landscape-painters of undeniable power. In marines **Gedney Bunce** has portrayed many Venetian scenes of charming color-tone, and De Haas[28] has long been known as a sea-painter of some power. **Quartley**, who died young, was brilliant in color and broadly realistic. The present marine-painters are **Maynard, Snell, Rehn,Butler, Chapman**.

[27]Died 1896.
[28]Died 1895.
[274]

FIG. 110.—CHASE. ALICE.

PRINCIPAL WORKS: The works of the early American painters are to be seen principally in the Boston Museum of Fine Arts, the Athenæum, Boston Mus., Mass. Hist. Soc., Harvard College, Redwood Library, Newport, Metropolitan Mus., Lenox and Hist. Soc. Libraries, the City Hall, Century Club, Chamber of Commerce, National Acad. of Design, N. Y. In New Haven, at Yale School of Fine Arts, in Philadelphia at Penna. Acad. of Fine Arts, in Rochester Powers's Art Gal., in Washington Corcoran Gal. and the Capitol.[275]

The works of the younger men are seen in the exhibitions held from year to year at the Academy of Design, the Society of American Artists, N. Y., in Philadelphia, Chicago, Boston, and elsewhere throughout the country. Some of their works belong to permanent institutions like the Metropolitan Mus., the Pennsylvania Acad., the Art Institute of Chicago, but there is no public collection of pictures that represents American art as a whole. Mr. T. B. Clarke, of New York, had perhaps as complete a collection of paintings by contemporary American artists as anyone.

[276]

POSTSCRIPT.
SCATTERING SCHOOLS AND INFLUENCES IN ART.

In this brief history of painting it has been necessary to omit some countries and some painters that have not seemed to be directly connected with the progress or development of painting in the western world. The arts of China and Japan, while well worthy of careful chronicling, are somewhat removed from the arts of the other nations and from our study. Moreover, they are so positively decorative that they should be treated under the head of Decoration, though it is not to be denied that they are also realistically expressive. Portugal has had some history in the art of painting, but it is slight and so bound up with Spanish and Flemish influences that its men do not stand out as a distinct school. This is true in measure of Russian painting. The early influences with it were Byzantine through the Greek Church. In late years what has been produced favors the Parisian or German schools.

In Denmark and Scandinavia there has recently come to the front a remarkable school of high-light painters, based on Parisian methods, that threatens to outrival Paris itself. The work of such men as **Kröyer, Zorn, Petersen, Liljefors, Thaulow, Björck, Thegerström**, is as startling in its realism as it is brilliant in its color. The pictures in the Scandinavian section of the Paris Exposition of 1889 were a revelation of new strength from the North, and this has been somewhat increased by the Scandinavian pictures at the World's Fair in 1893. It is impossible to predict what will[277] be the outcome of this northern art, nor what will be the result of the recent movement here in America. All that can be said is that the tide seems to be setting westward and northward, though Paris has been the centre of art for many years, and will doubtless continue to be the centre for many years to come.

Printed in Great Britain
by Amazon.co.uk, Ltd.,
Marston Gate.